FINANCIAL
PASSAGES

Also by Benjamin J. Stein

THE MANHATTAN GAMBIT
'LUDES
THE VIEW FROM SUNSET BOULEVARD
BUNKHOUSE LOGIC
DREEMZ
THE CROESUS CONSPIRACY

and with Herbert Stein

MONEY POWER
ON THE BRINK

Financial
Passages

BENJAMIN J. STEIN

Doubleday & Company, Inc.
Garden City, New York
1985

Library of Congress Cataloging in Publication Data

Stein, Benjamin, 1944–
    Financial passages.

    Includes index.
    1. Finance, Personal.   I. Title.
HG179.S82   1985   332.024
ISBN 0-385-17938-3
Library of Congress Catalog Card Number 82–45309

For Lois Wallace

CONTENTS

Foreword by Herbert Stein ix

ONE
Understanding the Journey 1

TWO
The Roaring Twenties—Lift-off Time 11

THREE
Building That Nest and Feeding Those Chickadees 27

FOUR
Not for Singles Only 45

FIVE
The Laws of Economics and How to Break Them 65

SIX
The Thrilling Thirties 73

SEVEN
Savings, Insurance, and Other Real-Life Aggravations 93

EIGHT
Thirtyish Singles—Agony and Ecstasy 101

NINE
The Late Thirties—The Income Apogee Passes 111

TEN
The Married Forties: Self-Help in a Time of Deceleration
and Transition 121

ELEVEN
More on the Married Forties—of Numbers, Exponents,
and the Future 135

TWELVE
The Single and the Forty—Good News and Bad News   141

THIRTEEN
The Fifties and Beyond   155

FOURTEEN
A Few Notes on Singles at Fifty   179

FIFTEEN
The Sixties and Seventies—Retirement Without Blinders—
and with a Smile   183

Conclusion   195

Appendix   199

Index   221

FOREWORD

William Shakespeare tells us that "one man in his time plays many parts, his acts being seven ages." Most of us will recognize, although few can recite, the seven parts from the mewling and puking infant to the second childishness, sans teeth, sans eyes, sans taste, sans everything. But Shakespeare, as far as I can see, draws no lesson from this observation, unless the lesson is that we should accept the several parts we play. Certainly he offers no advice about how to play the parts. But if we do only what comes naturally in each of the acts, there will surely be many anxieties and even crises.

We need advice—if we can get it. One of the subjects on which we need it most is the management of our financial affairs. Probably it is just as well that Shakespeare did not try to advise us on this. His best remembered bit of financial advice is "neither a borrower nor a lender be." That is bad advice, as this book shows.

My purpose in bringing up Shakespeare is not to claim that my favorite writer, the author of this book, Benjamin Stein, is a better writer than William Shakespeare. I am only pointing out that he deals with neglected implications of an important proposition. Good financial advice is not good for all seasons. What is good financial practice for a twenty-five-year-old is not good for a fifty-year-old. There is a corollary of this, which has become increasingly significant as life-styles have become more divergent. What is good for a couple in their thirties with two children is not best for a single childless woman.

One contribution of *Financial Passages* is that it gives suggestions for managing one's financial affairs that are tailored to the different acts of life, differentiated by age, sex, and family status. But there is another point at least as important. We go through these acts in a certain timing and sequence. The twenty-five-year-old will, in all probability, be thirty-five in ten years. The single man will in all probability become the married man and then, in a relatively short period, the father of young children and then the father of older children. We remain in each stage only briefly and then move on to another whose nature is rather foreseeable.

The key lessons, in which this book instructs us, are to adapt and to prepare. If it takes us ten years to learn how to live as a twenty-year-old, we are in trouble, or at least missing a lot. And if we live as twenty-year-olds without preparation for the fact that we will be thirty-year-olds, that will also be a great mistake. We will enter our thirties with the assets, liabilities, earning power, and consumption habits that we carried over from our twenties. This book provides not a set of separate guides for twenty-year-olds, thirty-year-olds, and so on, but a road map for twenty-year-olds who are soon going to be thirty-year-olds and then forty-year-olds and on to the end.

There are two turning points in our economic lives that almost everyone recognizes and for which almost everyone makes some preparations. These are death and retirement. Thanks to the ministrations of our eager life-insurance agent, we tend to acquire life insurance. Thanks to the paternalism of our government and our employers we almost all have some provision for our retirements. But even for death and retirement we cannot count on these provisions being right for our individual circumstances unless we individually invest some thought in the matter. And there will be many other changes in our economic circumstances to which we must adapt. There will be the costs of setting up a home, of educating children, of caring for parents, of meeting newly acquired tastes. All the changes will not be "problems." Some will be opportunities. Mainly the opportunities will come from the increase that an individual may expect in his or her income as he or she moves through the twenties and thirties. But they will also come, for example, with the reduction of basic living costs as children grow up and become self-supporting. Both the problems and the opportunities require adaptation and preparation.

For many years economists have been studying the ways in which people adapt their behavior and the ways in which they should rationally adapt their behavior, as they move through the phases of their life cycle. They have tried to take account of the changes in income levels, family status, and tastes in these successive phases. Particular attention has been paid to the important fact that incomes saved earn interest, so that people with equal lifetime earnings can have different lifetime consumption expenditures, depending on whether they consume early or late in life.

It is now possible to go beyond this theoretical analysis. Thanks to the efforts of many governmental statistical agencies, notably the Bureau of Labor Statistics, we know much more in quantitative terms than we used to about the economic stages of a typical person's life. We know how rapidly he can expect his income to rise as he gets older. (This information was presented and analyzed in the Annual Report of the Council of Economic Advisers for 1974, when I was chairman of the council.) We know how much of their income people of different ages and family positions spend on housing, automobiles, education, medical care, and so on. We know by how much (very little) living costs decline upon retirement.

Benjamin Stein mines and synthesizes this body of economics and statistics to provide us with guidance for the management of our financial affairs. He wisely does not pretend to offer a precise rule for every individual. No book can relieve us from considering our own circumstances and using our own judgment. But it is exceedingly helpful, indeed essential, to know as precisely as possible what opportunities and problems will be encountered in the world as we move through it, how other people deal with them, and what is prudent behavior in general.

This book is not a prescription for living on bread and cheese in an attic and leaving an estate of $10 million. It is a guide to enjoying the opportunities that this time and this country offer. Much attention is given to the avoidance of pitfalls. That is because the avoidance of pitfalls will have a large payoff in happiness achieved. *Financial Passages* can help you to achieve the happiness without being obsessed with the pitfalls.

HERBERT STEIN

FINANCIAL
PASSAGES

ONE

Understanding the Journey

Life is short. It is far too short and too precious to spend even one minute worrying about money at three o'clock in the morning. Even the most blameless lives can be ruined by wondering where the money will come from to pay for a set of braces or for the first year at Smith. The most noble soul can be cast down into a pit of anxiety and self-loathing by wondering how and from where the money to put on a new roof will come. Men and women who are kind to their children, loving to their dogs and cats, and unselfish with their time when friends are getting divorced still find that their peace of mind—the only really meaningful asset in this world—can be snatched away by an unexpected letter from the bank with the callously printed words *"Your account is overdrawn."* When perfectly fine people look back upon the last ten years of their lives, those ten years seem like a blur of falling leaves, gray afternoons before a fireplace, crowded trains and freeways, and—like a horrible scar cutting across it all, blotting out the blue sky—mornings and afternoons and nights of wondering where the money to pay for life's necessities or treats would come from.

That need not happen, which is, of course, what this book is about. Life should be for living and enjoying under those blue skies, not for worrying and sweating about money. Of course, in every life, there will be totally unexpected financial crises and windfalls that no amount of preparation could have prevented. An aunt will die and leave you her entire estate of one cottage in Thetford, Vermont. While you are fixing it up, you will fall into a well and have to spend one month in traction in the Thetford hospital. Your son will run over a prize miniature deer in his ATC on Christmas Eve at Lake Arrowhead, and you will have to take off from work for two weeks to beg the late deer's owner not to sue your son or press charges of cruelty to animals against him. Then your son will fall in love with the daughter of the deer's owner. The lucky couple will elope, and you will be able to spend the money you had been saving for a wedding on a trip to Cartagena. These things happen. The nature of life is to be unpredictable in all its small details and even in some of its large ones. No one can control all events.

But for most Americans, those nights of lying in bed hearing the neighbor's dog bark, while you wonder how you will tell your wife that her mother will have to move out of that good private nursing home into a miserable public hellhole, and all other bouts of terror about financial crises, are the result of poor planning or no planning. They should not happen and need not happen, which is also what this book is about.

The financial ups and downs of most Americans' lives are highly predictable, much like the phases of the moon or of the waistline. With some degree of understanding of what the future holds, both in kind (college educations, down payments on houses) and in amount (How much will they cost? How much do I have to start putting aside for them to have enough when the time comes?), the ordinary American family and individual can face the future with confidence. There will never be perfect confidence, because life is too complex. But with some understanding of the nature of life's financial crises and how they can be anticipated successfully and fairly painlessly, life will hold fewer terrors and far more peace of mind—at least in the financial area of the brain. That, too, is what this book is about.

For every American, life holds a series of financial crises just as surely as it holds a series of emotional crises. This is also just as certain as that there will be warmer weather in August than in February. All of the events—financial, emotional, and meteorological—can be prepared for. Preparation for weather is ancient and commonplace. Few grown people go outside in Boston in March in shorts and a T-shirt. Even in Los Angeles, people know they should put up their convertible tops when rain threatens. By now, men and women are aware that they ought to prepare for their predictable emotional crises as well. The loving wife can sense when her husband is going through mid-life crisis and tries to smooth the passage. The caring husband sees the pain when the wife starts to notice a few more crow's feet after Junior leaves for college. But preparation for the predictable financial crises of modern life is still astonishingly crude. This is wrong because it wastes the human spirit.

Most Americans still try to put something aside for a rainy day. But few of them have an accurate idea of just when that rainy day will occur or how much rain will fall—despite a wealth of data compiled over decades telling precisely what most families and individuals can expect in the way of rain and umbrellas. Most Americans know that if their children want to go to college, it will be expensive and that some provision should be made for the event in terms of saving or borrowing. But almost no one has a clear idea of just how much college will cost at different kinds of institutions, at different times in the future, despite a mountain of information on that subject for the past, the present, and the future. More sadly, almost no one has any very good idea of what amount of money, put away at what rate of interest, will be necessary for Junior to be able to pay his first tuition bill at State or Stanford. Yet there is also a great pile of material on that very subject. What a waste that the people who need the information and the information hardly ever meet. And that too is what this book is about.

Most couples starting out in wedded life have the idea that they would like someday to hear the patter of little feet around the house. Those same couples also know that raising children is not free. But they have only a vague idea as to how much the bassinet and diapers (or Pampers) will cost or, as time passes, how much car and college will cost. They remain unaware of the actual cost of raising a child despite the warehouses filled with data on how much it costs to raise a child at different economic circumstances, in different size families, and in varying regions of the nation.

Most people in good health anticipate that they would some day like to retire. They know it will take a certain sum of money to afford a vacation home and the membership in the country club. They also know that it is foolish of them to count on Social Security. But they have no more precise idea than that of what retirement will cost under varying circumstances or how much they need to put aside so that the golden years will not be leaden and fearful. Yet, again, the statisticians and sociologists of America have been tireless in figuring out exactly those facts.

The sad fact is that the overwhelming majority of Americans know that certain financially meaningful events lie in store for them, but have only a hazy idea of just what those events will cost. In view of how much information is available on just that subject, such lack of awareness is tragic. It does not have to happen. It can be avoided, and should be avoided, by learning about when the inevitable financial crises will come along and how much they will cost. To stay away from that kind of helpful information is very much like leaving an umbrella in the hall closet after hearing a forecast of continued rain. I wouldn't do it and you wouldn't do it, so let's not do it.

Think of this book as a convenient, accessible weather report telling you what to expect in the way of heavy financial weather over the course of a lifetime. Use it to know when to put up that old bumbershoot.

There will also be sunny financial days and years, and those too can be anticipated. Just as it can be clearly foretold that at certain times in a lifetime, there will be spells of crisis, periods of personal financial boom can also be sighted in advance. For most Americans, there will be years when money comes pouring in, expenses are low, and even the Nakamichi stereo, even the Jensen sports car with five-speed manual transmission suddenly look affordable. For most Americans, either families or singles, there will be periods when income rises magically, gracefully, euphorically, seeming to offer a lifelong escape from those years of pinching pennies.

For most Americans, those epochs seem to be either once in a lifetime freaks or the harbinger of astronomically rising income for the rest of recorded time. The paychecks grow fatter, and the trips to Europe or to the jewelry store or to summer homes become more frequent. Spending rapidly rises to meet expenditure, and the looming years of the locust are forgotten in a blizzard of charge receipts. Most people make no systematic effort to relate those good years of high earnings to days when paychecks will be small refuge against avalanches of expenses. For most families, little or nothing is done to make certain that the fat years are used as hedges against the lean years that will inevitably follow. The days of wine and roses are treated by a great many intelligent people as if they had no relation to any time that will come after them. The good times come and go and for most people make no contribution to the lasting peace of mind that they could shore up so mightily.

It is as if a day of warm weather in Minneapolis made everyone throw away his overcoat and snowshoes. Sensible people would never be so foolhardy as to expect that good weather would last forever. But grown, educated people fail to make any connection at all between the highly predictable needs of the future and the highly predictable valleys of earnings. It is not those people's fault, because they generally do not know that those needs or resources can be predicted. Nevertheless, failure makes for too many Valium prescriptions and cases of high blood pressure. The ordinary citizen can and should match up his earning and his spending over a lifetime to get the least possible money worry from life. Alas, too few ever do it, mostly because they simply do not know that it can be done.

Yet the raw materials are at hand. Economists and statisticians can predict—basing their forecasts on decades of observation—what the financial peaks for earnings will be for most Americans. They know very well what periods of a lifetime will see rapidly rising earnings and what years will see flat or even declining earnings. Knowledge about the earnings "function" over a lifetime can be counted by the ton in academic libraries, just like information about spending on various highly predictable needs.

Economists know all about consumption functions over a lifetime. The tragedy is that the ordinary middle-class citizen and his or her family do not know it. If the ordinary middle-class American could do what economists do—stay aware of the lifetime earnings function and the lifetime consumption function (as the economists call them)—the ordinary middle-class American would have taken a giant step toward true financial security and mental serenity.

That is what this book is about, too: helping the ordinary middle-class citizen to take that giant step.

The American salaried worker has an opportunity to improve his or her life dramatically by making use of what economic scientists have found out about lifetime earnings and lifetime expenditures. It is just as accessible and just as available for use as medical information that eating too much saturated fat is harmful or that smoking cigarettes is often hazardous. The problem up to now has been that this economic information has not been adequately publicized. News of the latest medical findings on cigarette smoke can be heard on television or read about in newspapers and magazines daily. But economists' findings on the average middle-class American's expected increase in income throughout his lifetime do not receive nearly as much exposure.

And, even more annoying than that, while the past ten years have seen a successful effort made to explain up-to-the-minute medical research in laymen's terms, no such effort has been made toward economic journalism. Statistics on tar and nicotine content are printed right on the packages. Yet one is hard pressed to find vital economic and financial statistics compiled in a comprehensive guide for the American public. That, too, is what this book is about.

If the American family or individual can take the scientific data that has been accumulated on how to maintain economic health—much of the data admittedly stashed away in boring research journals—the American family can make just as good use of that data as if the family learned how to eat properly or exercise regularly.

Think of this book as a plan for economic health, something like a medical text for your own family or individual economy, and you will understand what it is about.

The basic principles are quite simple and straightforward. To match up your lifetime earnings with your lifetime expenditures is no different in theory from matching up your monthly income with your monthly expenditures. In this instance, we are simply taking a much longer time horizon. Instead of trying to match up one month of spending on rent and meals and gasoline and baby-sitting and cosmetics and clothing and shoes and telephone with one month's paychecks, we are doing something far more ambitious—but no less possible: matching up a lifetime's probable spending on a house, college educations, trips to Europe, major surgery, automobiles, and retirement with a lifetime's earnings from hard labor on the job, investments, and interest income.

To do that we need a road map of what the usual expenditures are for middle-class Americans and a survival guide for what the years will bring in the way of income. You also need to know one crucial additional concept—that certain sums of money, put at interest for certain periods of time, yield certain sums at different rates of interest. The lucky fact that in our society families and individuals can put money aside and have that money grow to certain heights without further tending is one of the key bridges over troubled waters in matching up the earnings function with the spending function. The other key pontoon is something that makes a great many people queasy—borrowing.

The queasiness that comes with the thought of borrowing is a basic flaw in our economy. For a great many law-abiding citizens, the thought of going into a bank, sitting down, and asking for a loan, which may be turned down, is enough to ruin a perfect day. However, getting loans is a basic part of modern economic life for all large and small businesses. It must and should be a part of the life of the individual who wants to harmonize his economic condition with his natural desire for peace and serenity. There is absolutely no alternative to occasional borrowing. Borrowing is an essential tool for economic wellness in this world. Once you get used to it, you will take to it with perfect calm, seeing it rightly as no different from using a credit card. Borrowing is not the path to perdition, nor is it a way to lose your reputation and your worldly goods in an orgy of uncontrollable indebtedness. That is a medieval fairy tale. Borrowing is a sensible and appropriate tool of economic survival. It is just as necessary and appropriate as saving. Properly used, it can add confidence and security to your economic life and become indispensable for making your life work properly in the financial sphere.

The four parts of getting your financial life's crises ironed out are no more than having (1) an idea of how much predictable events will cost, (2) some notion of how much you are likely to earn at different stages of your life, (3) a basic knowledge of how much money to save and when, (4) some grasp of when and how much to borrow. Even more briefly, let's say that the book will try to tell you how much things will cost and how you can arrange to pay for them. Think of it as a user's manual for your economic life, and you have an even clearer idea of the purpose.

Now, before beginning to chart the path of life earnings and expenditures in the youthful decade between age twenty and age twenty-nine, a few cautions are in order.

First, the road map to New York City from Boston is also useful for getting to Yonkers. By that, we mean that if and when you see something in this economic guidebook that strikes you as not exactly, precisely on target for your life, bear in mind that it still may have some value. For example, if you are a divorcee with two children and you are planning to send them to college without the help of your no-good former husband, solely on your income plus whatever can be borrowed or saved, and if the book's example of a college education involves a husband and wife sending their children to college, you should on no account think that irrelevant to you. The same calculation a *couple* uses about how much to put aside to yield the needed money by the first week of college registration is absolutely vital for the divorcee and the widow. If you need to make a slight adjustment up or down for your personal circumstances, do so, just as if you were thirsty and had to drink Canada Dry instead of Perrier. It is not possible to include every possible personal situation in this book. What we can do is give a range of situations, how to cope with each, and then you, the reader, can adjust the example to correspond to your particular life.

Again, for example, if you see that a man and woman in their mid-twenties should be saving a certain sum each year to put down on a house, and if you already have inherited a house, do not think that frees you from any obligation to make further financial plans. Take the money you have saved and put it to work for the other financial needs and crises that will inevitably arise, just as you would make the best of it if you were moved from a coach to a first-class seat by sheer accident. Use your imagination to see how each particular financial stratagem applies in your own life. This book is a guide, but not a drill sergeant. Have fun with it. The free play of imagination and adaptation is what saves us from being computer chips and puts the finishing touches to each one of our financial salvations and our personalities. Your under-standing and imagination *plus* the weight of financial information avail-able to you here will carry the day.

Next, money is counted with numbers. We do not see a pile of money and say how good it smells. (Well, most people don't. . . .) Nor do we see a bill for a semester's room and board and remark on the texture of the paper. We talk about how *much* things cost. As for calculating how to wring peace of mind out of life's predictable financial crises, the watchword is not *how* but *how many*.

That means some numbers will be involved. For most readers, this will not be a problem. But for anyone who is worried about complex computations involving regressions and multivariate analyses, stop wor-rying. The calculations here have already been done. You only have to read the results. Persons far smarter than you or I have done the tables in the back and the complex charting of waves of income ebb and flow. We need only enjoy the fruits of their labor. It is not necessary for you to understand how a stereo works to enjoy a Tchaikovsky recording. By the same token, you do not need to know mathematical statistics to understand how much you will need for the third child you may be planning to have. You paid for the book, and the basic calculations have already been done for you.

Finally, the game plan in this book involves a modest degree of discipline. Obviously, if you are completely and psychopathically unable to do anything with your money except spend it the minute you get paid, you may have a problem. But for most people, the change will be slight. Most people already know that they will have to save something for the contingencies of life. They simply do not know when and how much. That is what this book is for. You will be told what changes to make in your life-style long enough in advance so that you need fear no hairpin turns and no sudden death stops. Nothing in this book requires days of eating gruel, taking in laundry, or selling your wife's hair.

This book's purpose is *precisely* to ensure that you do not have any nasty surprises, jagged bouts of money anxiety, and days of miserable scrimping.

As you begin your cruise through this book, you may find that the whole idea of really taking charge of your financial life is frightening. After all, money is a frightening subject and so is life. But when that feeling comes over you, bear in mind this true story. Once there was a man who was learning to fly airplanes from aircraft carriers. After long training, he had to make his first solo night landing on a carrier deck. As he approached the deck, he panicked. The deck looked so small, pitching and rolling in the cold water. "I thought, 'I'll never do it,' " the man told me. "Then, I saw that the man in front of me had just done it. I had always thought that he was an idiot. I figured that if he could do it, I could do it, and I did."

Many people much stupider than you or I have taken financial charge of their lives, ironing out the predictable crises of financial life. They had the right data, and now we do too. If they can do it, so can we.

TWO

The Roaring Twenties—
Lift-off Time

Productivity and You

Imagine a dramatic ski slope above Aspen. Imagine that you can turn that ski slope upside down, so that it angles sharply upward at a slope which would be steep even for Jean-Claude Killy. That sharply angled slope represents something very good in most young people's lives. It is the curve explaining all that statisticians have learned about how real income moves in the first nine years after a young man or woman enters the labor force. Except for one other period, that first nine years will show the most exuberant upward movement in a lifetime of real earnings.

If you understand why income rises so dramatically in the first years of a career, you can understand why it is so important to seize upon those blessed years as the launch pad for a financially secure tomorrow. Of course, getting your act together in the first nine years of work is not indispensable, just as being born as a Rockefeller is not indispensable. But in both cases, the money will come in handy. In fact, if you act upon how to treat the first nine years of work financially, you will find that, in effect, you have given yourself a trust fund to draw upon for the rest of your life.

But first, it is helpful to see why your income generally rises so marvelously after you first enter the labor force.

Try to think of yourself as an employer. You own the Pygmy Athletic Shoe Company. You have an office where you handle the incoming orders for athletic shoes before the orders are sent to the factory. Along comes Jane Q. Colgrad, a recent graduate of the local junior college, Franklin Pierce J.C. Jane is a personable, intelligent woman of twenty-one. She is eager and willing to work hard.

Unfortunately, she knows nothing about the athletic shoe business. Nor does she know anything about how to file or how to keep accounts for your particular business. She does not know how to use your elegant new Monroe office computer. Nor does she know the names and idiosyncrasies of your salesmen and their customers. However, she is eager and willing to learn.

In her first year at the office, she makes a great many mistakes. She files the orders from Dayton in the drawer for Des Moines. She forgets to send checks to the bank the very minute they come in, thereby losing interest. She forgets that a certain salesman needs to have a certain kind of rental car when he travels the territory around Palm Springs. But little by little, she learns. In fact, the athletic shoe business is not really that complicated when you get down to it. A smart woman like Jane Q. Colgrad can pick it up at a basic level within two years. By the third year, she knows the name of every salesman's wife. She knows where to go to get a super buy on a new, even more efficient office computer. She has even figured out a way to process the checks so that they are credited to a money market fund before they are physically in the office. She becomes a key part of the enterprise. You, her employer, realize that she is vital to the successful running of the office and that Pygmy would be in deep trouble if she left.

Whatever you started paying her at the beginning is nowhere near enough any longer. By the end of the first year, she has had an intense course in the athletic shoe business. In particular, she has had a crash course in the Pygmy Athletic Shoe business, which makes her worth quite a lot. So you give her a good raise. Then, after the second year, she knows the business better than all but a few Pygmy veterans. You begin to get scared that Jane Q. Colgrad could leave and take her skills with her to the Watusi Athletic Shoe Company across town. You give her a really excellent raise after that, just to keep her heart in the right place. By the end of the third year, Florence, the office manager who has been with you since you started Pygmy, has retired to collect butterflies in Montreux. Jane has taken her place. If she left now and you had to train someone else, the sales office would be chaotic for one year. Now you give her a truly huge increase in pay.

After the fourth year, she meets a man at Shaughnessey's Bar and Grill. It so happens that the man is the founder of a new athletic shoe company, Maori Shoes. When he talks to Jane Q. Colgrad, he realizes that she knows the business the way a dog knows sleeping. He offers her a management level position at Maori. Jane Q. Colgrad comes to you and says that she is sorry, because she really loves the Pygmy people, but she would not be fair to herself if she did not take a management level position at Maori. Your heart sinks. You tell her that Maori is a flimsy operation. She might be making the mistake of her life if she left Pygmy. Whoever heard of Maori? Pygmy is an old established organization. She would make a great mistake if she did not stay. Besides, how much is Maori offering her? Pygmy has had a good year and might just be able to meet the offer. Jane Q. Colgrad walks out of the office with a management level position at Pygmy and a fat pay increase.

This is an *idealized* schematic of how life works. To be sure, there are bosses who will tell you to get lost if you tell them you are going to a rival. There are also bosses who are so ignorant of the workings of business that they will not pay anything extra for your fine work and your accretion of skill and knowledge. And there are businesses that are suffering so badly from recessions or foreign competition or bad management that they simply cannot afford to pay a sizable wage increase or any at all. But by and large, as the young worker starts at a position, gains skill and knowledge of how the business works, and makes himself or herself more valuable to employers, his or her pay rises dramatically. Since most businesses are not terribly complicated, most of what needs to be learned can be learned fairly quickly. The employee's increase in skill and knowledge can be translated into increases in productivity extremely quickly, generally within a matter of months and years. As productivity rises, employers will pay more, and once again, that is because the employee is worth more.

The curve of increased learning and skill tilts very sharply upward in the first years of work and so does the curve of increased production. That is the way an economist would look at it. To you and me, this means simply that pay increases very rapidly as you learn the ropes and become worth far more to your employer.

In numbers, pay increases at a rate of about 8 percent a year for both blue- and white-collar employees and has continued to increase at roughly the same rate for twenty-to-twenty-nine-year-olds for almost fifty years. The rate of 8 percent does not include inflation, which lifts the nominal rate still further.

Of course, for some workers, the rate of pay increase will be faster than 8 percent per year. For others it will be slower. But as an average number, compiled over decades by statisticians, 8 percent is right on target. Again, remember that the 8 percent number comes about as the result of extraordinary increases in skill and knowledge and productivity during the first years in the large and not at all exclusive group called the labor force.

Eight percent each year may not seem like a great deal in an age when certificates of deposit often offer 13 percent. But in fact, real wage increases of 8 percent, after inflation (or on top of inflation, as one might say) are genuinely staggering. If you imagine that your first job out of school at age twenty-one paid $15,000 per year to start (which is near the average for college graduates in 1983), you could see a pleasing chart of income growth from age twenty-one until age thirty. If you look at the growth in terms of real, constant dollars, the numbers are impressive. If you imagine a rate of inflation of 7 percent and then add the growth of your real wages on top of that, your increase in nominal pay is phenomenal.

Age	Income in Constant Dollars (inflation-adjusted)	Income in Current Dollars (including inflation)
21	$15,000	$15,000
22	$16,200	$17,250
23	$17,496	$19,838
24	$18,896	$22,813
25	$20,407	$26,235
26	$22,040	$30,170
27	$23,803	$34,696
28	$25,707	$39,900
29	$27,764	$45,885
30	$29,985	$52,768

Not bad for a beginner. The column on the far right looks impressive indeed, but remember that if inflation goes on for nine years at the rate of 7 percent, by the end of those nine years, a Big Mac will cost about

$2.50 and a gallon of gasoline will cost a minimum of $3.00. The figure to keep your eye on is the number for inflation-adjusted income. It tells you that your income will approximately double in the first nine years of your participation in the labor force. Since the dollars are inflation-adjusted, they also mean that your standard of living will double. For most young Americans, then, real income will approximately double by the time they have blown out the candles on their thirtieth birthday cake. Again, this does not happen by magic, but only because your skill and productivity at your job increases.

Happy Days

Now for the expenditure side. Of course, expenditures can and will vary wildly from person to person in this large country. Some workers will live at home with Mom and Dad for several years after they begin work. Those people may well take the bus to work, brown bag it for lunch, and go on vacation with Mom and Dad at the old shack at the beach or not go at all. For those persons, expenditures will rise only slowly above what they were when the worker was in school.

Then there will be other workers who will take the first paycheck and get an apartment in the Rittenhouse Square area. With the second paycheck, they will buy a complete set of modular furniture at a futuristic store they have seen advertised on late night television. With the third paycheck they will buy a black-on-black Corvette. Paycheck number four goes for an airplane ticket to Hawaii. All of these goodies are bought on time, of course. For those persons, expenditures will shoot up dramatically and indeed hopelessly.

But for the ordinary citizen entering a career of toil, a middle course will be taken. There will be expenditures for one's own or shared dwelling, usually for a car (often used), and for a very substantial increase in the stock of clothing. There will be a large increase in the cost of "food eaten away from home," as statisticians call restaurant meals. There will also be a noticeable increase in the cost of vacations.

For all too many persons, those increases will exceed even the very significant rates of increase for income in the first nine years of work. Obviously, if a worker begins by spending 100 percent of his or her income on clothes, cosmetics, an apartment, ski trips, and a sports car, and if those expenses rise by an inflation adjusted 9 percent per year, then the worker will be in a state of constant deficit financing. This may be all right for a government, but it puts a tremendous strain upon a human being. On the other hand, if a worker can restrain his expenditures so that they rise less rapidly than his income, he will soon see savings and security for other, more pressing times.

This does not mean that there is no place for borrowing during the early years of work. There definitely is a sensible time and place for borrowing, but before that time arrives, it would be helpful to take some stock of what the results would be if you, the worker, had a real wage increase of 8 percent per year and were able to keep your spending increase to only 4 percent per year adjusted for inflation. Notice the amount of savings and how it grows as it is compounded by the interest it earns. Again, for the purpose of this example, imagine that a worker begins his work career at age twenty-one with an income of $15,000 per year.

(The following chart is for purposes of example only. If a worker or his family or her family begin a lifetime financial planning program after the first years of work, it is entirely possible to establish fiscal peace of mind in the home. Do not kick yourself if you are thirty-eight and wish you had started this program when you were twenty-one. There will be other opportunities.)

On Your Mark, Get Set . . .

Age	Real Income rising 9% per year	Real Expenses rising 7% per year	Savings per year	Cumulative Savings at 11% interest*
21	$15,000	$15,000	—	—
22	$16,200	$15,600	$600	$600
23	$17,496	$16,224	$1,272	$1,938
24	$18,896	$16,873	$2,023	$4,174
25	$20,407	$17,548	$2,859	$7,492
26	$22,040	$18,250	$3,790	$12,106
27	$23,803	$18,980	$4,823	$18,261
28	$25,707	$19,739	$5,968	$26,238
29	$27,764	$20,529	$7,235	$36,359
30	$29,985	$21,350	$8,635	$40,358

* Here and following, interest rates are for example only. In your experience, you may not have the benefit of such high interest rates unless there is some inflation or expectation of inflation.

Once again, not bad for a beginner. Remember that those figures are adjusted for inflation and that in a time of 7 or 8 percent inflation, the dollar figures would be more than twice as large by the end of the ninth year (although the amount of buying power would not be different—that is what adjusting for inflation means). By managing to restrain buying by only a small amount, allowing it to rise but not as fast as income, genuinely impressive results can be achieved. Of course, one cannot count on 11 percent interest, but even without *any* interest, the total savings for those years would be over $37,000 in inflation-adjusted dollars.

Averages and the Law of You

But before you rush out and begin to save your pennies and yell at your wife (or husband) for spending too much money, remember that there is a joker in the deck for the unwary. *It is not easy to restrain your spending while your income rises.* A great many Americans have tried to do it. A much smaller number succeed. The temptation to spend every cent you earn and more is enormous. There are a great many Honda motorcycles, Pan Am flights to Europe, Barcalounger chairs, and Gloria Vanderbilt jeans out there, millions of advertisers using their wiles to persuade you to spend, and very few people grasping your shoulder and telling you to be careful to keep your spending to only a 4 percent increase each year.

To get some rough idea of how you might succeed at that kind of self-restraint, it is important to have some idea of what you should be spending your hard-earned money on. That way, you can know if you are overspending on some things that might be controlled—or underspending on some items where you might indulge yourself further.

(A note of caution: Personal spending decisions are extremely personal. The totals are what count, not whether you had steak one night instead of hamburger. But within those homilies, it is still useful to know how families in the twenty-one-to-thirty-year-old age bracket spend their money. It is especially interesting to know how families spend their money if those families are able to save money. If you are slightly apart from those figures, it hardly matters. But if you are vastly overspending the norm on one or another category, that means to beware.

(As a general rule, families or individuals in which the head of the household was under twenty-five were unable to save at all. But for those who did save, there was a consistent pattern of careful restraint in the general areas of transportation, recreation and vacations, and house furnishings. In other words, the young families that lived without the Winnebago, the ATC, and the top of the line Henredon bedroom suite tended to be able to save. But these are highly individual decisions, and some families who substituted Hamburger Helper for salmon filets also came out well.)

After decades of study, economists and statisticians have found that in general, the following percentages of total family expenditures went for the following goods and services. As you can see, there are major differences in spending, depending upon whether the family head was twenty-one-to-twenty-five or twenty-six-to-thirty.

For Families in Their Twenties—
Percentage of Total Consumption Expenses After Taxes
(not including savings except for pension and insurance)

	Age 21–25	Age 26–30
Food—total	16	18
Food at home	10	13
Food away from home	6	5
Alcohol and tobacco	3	3
Housing (rented or owned)—total	34	34
Utilities	3	4
Telephone and other household operations	4	6
Home furnishings and appliances	5	5
Rent or mortgage and property taxes	22	19
Clothing	6	7
Transportation (including auto purchase)	24	19
Health care	4	5
Recreation (including vacation and recreational equipment)	6	7
Insurance and pension contributions	7	8

(Totals here and subsequently may not be 100 percent because of rounding.)

The typical family headed by a person twenty-five or younger was in debt by an amount equal to about 6 percent of its yearly income by the time the head of the household reached twenty-five. The family that had reached thirty was, on the average, able to save a total of about 30 percent of one year's income in all of that time. Again, these figures are for general guidance only, but if your household budget diverges from these numbers by a huge amount, there may be a problem. Read on.

There is something going on here in the category of automobile expenses that is dramatic and important for the young family to understand. While there is great similarity in that expense in the same age groups, there is a sharp drop as the family grows slightly older. That drop in relative spending is what enables the family to save. Statisticians have found that if a family merely increases its spending on automobiles slightly, but does not go hog wild, the family can make its first breakthrough into savings. That means that when the breadwinner comes home with a fat pay increase, the family does not all run down to the Cadillac dealer to get a new Coupe de Ville. Instead, they buy a higher quality Chevrolet or a used car. Sometimes, if the family car can take it, the family sticks with the old Ford for a few years longer than would be prestigious.

Automobiles—and automobile owners—lose a large sum in the first year after buying a new car because of depreciation as the car shifts from being new to being used. If that depreciation loss can be forestalled for a few years, the savings to the family will be worthwhile indeed.

A potential savings is also "concealed" within the overall statistic about recreational expenses. The "older" family (twenty-five-to-thirty) spent a large part of its total recreation dollar on buying vacation property or a second home or boat or something with resale value. In a word, that meant not all the money spent on "recreation" was completely gone after it was spent. This also added to the savings of the families between twenty-five and thirty.

Finally, the fact that spending on furniture and other household expenses did not increase over time more than income increased was also a lifesaver. The temptation to buy drastically better sofas, ottomans, wallpapers, and loveseats is strong when one's paycheck rises. If one can defer that joy of having really expensive furniture for another two decades (if not forever), one can reap the benefits of peace of mind instead of giant furniture bills.

Keeping the Lid On

In fact if you are searching for the key difference between families that were able to save and those that did not, it would be that *the saving families were able to do without most large vanity and prestige items.* Cars, furniture, and recreation expenses, the items which allow young people to display their wealth and their prestige, are also the items that can wreck the possibility of savings.

Many people consider extravagance a sin. But morality has nothing to do with economics. If a family or an individual can save during the period of the first decade of work, that is the key, not almanac clichés about pennies saved and earned. If the family or individual can save while driving a Rolls convertible, the family should by all means keep driving what they have been driving. If the family can save while spending two months each year in Europe, more power to them.

The trick is to manage your affairs so that you can save during the vital decade when income is rising very dramatically. The twenties offer an opportunity too precious to be blown by having to show the neighbors that you can afford a four-wheel-drive vehicle and an Advent. Try to put aside all the excuses for buying yourself into permanent indebtedness. (My particular favorite lie is "In the long run it costs less to buy the best." Who says?) Then you can build the foundation you need and must have for two giant superexpenses that will come up toward the end of the decade of the twenties if you are planning to buy a home and have children.

Before we get to children and mortgages though, let's take a look at what situations call for borrowing even in the decade when savings should be possible.

How Not to Borrow Trouble

First of all, any short-term borrowings that can be arranged so that the proceeds are used for something *necessary and so that repayment can be accomplished quickly* make sense. For example, a young man or woman in his or her first apartment should not be expected to sleep on a sleeping bag. He or she should not expect to entertain guests on beanbag chairs. In a society like the United States, under ordinary circumstances, the young member of the labor force should have furniture.

It need not be from Herman Miller. But it should be sturdy, serviceable stuff. Very few persons can afford to pay for their new bed or couch out of their first paycheck. Yet, the need for furniture cannot wait until you have saved enough to pay for it. In that situation, it makes perfect sense to borrow for the furnishings necessary to fill up your apartment or house. As long as the expenses for furniture and appliances—including paying off the loans for the Frigidaire and the Sony—are kept to about 5 percent of net income, the budget ain't busted, and plans for saving can go along in an orderly way. Again, if you can save far more on some other category, you can let your furniture expense rise accordingly.

By the same token, only the cruelest skinflint would deny that the best time for travel is when the traveler is young. But few new families can pay for a trip to the Bahamas out of current income. In that case, the necessity for short-term borrowing is obvious. Both travel and furniture can usually be paid for with credit cards, often the fastest and most efficient way to borrow. In other cases, stores or travel agencies will arrange loans. But no matter what the source of borrowing is, the sum of all travel payments (including loan) should not be more than 6 or 7 percent of net income—unless you know you will be able to save very substantially on some other categories of expense.

It may be that you will need to go into a bank at some point in your young life to borrow for furniture or for a vacation or even for a home (q.v.). There are a few simple principles that should govern your conduct in asking for a loan. First, remember that most bank lending officers are just people like you. They want very much to get through the day without any unnecessary aggravation. If their job is to make loans, they want to follow the bank guidelines and not get themselves in trouble. They have no feelings about you personally. Do not confuse them with your uncle or your best friend. They will absolutely *not* lend to you because they like your face or your smile. They will lend to you if you meet their criteria. If you do not meet their criteria, they will not lend to you, pure and simple.

Put yourself in the loan officer's place. Would you grant yourself a loan *if* you might lose your job should the loan go sour? Try to find out what the bank's specifications are for getting the loan in question, and then try to put yourself in the position of meeting those specs. Remember, banks live and die by making loans. They do not want to turn down a loan application. Your assumption—upon entering the lending department—is that you are there to do something that will be mutually beneficial. The bank will make money from its loan to you. You will use the money profitably. The general idea is to work with the bank in a joint venture to get the loan. The loan application process should not be a confrontation or an opportunity for you to ventilate your grievances against capitalism. It is more like trying to make friends with someone who can—and wants to—help you.

Lenders generally base their decision about you and your loan on what is still called the three C's: collateral, creditworthiness, and character. Sad to say, in this mass society, character is usually unknown to your banker. By the same token, when you are starting out in adult life, your collateral is likely to be nil. But you still can and should show creditworthiness—the ability to repay the loan.

The bank wants to see—as a general rule—that you can lump all of your installment debt together and that it will still not exceed 25 percent of your pretax income. (This does not include mortgage debt.) If you are not going to be able to show that, you should have a good explanation of why not. When you fill out your forms, you should try to arrange the data, ahem, ahem, so that you seem to be able to meet that 25 percent rule.

(This does not mean fudging the papers. It does mean that you should be alert to what is considered the margin of safety for repaying loans—for your sake and the bank's.)

When you are shopping for a loan, do not make the easy mistake of thinking that all loans are equal. Loans can cost wildly different amounts of interest and origination fees. For example, at this writing, three banks here in Los Angeles are offering auto loans that claim to be the lowest in town. Despite that claim, their rates range from 11½ percent to 18 percent. The difference over a four-year loan on a new car can be in the tens of thousands of dollars! Momma told you to shop around, and it was good advice. Banks can and do compete on loan rates. It is often the best paid hour of your life to call around to various banks to find out just exactly where you can get the best deal.

In that vein, banks should always be the first place to look for a loan. Their rates are almost always lower than rates at finance companies. Their rates are always lower than rates at the furniture store or the appliance center.

You are, in your twenties, in a period of high income growth, but growth from a low base. You owe it to yourself to burden yourself with the smallest possible interest payments, so that you can have the widest possible gap between what you earn and what you spend. In turn, this will give you the maximum savings with which to meet the well foreseen financial pitfalls coming down the pike of life.

Shop around for loans. This is essential. Do your shopping in a cooperative and self-helpful way, but do shop around.

Triumphs and Tragedies

This principle goes back to the basics of the lifetime plan for harmonizing the earnings function and the consumption function.

1. It is fine to borrow as long as you borrow for something useful and necessary at a sensible price.

2. Within that free and easy guideline, it is crucial to keep total expenses at the correct level over a period of years.

3. Unless there is a sensible and well-thought-out relation between income and expenses, one which yields a financial cushion, all of the hopes in the world will not tide you over the rough waters that lie ahead for almost all individuals and families as they progress through life.

In terms of the first years in the labor force, this means keeping track of your expenses and making certain that they lag your income by a small but growing amount each year.

Look at it with examples to see how all of this translates into real life. The Millers and the Grahams are two young, childless couples. Both Harvey Miller and Edward Graham are twenty-nine-year-old sales reps for an established electronics manufacturer in San Jose. They are earning exactly the same amount, $29,900 per year. Their wives, Elaine and Lydia, are receptionists at different doctors' offices, and also earn the same amount as each other, $17,000 per year. It is here that the similarities end, however. Right now, the Millers have savings of $16,000, two cars (one new and the other four years old), a lovely apartment, and a down payment on a cozy little condominium in Lake Tahoe. They are in excellent financial shape, with enough savings to afford having a child without severe anxiety, as well as the security of investing in property which (1) could possibly increase in value, (2) can be a source of added income (if leased or rented), and (3) will provide them with enjoyable, lower cost, and more frequent vacations.

The Grahams however are in deep and serious financial trouble. Heavily into debt, Ed Graham has been forced to sell the brand new Porsche 944 he recently bought his wife, at a great loss. He has also had to borrow money from a high interest finance company, since the bank classified him a risk and refused to grant him a loan (because the Grahams' ratio of indebtedness to income is beyond the bank's lending limits). Absolutely nothing he owns is actually paid for. To keep up his life-style, each paycheck immediately goes to pay outstanding bills. Unable to save a dollar, the Grahams are facing what seems like a hopeless financial future.

How is it that the Millers have succeeded where the Grahams have failed? Simply because the Millers paid attention to what the proper balance is between savings and spending. The Grahams acted as if there were almost no relation between what they earned and what they spent. If we examine both families' expenditures in different areas and tally up the results, we will see how the Millers were able to save money without undergoing any real hardships or deprivation, by following a plan of restraint, saving, and borrowing intelligently. Instead of buying two new cars right away when they began work, the Millers waited several years and instead drove old VW Rabbits. They saved the money they would have spent on the cars. These savings were what enabled them to afford the down payment on their condominium.

For their first vacation before buying the condominium, the Millers saved up two years' worth of vacation time and took one long trip, a cross-country road trip to New Orleans. They could explore unique antebellum mansions throughout the country, leisurely and at much less expense than an organized overseas excursion. It was the kind of vacation well suited to their youth and sense of adventure, as well as to their sense of self-restraint.

The unfortunate Graham family never took time to plan a financial strategy. They viewed each paycheck as a gift, to be spent on whatever they wanted. Ed knew that Lydia had dreamed of going to France for their honeymoon, but at the time it was completely unaffordable. But as soon as he had worked long enough to earn two weeks' vacation, he rushed out and bought two tickets to Paris. Lydia gained seven pounds and all of their luggage was rerouted to Brussels, but all in all the trip was wonderful if you ignore its cost.

Ed wanted a sports car, not an old clunker. So he traded in his old car and his wife's (the two of them were worth one third the price of the new Jaguar) and bought a brand new Jag, which Lydia drove to work during the week, and he used on the weekends. It was inconvenient when Lydia broke her ankle and couldn't drive the new car because it had a five-speed manual transmission. But Ed sure did love the way the XJ6C looked, parked in front of their apartment building.

With these two expenses alone the Grahams had already spent about half their first year's after-tax income, except that the Grahams' purchases were still mounting. Suffice it to say that Ed and Lydia also invested quite a bit in furniture from Roche Bobois, an expensive new Hitachi stereo, and a JVC home video recorder. They hadn't saved to pay for anything, but instead made small initial payments on each item. Thus, each month brought in a slew of ever-increasing bills, while the size of their paychecks increased at a much slower rate. In a word, the Grahams' spending began and remained out of control. It bore no relation to their income.

The really amazing part was that, for such a long time, the Grahams managed to continue to sever the connection between what they earned and what they spent. In itself, their ability to obtain loans for the VCR, the Porsche, the second and third trips to Europe, is a testament to their ingenuity. *Unfortunately, the ingenuity was mercilessly directed against themselves.* By their craftiness, they managed to dig themselves into a hole of debt and interest payments which is by now well above their heads. To get out will require almost superhuman effort. To have stayed out in the first place would have required only a modest effort. The Millers made that effort, and the result will give them shelter for the rest of their lives. It is a simple lesson, but no less important for its simplicity.

To return from the world of the Millers and Grahams to our world, the exact amount of savings that should have accumulated by the age of thirty will vary from family to family and from individual to individual. The family who plan to have several children and a home big enough to house them all will quite naturally have different savings needs from the family who plan to stay childless until their mid-thirties, have one child, and live in a rent-controlled apartment until age forty.

Tables in this book give a range of costs for the larger family. That will give you the numbers you need for calculating how much to save year by year. The tables at the end also will tell you exactly how much future value you can arrive at by saving certain sums each year at different rates of interest. Those are your precise coordinates for saving and spending.

Simple Dreams

For the decade of the twenties, the first years after most persons enter the labor force, there need be only two more general guidelines:

1. The phenomenon of rapidly rising income more or less as a matter of course will not continue forever; bear it in mind;

2. While it lasts, if you can restrain your spending to create a foundation of savings for the two blockbuster expenses of young adulthood—children and a home—you will sleep much better in your thirties.

An economist would explain the decade of the twenties as a time of a leftward tipped and highly angled income function. It should also be a time of a less highly angled consumption function tipped more to the right.

In laymen's words, try to forget the prestige of spending everything you make when you first start to work. Instead, concentrate on the peace of mind you get from having a few bucks in the bank.

NEXT: Children and Houses—How to Love Them and Pay for Them.

THREE

Building That Nest and Feeding Those Chickadees

Bricks and Babies

There has probably been more confusion written and spoken about the cost of having children than about any other financial subject except one: the cost of owning a home. Taken together, the general pool of misinformation, missed connections, and just plain ignorance about two of life's most crucial decisions approaches an almost overwhelming level. It is no wonder that the ordinary citizen and citizeness contemplate homeownership and bringing up baby with a mixture of terror and blind hope.

In even the most respected publications, learned economists, and columnists suck their teeth and announce that homeownership is now out of the question for (pick one) 90 percent of the families in America, 80 percent of the families in America, 92 percent of the families in America.

On television shows and in magazines, wise men and women draw in the smoke from their pipes and earnestly assure the world at large that now is (1) the best possible time, (2) the worst possible time, (3) not sure, to buy a home in America. They also promise that mortgage rates will (1) stabilize, (2) skyrocket upward, (3) collapse before the next turn of the moon.

Similarly, on the pages of mass market magazines, free-lance writers pour out their wisdom about the cost of raising children. According to their pronunciamentos, you can make the price of reproducing the race manageable if you buy baby food only with coupons from magazines and if you engage the services of a holistic doctor. Alternatively, say the "experts," you can afford to have children if you can only find a neighborhood where the public schools are safe and decent. And then there are the articles in newspapers and magazines which assure the reader that the real key to affording offspring is the selection of exactly the right Scottish nanny, who will actually save you money in the final analysis by allowing the young mommy to go back to work at Citicorp, where she was destined to become the head of international banking until hubby got that gleam in his eye.

Somehow, in this mishmash, a basic and well-documented truth has been lost. Yes, owning a home has gotten to be more expensive than anyone would have imagined a mere ten years ago. And, yes, having children has gotten to seem to be crushingly expensive. These are not the products of a disordered imagination. They are real world phenomena. But the critically important connection between the two facts— higher housing costs and higher child rearing costs—has apparently been overlooked by the general media coverage of consumer finance.

In fact, the reason that raising children has become so very expensive is exactly and precisely because the cost of housing has risen so high. The single largest expense in raising children is the cost of their housing. Moreover, this is the one expense that has grown the most rapidly in the last ten years. The additional cost to a family of two when that family grows to three or four or five is made up of many expenses, but the cost of the bricks, mortar, wood shingles, wall-to-wall carpet, and land for the house big enough to fit little Jason and little Debbie is by far the largest item of additional expense.

Figure it out. When a couple in their twenties begin life in this particular era, they rarely do so in a large old house with a wide porch bequeathed to them by a maiden aunt. Instead, they begin wedded bliss in a tiny apartment with fiberboard walls and one bedroom leading into one living room overburdened by a color television set. When baby comes along, that apartment is too small. It can and must give way to a larger dwelling. With only one infant child, that dwelling may well be a two-bedroom apartment. The average difference in costs between a one-bedroom and a two-bedroom apartment, however, can be extremely significant. If a family in Cleveland moves from paying $350 per month for a one-bedroom apartment to paying $460 for a two-bedroom apartment, that is an increase in their housing costs of almost one third. And, indeed, such an increase is commonplace when a first child arrives.

If, after the arrival of a second child, family housing needs dictate that the family buy a free-standing house or rent a home as opposed to an apartment, housing costs can rise by an even greater amount, sometimes doubling or tripling.

For example, if a family is paying $450 for an apartment and then decides it must have a home (which we will get to in a moment), and if that home costs the typical average amount in late 1984, that home will cost well over $80,000. The cost of paying for such a home will be over $1,000 per month at current mortgage interest rates. That represents an *increase* in housing costs of 122 percent, for a total housing cost more than two-and-one-fifth times greater than when the family lived in an apartment. If we assume that the family in question has one little Joshua and one little Jessica, then each child has added a minimum of 60 percent to the family housing budget.

No other cost tends to rise as dramatically as that housing cost. A family's total food budget, for example, actually often *declines* as children come into the picture. For one thing, all those meals at Chez François tend to become meals of meatloaf and mashed potatoes when baby appears. For another, those gourmet meals cooked at home for eight of one's closest friends tend to become reheated fried chicken from Pioneer when the baby has finally fallen asleep.

The same principle applies to transportation. The huge majority of young families in America spend most of their transportation dollar on automobile expenses. When little Timmy comes along, even the most humble Dodge Omni Miser is still plenty adequate to take him to or from the grocery store. Even when little Tracy comes along to keep Timmy company, the old family Fairmont is still more than big enough. In fact, once again, it is usual for the family transportation budget to *shrink* when children appear. Mom and Dad tearfully give up their old TR-7 and shift to a used Chevy station wagon, saving insurance premiums, maintenance bills, and traffic tickets on the way.

But Junior and Sister cannot sleep in the car. They need bigger quarters, and for that, a major increase in housing budgets simply cannot be avoided if normal standards of family housing are to be maintained—

which is, if Mom and Pop do not want to share the bedroom with Junior and Sis.

Federal government surveys have found that in general, when a two-person household becomes a three-person household and in the process moves from rented to owned dwellings, housing costs increase per family by about 30 percent. When the family becomes a four-person unit and moves to owned quarters, housing costs shoot up by over *80* percent.

To restate all of this data about housing costs and child raising costs another, even more persuasive way, federal statisticians have found that for the first eight or nine years of a child's life, the increase in housing costs associated with that child *are almost as large as all other costs of having a child put together.*

What this means, pure and simple, is that the family that wishes to avoid a financial crisis when the patter of little feet becomes heard should and must get a good grasp of how to keep their housing budget under control. If the shock and surprise can be taken out of the shelter element of a family's budget as that family expands, the family is in Fat City.

Laying Foundations

There is, alas, no simple answer to how to control housing expenditures except for a watchword: As in all expenses, when a family is starting out, housing costs must bear a well-thought-out relation to present and future income. The family that earns $400 each week should not plan to live at Sixty-second Street and Fifth Avenue any time soon. The family that plans to spend half of its current income on a new Ferrari should not expect to buy a house as well.

But while there is no master plan that is applicable to all families, there is definitely a method by which families in their twenties can improve the odds on their financial survival when babies and mortgage bills both begin to come around. Basically, that method is to plan well in advance for both eventualities and to start the expansion of their housing well before the bassinet needs to be put into the second bedroom. If you can start to segue into that larger house or apartment when it is still so big that just the two of you rattle around in it, you are on the right track to keeping sane when Junior arrives.

That is, the first years of work and marriage are generally the years of the most discretionary income for decades to come. If you can divert some of that discretionary income into housing even before you really need it, you can and will be doing two crucial acts.

First, you will be performing a sort of saving. In the period since the end of World War II, the price of housing has generally risen well in advance of the average returns on stocks and bonds. The price of housing has risen approximately by a factor of seven since World War II on a weighted nationwide average. That means that money invested in housing has paid a real, inflation-adjusted return of almost 6 percent year in and year out, which is excellent considering that the Dow-Jones Industrial Average, the return on savings in a bank, or the return on Treasury bonds would all have paid less.

More to the point, in most parts of the postwar period, your savings would have been added to by the leverage involved in buying a dwelling. As most Americans know, a house or condo or co-op is bought with mostly borrowed money. That money, called a mortgage, has generally been available at interest rates considerably less than the annual increase in value of the housing in question. That means, for example, if Bob and Betty Jones buy a home in Oak Park, Illinois, they are likely to pay, say 12 percent on a mortgage. (This is a number for illustrative purposes only. In the last two years, interest rates have been extraordinarily and uniquely high relative to inflation. There is no historical precedent for their remaining so high for long.) At the same time, their home may well increase in value by, say, 14 percent per year. That means Mr. and Mrs. Jones will be able to make the difference between 14 percent and 12 percent on the bank's money. In other words, they will be making money with other people's money. Bob and Betty will not only be *saving* by putting money into their house each month. They will also be able to earn money on the savings of bank and savings and loan depositors, which have been lent to them for their mortgage. In that miraculous way, they will get the benefit of both their own saving and the savings of total strangers.

So, by putting money aside into a house or other owned dwelling, the ordinary citizen will be able to get the kind of leverage that young people can hardly get in any other way.

There is yet another advantage to buying a dwelling before one is needed. It is a homespun point but real nonetheless. A home or condo or co-op, once bought with a mortgage, requires that payments be made on a regular basis, generally monthly. These payments must be made or a legal penalty will be incurred. Possibly, the mortgage will be in default and the home can be sold by the lender if payments are not made in a regular and timely fashion. That means the young couple's payments for the home are not only a form of saving but also a form of *enforced* saving. The couple is simply not allowed to *stop* saving in this form without severe penalties and complications.

However regular in habit a young couple may be, however conscientious they may be, whatever plan they draw up, they may and will still be tempted to get off the wagon from time to time. The Kenwood stereo beckons at the electronics show. The new Mustang GT, with its "muscle car" acceleration, winks at them from the showroom floor. The Love Boat, seen regularly on television, is offered in the flesh to the couple by a travel agent. The parents-in-law demand that they be visited back in Little Rock over New Year's. In a word, the temptations to leave the savings plan for a few months only are enormous. If you rely solely on your own discretion to keep saving, you may succeed and you may not. When you are saving as enforced by law and by contract, with the underlying penalty of losing your home, you tend to be far more regular in habit.

Of course, there are dangers in home buying. Should you buy a home into a rare falling market, you will find that your "savings" are locked up for some time in a trap of illiquidity and loss. But even so, you will still find that the market generally turns again, this time in your favor. Indeed, in the postwar period, there has never been a time when average home prices in year one were not exceeded by prices in year four. That is, even if prices dip for one or two years, by the end of the fourth year, they have always made up their loss and shown a gain. There is no promise that such a gain will happen in the future, but the past is generally considered the best guide to the future. Enforced saving by buying a home has tended to be an extraordinarily good way to save and to invest, especially for young people. It also tends to allow good long-term preparation for having and raising children.

Shelters, Storms, and Sunny Days

The second large advantage to buying a home at a young age, even before children come along, is that owning a home with a mortgage is one of the best tax shelters available to young persons of moderate means. The Mellons and the Rockefellers and even Doctor Lipschitz can afford to buy into cattle feeding programs or oil-drilling programs or to own municipal, tax-free bonds. But for young Bob and Betty Jones, who have basically no sizable assets besides their ability to work, there are few ways around that giant tax bite. Except for buying a home, there are few ways indeed for the family without capital to buy tax shelters. In the era of permanent high taxes, a tax shelter is a very good thing to have.

When sheltering income can be combined with sheltering body and soul inside bricks and mortar and saving for future needs, that kind of tax shelter is an *extremely* good thing to have.

The tax shelter involved in buying a home with borrowed money is basically that interest on the mortgage is deductible from income for purposes of computing state and federal income tax liability (as is property tax). In the first few years of a mortgage, almost all of the payments are for interest and very little for reducing principal. In turn, that means almost all of your payments to the bank or savings and loan will be deductible from your income for purposes of computing tax.

If the young couple buys a home in a rising market (which all markets have turned out to be in the long term), the savings as compared with renting can be truly impressive.

For example, suppose that Bob and Betty Jones buy a two-bedroom apartment condominium right on the main drag in Oak Park, Illinois. The condominium costs $65,000. The seller is determined to sell, so he allows the condo to be bought with 10 percent down, or $6,500, which Bob and Betty Jones have saved in their first three years of marriage. That leaves a mortgage of $58,500. The lucky couple have gotten a mortgage from the seller at 11 percent, amortized in equal monthly installments payable over thirty years.

That means Bob and Betty will have to make equal monthly payments of $557.11. In the first year of that mortgage contract, the total interest paid will be $6,422. The total payments will be $6,685.28. Remember that the interest paid is tax deductible. If Bob and Betty Jones pay a combined state and federal tax rate of 30 percent (which is about average for a young couple), the tax savings realized by deducting the mortgage interest will be $1,927 in the first year. That can and should be deducted from the total amount paid for the mortgage payments, leaving a real, out-of-pocket cost for the first year of $4,758 for servicing the mortgage. That, in turn, means a monthly cost of $397 for the two-bedroom condominium, which is by no means out of line even in Oak Park.

But the best part of the housing/tax shelter/saving equation is that the house will generally rise in value by about 2 to 3 percentage points faster than the mortgage interest rate. (Again, this is a long-term average and not a promise for any given year.) In Bob and Betty Jones's case, that will raise the value of their condo to $74,100 at the end of the first year. If you compound that rate of increase over five years, the condo will have doubled in price in current dollars in just over five years.

(Again, this assumes a 14 percent rise in home prices and an 11 percent mortgage rate.)

Even after we have taken out $2,000 for taxes and for upkeep of that condo, Bob and Betty Jones are still far ahead of the game. They have laid out $4,758 and have a paper profit of about $7,000. In fact, in this example and in tens of millions of real-life examples, the Joneses got a place to live and were able to use the tax shelter/leverage force of homeownership to make substantial savings.

Further, they were able to make preparation for the day when Betty comes home from the ob/gyn office to announce that she has wonderful news.

What About Me?

The alert reader may well stroke her chin at this point and say, "Well, all well and good for the couple who have managed to save enough for a down payment. All well and good for the couple who have enough earning power to pay for the additional monthly payments needed to buy rather than rent. But what about people like me who are barely getting by on what we earn right now? We can't afford to buy rather than rent. What about us?"

There are two answers to that line of inquiry. Answer number one is that it is simply true that there are some couples who cannot buy a home in the first decade of their work lives. After all, some people earn more than others. A schoolteacher tends to earn less than a lawyer. An artist tends to earn less than a plumber. There are many young people (and quite a few older ones) who are living frugal lives, not wasting money on Advents and 300 Z's and trips on the Orient Express when they should be saving, who nevertheless simply cannot afford to pay any more for their shelter than they are now paying. In other words, even with the equity buildup, the tax shelter feature, and the enforced saving, they still cannot afford to buy a dwelling.

If those people choose to remain in their current lines of work, they should not plan to buy a house with money they do not have. After all, the point of the exercise is to enhance peace of mind, not to wreck it. But that has an important real world consequence. If the family who cannot afford to move to larger quarters in advance of having children plans sensibly, they can anticipate that their incomes will rise through the twenties and thirties. At some point, even if that point is not in sight, they will certainly be able to move to larger digs, rented or owned. (While owning has many advantages, there is no disgrace in renting either.) The rise in their incomes at some point before they are thirty-five will generate enough extra cash so that they can move upward and outward.

At that point, they should be ready to start a larger family. That is, it makes excellent sense for the couple to plan that just as the child should be wanted in terms of love and the emotional maturity of the parents, the child should be arriving when there is enough space for it in the home. But, again, that means the couple must keep a careful rein on every other item of expense so as to save enough for the down payment or the larger rental payment. It is usually not possible to spend as much as you want on movies and video tape players and home computers and also save enough to have a decent home if income is rising slowly from a low base.

Masters and Fates

Answer number two for those who fear that they will not be able to buy a house in time is that their incomes are not fixed in stone. This is extremely important.

Ever since there have been societies and marketplaces for labor, workers have been striving to upgrade their earning capacity. The secretary goes to night school to learn accountancy. The accountant goes to extra classes to add a law degree to his accounting tools. The plumber takes that course in office management so that he can open his own shop. More than that, sometimes people work at two jobs. It is commonplace for even college-educated people to moonlight to add to their incomes. The schoolteacher takes a job demonstrating computers at

Computeria. The nurse takes part-time work in the home of a wealthy invalid. The fledgling woman lawyer who loves clothes takes a job in a dress shop. The economist takes on extra work teaching a night-school class in economics for businessmen. In short, the hours that might have been spent watching Morgan Fairchild and Carroll O'Connor turn into a few extra bucks.

This, indeed, has been the major occupational story of the past ten years. In the decade from 1970 to 1980, there was only slight growth in the overall population. But there was a whopping one-third increase in the number of married women (with spouse present) who entered the full-time labor force. There was an almost 30 percent increase in the number of married women who entered the labor force on a part-time basis. The number of workers with full-time jobs who also obtained part-time work rose by about 15 percent, a vastly greater increase than the increase in population. In the decade which saw hyperinflation stay on like the man who came to dinner, there was an immense effort made by Americans to increase their incomes by improving their skills and by working harder.

For the young couple preparing to start a larger family, eager to collect the savings necessary to buy a larger home (or rent one), the option of increasing earnings by getting new skills or by working more hours should be a lively option. It is wrong to assume that there is an eleventh commandment requiring that workers have their evenings free to play video games and watch television. There is no such law. (Indeed, many of the young people I know find greater amusement and pleasure in working than in sitting and watching the ten millionth TV car chase of their lifetimes.) When a couple is young and strong, they should actively consider trying to boost their income. There will be plenty of time in the future when they need the money and are not so well prepared physically or mentally to earn it. Night school leading to a better job is no crime. A part-time job at the local Safeway or Pathmark checking out shoppers is not a prison sentence. Indeed, these acts can bring on the kind of financial ease which makes marriages closer, makes nights more snuggly and sleepy, and gives young people that safe, secure feeling.

The money mounts up in a way that will be especially helpful when baby has arrived and Mom may want to take a short, long, or permanent breather from the labor force. If the couple can increase their

savings by only $1,500 per year for a few years, and bank the money at
10.5 percent interest, look at how much better off they will be:

Year	Total Savings
1	$1,500.00
2	$3,157.00
3	$4,989.04
4	$7,012.89
5	$9,249.24

(All figures for the end of the year.)

Even in the inflated housing market of the eighties, four or five years'
worth of part-time work, even very part-time work, will yield the down
payment on a house or condo.

Of course, part-time work or school is not for everyone. Some persons work such exhausting days that they simply lack the strength to
work on a second job. Moreover, some persons love their leisure so
much that they cannot bear to tear themselves away for a class in
accounting. That is the infinite variety of human preference at work.
Just as there is no shame in *working* a second job or taking classes, there
is no shame in *not* doing so. But the young couple should be aware that
working more than one job or improving skills and productivity
through education is a time-honored way to prepare for financial need.
The fact that you went to an ivy-covered college or did not, the fact that
your dad never did or didn't, the fact that your friends are or are not
should not make a difference. If you need more money for a useful goal
such as preparing larger quarters for the arrival of baby, part-time work
can be a godsend.

Planning for Yourself and Against Yourself

To return to where we started, the largest single additional cost of
having children is the increase in the cost of shelter. In most regions of
the United States, the additional cost of having a larger dwelling for
children is equal to *all* other costs. (See above.) That cost, combined
with the wife's leaving the work place for a greater or lesser period of
time, is a large shock to most young families with children.

If, by careful planning and by judiciously restraining other expenditures, the young couple can buy a home before children arrive, that
couple is far ahead of the game. Figure it out. If a couple, our pals Bob

and Betty Jones, can work a home purchase into their budget three years before Bob, Jr., comes along, they will not be stunned at the cost of finding and buying a new house with Bob, Jr., in the car (screaming). They will already have adjusted to that shock. Besides, they almost certainly paid less for the house than it would now cost.

But probably the most important benefit of buying a home before the need for a dwelling of that size arrives is that Bob and Betty Jones now have a few years for their incomes to rise *while their housing costs stay virtually constant.*

Look at it with numbers to see the advantage of starting early to buy a home. Take two couples as paradigms of how to do it right and how to do it wrong.

First, there are Jim and Janet Thompson. They are doing everything wrong. They spent every cent they could on a truly epic collection of memorial medallions from the Franklin Mint. Next, they insisted that Jim buy a 1967 blood red Ferrari Dino, because Jim had always wanted one and the '67 was "a good buy." As it happened, the Ferrari ran once around the block and ever since has been in the San Jose Ferrari Repair Shop, near the Thompsons' apartment in San Jose. It costs the Thompsons $225 each and every month just to have the repairmen tune it enough to keep trying to locate the cause of the problem.

By dint of hard work, Jim and Janet Thompson earn over $600 per week. Jim works as a tester of diodes at Intel. Janet works as a preschool teacher in Walnut Creek. Jim even works two nights a week at Foothill Junior College teaching about semiconductor testing. But by dint of endless gratification of the need to show off, Jim and Janet have used airplane tickets to Acapulco twice a year, American Express bills in the hundreds for restaurant meals, whole closets filled with clothes that are now too tight for them, and only $4,600 in savings on the day that Janet started trying to become pregnant.

One year later, when Janet was shown the little baby Jim-Bob (after an ancestor of Jim's from Texas) in San Jose Dominican Hospital, she told the nurse that now she and Jim would find a home suitable for little Jim-Bob to grow up in.

Jim, Janet, and Jim-Bob found that times had changed. They had been paying $410 a month for an apartment with one bedroom and a tiny den. This amounted to almost exactly one week's paycheck for both of the adults after taxes. They had hoped to find a home that would cost about the same on a monthly basis.

Instead, the very cheapest house they could find (actually a two-bedroom, one-and-a-half-bath condo at Silicon Valley Arms) was for sale for $81,000, with only 10 percent down and a 12 percent mortgage for thirty years.

What that meant was that the $4,600 in savings was gone in a flash. What with closing costs and taxes, Jim and Janet had to borrow another $5,400 from the Intel Credit Union just to turn the key in the front door (made of particle board stained at the factory to look like cherry wood). The loan bore interest of 18 percent and had to be paid back in five years.

Not even counting taxes and the condo fee, Jim, Janet, and Jim-Bob were now obliged to pay total loan payments of $1,058.90 each month for at least the first five years.

Of course, the blood red Ferrari Dino went immediately. But by then it was only usable for parts, and Jim lost almost every penny on it. He was not even able to pay off his loan on the machine.

Further, of course, both Jim and Janet wanted badly to stay at home with the little Jim-Bob, or at least for Janet to be a proper, old-fashioned mother and stay home with Jim-Bob for a few years. That meant that the weekly net pay went from $425 each week to $345 per week. (The fall was cushioned because Janet's salary had been only $150 per week, and she had allowed overwithholding. When she stopped work, her last paycheck had been for only $90 net pay. Further, because of Jim-Bob's arrival, Jim's withholding decreased, leaving Jim and Janet with a net decrease in after-tax earnings of $80 per week.)

Jim, Janet, and Jim-Bob were spending 23 percent of their total consumption expenses on housing when they were back in their apartment. Now, with the condo at Silicon Valley Arms, and with Janet not working, they are up to an astounding *73 percent* of their total spending going for housing before counting taxes. That compares with a desirable range of from 25 to 35 percent. Because of the tax deductibility feature of the interest payments on Jim's mortgage and credit union loan, Jim's real after-tax housing costs are really "only" about $775 per month, or 53 percent of the family's total consumption expenses after Janet has stopped working. That is still more than 50 percent higher than the upper limit of desirable spending on housing in a young family's budget.

In a word, Jim, Janet, and Jim-Bob are going to be extremely strapped for many years to come. If Jim's income rises, in real dollars, at 8 percent per year (inflation adjusted), it will still take him *ten and a half years* before his income is as high relative to his housing costs as it was before he, Janet, and Jim-Bob moved into that condo. Those will be ten and a half lean years indeed. Of course, if Janet goes back to work, the lean years will be fewer. But even if she goes back to work at the same rate of pay and has 8 percent increases per year for each year in real dollars, Jim, Janet, and Jim-Bob will still have almost *eight* years before they can restore the same balance that existed before Jim-Bob and Apartment 2-G at the Silicon Valley Arms entered their lives.

Jim, Janet, and Jim-Bob have let every economic trend be used against them. They rented when they should have bought, letting housing prices move up to a stratospheric level. They frittered away their earnings when they had a chance to accumulate savings. In specific ways, they failed to think through the absolute necessity of establishing a sensible relation between how much they would earn and how much they would need to spend. They poured money into San Jose Ferrari Repair while they should have been buying bricks and mortar. They let the IRS take far too much of their income. They brought Jim-Bob into the world with no serious thought about how they were going to put a roof over their heads. They completely ignored the possibility of letting home price increases work for them instead of against them. They paid no attention to the likely increase or decrease in their earnings relative to the likely increase or decrease in their spending. Alas, while it all sounds academic, this kind of thoughtlessness leads to sleeping problems, daily misery, and divorces. Junking any careful preparation in favor of living on whims is an excellent way to junk peace of mind and serenity. Jim and Janet, now divorced, found that out for themselves.

The facts were there for them to see, just as they are being laid out here. The Thompsons chose to believe in Never-Never Land and paid a weighty price: their marriage and their happiness.

Everything could have turned out differently, as the case of Bill and Jean Wright shows, if the Thompsons had just used the information around them, and planned sensibly.

Bill and Jean Wright also worked at Intel and at Walnut Creek preschool. By coincidence, Bill also worked as a part-time teacher at Foothill Junior College. Bill and Jean earned almost exactly the same amount as Jim and Janet, roughly $600 each week, by the time they were twenty-seven.

But Bill and Jean had done a number of intelligent things to prepare for the arrival of Willie Jr. when Jean was going to be twenty-eight.

First of all, two years before they turned twenty-seven, at the young age of twenty-five, Bill and Jean decided to start preparing for a time when baby would make three and when Jean would want to stay home. That meant they got rid of one of their cars. Bill and Jean alternated using the one car they kept, an ancient VW Rabbit. Whichever one did not take the car rode on a bus and actually learned how to cook Italian food reading on the bus—in Jean's case—and about the history of Etruscan Italy—in Bill's case. Having only one car represented so much savings in just one year that Bill and Jean were able to get together $4,000 by their twenty-fifth birthday plus six months. (Much of the savings had accumulated earlier, when they took their vacations in Yellowstone National Park instead of accepting Jim and Janet's invitation to come along to Acapulco.) At that time, they were able to find a house that was small but adequate near Boulder Creek, for $57,500, with 10 percent down.

The mortgage was at 9.75 percent, which was another lucky break, because in only a few months, home mortgage rates went up rapidly to 12 percent and above.

Since Bill and Jean had saved up only $4,000, they needed to borrow another $1,750 for their down payment. They carefully shopped around and found that through the local teachers' association, they could borrow the needed money at only 14 percent interest if they repaid it within four years. (Note that Jim and Janet did *not* shop for their loan for the down payment and wound up paying 4 percentage points more than Bill and Jean.)

Because Bill and Jean got their house at a price so much lower than Jim and Janet did, and because Bill and Jean also were able to borrow at a much lower rate, they were obliged to pay only $441 per month for their mortgage. (It was a thirty-year note.) Because they shopped around for a good rate on their credit union loan, they only had to pay $47.27 per month for that loan.

The total payments on the loans for the house turned out to be only about $488, or only slightly more than one week's take-home pay for the lucky Wright family. At that time, when they were twenty-five, they were earning $508 per week and about $380 after tax.

By the time two years had passed and Jean was in a family way, Bill and Jean's weekly income had risen to $600 gross. Now, when Jean went into the maternity ward to have little Willie Jr., there was virtually no financial squeeze at all. Jean left work, and the family's after-tax income fell from about $425 a week to about $345 per week. But instead of having housing costs that skyrocketed upward as Jim and Janet did, Bill and Jean already had their home. Their housing costs did not change by one penny. Because of the tax deductibility feature of the mortgage and credit union payments for interest, the real after-tax cost of Bill and Jean's house (not counting taxes and utilities) was only about $342, which is easily affordable with Bill alone working.

For all intents and purposes, by reducing consumption and buying a home as early as possible, Bill and Jean have defeated the shocks and problems associated with both raising their first children *and* with buying their first house. They

• made housing price inflation work for them instead of against them;

• made their increases in income over time a resource instead of a burden by saving out of income instead of raising their expenditures ever higher;

• established a relationship between their income and their expenses —especially their housing expenses—that would make their lives easier rather than harder as time went on and took full account of exactly what they were planning—i.e. that Jean would stop work to have a baby and that they would need a larger home.

Bill and Jean foresaw the financial journey that they would take. They made sensible and adequate provision for it. The journey—at least the financial part of it—went effortlessly and pleasantly. When Jean came home from the hospital, she and Bill could and did devote their full attention to providing the best possible environment for little Willie Jr. instead of worrying how long it would be until their MasterCards were recalled.

Jim and Janet thought they were having "fun." Instead, they were planting time bombs that would blow up just when they needed peace, quiet, and security. They disregarded the clear signs of the route of economic passage for them and for Jim-Bob. They paid for their neglect of the financial side of the journey with their marriage and their peace of mind. It was not fun.

A few hours of planning, a modicum of self-restraint, and a decent respect for their own futures brought Bill and Jean out of the decade of the twenties rarin' to go. For Jim and Janet, it's all uphill now.

(Minus the tax-deductibility feature, the exact same principles apply to those who have the foresight to set aside money to rent larger quarters when baby comes. Since the renter builds up no equity in the house, he loses the advantage of enforced savings through homeownership. But he does have the advantage of adequate dwelling space, arranged for at a time when he and his wife could afford it. That is, even if you cannot afford to buy a home, you should make some provision to set aside enough money to rent larger quarters when baby comes. If rents are rising rapidly, as they have in some parts of America [astronomically in New York City], it would even be sensible to rent the larger quarters well before the family expands. The loss on larger quarters than you need for two will be more than made up by getting a cheaper lease than you would pay if you waited.)

Again, whether renting or buying, the key is always, always, always to establish a sensible relationship between the *anticipated* future course of your earnings—bearing in mind that one of you may leave the labor force when babies arrive—and your urgent need for a larger dwelling for a larger family. Solving the housing cost equation is the key to solving the child cost equation. The x that turns the trick is always *planning in advance* for a highly predictable need.

A Note of Caution

Speaking of predictability . . . there is an extremely large problem in your life once you have a family and a home: You need insurance. If you are a single man or woman, even a young couple without children, you do not urgently need insurance. *But* once you have obliged yourself to put a roof over the heads of your children, you can and must provide some protection for them in case you or your spouse passes into heaven. Insurance is discussed more fully in the chapter on your thirties. Read that when you are about to have children and buy a home. You must be able to feel sure that you have provided for the kiddies if "something happens to you." There are many different ways to arrange that protection. As you did for loans, shop around. There is no reason at this or any other stage in your life to pay one dollar more for your basic protection than is absolutely necessary. Be protected so that the mortgage is paid off and so that the kids can get through high school. But do it smart.

NEXT: Singles, Swinging and Otherwise.

FOUR

Not for Singles Only

A Few True Facts

As of 1984, there were about 17 million single Americans between the ages of twenty and twenty-nine. Those people have needs for dates, for BMW 320 i's, for trips to Club Med, and for new clothes. But do they need to own their own dwelling, whether condominium or house? Just as buying a home is the key question financially for married couples in their twenties, so it is for single people as well. But for most single people, the calculations involved in whether or not to buy their own homes are entirely different from those of married couples. We will get to the calculus in detail, but right now, let's go back to square one.

In the first decade of work for most young Americans, there will be a steep increase in real, inflation-adjusted wages. Again, this is because the new worker gradually learns to do more and better work, much like a machine that is brought out in successively better, more capable versions each year. The employer would expect to pay more for the better machine, and he will pay more for the better worker.

As we noted before, the worker entering the labor force at twenty-one can confidently expect that his or her real income will have approximately doubled by his or her thirtieth birthday. Also, as we have noted before, it is easily—more than easily—possible for the new worker to spend every bit of his salary and more.

The temptation to expand consumption even faster than income is perhaps even more pressing upon the young and the (presumably) hip than among the married. After all, the married can clearly see that they have some responsibilities to each other and to their posterity. But the single see their responsibilities primarily as themselves. Further, married couples tend to take a longer time horizon in their spending decisions than single people. Again, that is probably because the single see their status as both more uncertain and also as requiring less planning, since fewer people's lives are involved. To be sure, there is a certain degree of myth surrounding the notion that every single person is a swinging guy or girl just waiting to get that paycheck to spend it on trips to St. Lucie or Atlantic City. There are many extremely frugal single men and women in this country who cannot be seduced by even the most tempting advertisements for 4711 cologne or Yamaha motorcycles or Hitachi digital stereos, who want to be sure that whatever the future holds, they are prepared with ample savings. *But* it is a fact that the propensity to consume noninvestment goods and services is higher among the single than among the married. When Suzuki wants to sell bikes, when Eastern Airlines wants to sell trips to Puerto Rico, when Calvin Klein wants to sell jeans, when L'Oreal wants to sell shampoo, they can count on single young Americans buying a disproportionately large amount.

Statistics bear this out richly. The ordinary married couple has about 30 percent of one year's income in savings by the end of the first decade of work. The ordinary single Jane or Jim has about *20* percent. Moreover, there are relatively far more single people with *no* savings than married people without savings in their thirtieth year.

Whether it is because of hypnotic sales pitches or the insecurities of single life or the ecstasy of single life or the torture of single life, single men and women in America as a group tend to get themselves into financial trouble with a particularly nagging frequency and regularity.

When we reach square two for young single Americans, that square is often stamped with a giant "past due" or "slow pay" in red ink: Income has risen faster than the worker ever thought possible, but by an evil miracle spending has risen even faster.

In order to get to the square in which the single person has the luxury of even *considering* whether or not to buy a house, the single person in

America must first make some real observations about single status in America. Those observations, once learned, will move the single worker to a more secure life.

What Happened to Rhett Butler?

First, the single woman in America, in the last 20 percent of the century, is by no means certain to get married. This is basically because the allure of marriage for both men and women has diminished so drastically that the percentage of Americans who remain single has risen by a factor of two, that is, doubled, in the last twenty-five years.

The woman who is twenty-eight, spending every penny and firmly expecting Prince Charming to come along and get her financial house in order with his huge inheritance from a cotton plantation in Louisiana should not count on it quite as firmly as she might have in 1958. (The number of single young men with the resources to bail out their fiancées is not large. Second, the man might not come along at all. Third, when he does come along, the woman may hate him.)

All of that means that the single young woman should count mainly upon herself to rescue herself from fiscal catastrophe.

Second, the future needs of both single men and women may be even more pressing than those of married people even if there is no child involved immediately. This is because it is likely that *some day* there will be a child involved and also because the income expectations of single people are not as rosy as those of married people for a variety of reasons.

Income tends to rise largely because of increased productivity. Increased productivity, on an individual basis, tends to be highly correlated with longevity on the job. For this reason, employers whether at the government or at the Acme Travel Agency like to pay more to employees who have been on the job longer.

This is a problem for the single, who tend to stay at their jobs for shorter periods and change jobs more frequently than the married. In the first decade of work, the difference is less pronounced than in later decades (largely because there are fewer changes among the single and more changes among the married). But in later jobs and later years, those differences can become quite significant.

The income trend lines of the single do not rise as fast as those of the married for yet another reason: The married tend to be promoted and paid as if they had more needs and more reliability than the single. In other words, they tend to be paid more. Of course, this is illegal under federal law in many instances. But law or no law, when salary committees meet, they take into account whether or not an employee has a wife and babies at home who need to be fed. Survey data have shown time after time that paymasters pay more when they know that a man or woman has a family to support. Also, when wages and salaries and promotions are considered, married workers often look more solid than unmarried workers. Every employer, even in Hollywood, even in the record business, likes a solid worker. The married worker often gets a promotion or an increased paycheck simply because of the perception that "family man" = solid, hardworking guy or gal.

Traps and Pitfalls

On the consumption side, expenses *per person* can often be greater for a single worker than for a married worker. Mainly, this is because of the economies of scale associated with two people living together. In other words, while two cannot live as cheaply as one, two can and do generally live as cheaply as 1.7. One can only live as cheaply as one by himself or herself. Rental for two persons is often no more than rental for one, since most rentals in this country are based on the size of the dwelling rather than on the number of occupants. While a husband and wife can split that rental, lowering the cost per person, the single man or woman must pay it all himself or herself. In theory and in fact, this means that housing expenses *per person* are higher for young single men and women than for any other group.

Another higher cost for singles is automobile insurance. To the city dweller without a car, this may seem like a trivial concern. But for many young singles in their twenties, automobile insurance can cost more than automobile payments themselves. It is not at all uncommon for young Americans to spend one out of every twelve dollars they earn for automobile insurance, far more than for life insurance and often more than for food.

Alas, automobile insurance rates are drastically higher for single Americans than for married Americans. This difference approaches 50 percent in many areas of the country. Again, while this may seem like a remote concern to the Manhattanite, it is a matter of life or death for the suburbanite in Dallas or Chicago.

All of these income and consumption problems are only possibilities. Also, all of them can be dwarfed by the pressures of trying to keep up with the young Joneses. A young life filled with promotions and good salary increases can be thrown into complete and total pandemonium because you are in with a crowd which has more money than you do. If you, a junior accountant at Macy's, find yourself among the heirs to Macy's, you may find that you have to go to Jamaica twice each winter, fly to Montauk at the drop of a hat, buy a suit each month at Paul Stuart, and generally live like a young merchant prince. The most well-constructed hopes and dreams for a solvent future are doomed before such an onslaught of showing off.

If you are a young woman in the advertising department at Donaldson's in Minneapolis–St. Paul, you may well find that keeping up with the buyers and the finance vice presidents at Dayton-Hudson keeps you running flat out. A new blouse from Cacharel, a new pair of Gelman shoes, a new pocketbook from Nazareno Gabrielli, a complete set of cosmetics from Clinique as they appear in *The New Yorker* week by week, a season ticket to the St. Paul ballet, an unlimited telephone budget for calling your pals from U. Minn., and next thing you know, you are so deeply in hock that you cannot even think about anything but your bills.

In other words, there are many ways and places to fall off the track toward having some savings.

Hey, but I'm Single . . .

But you may ask, "Why do I need any substantial savings? Why shouldn't I have just enough to tide me over in case I want to say Screw you to my boss and look for another job? After all, I don't have to think about putting Junior and Sis through college, do I? I don't have to worry if they foreclose the house. I don't even have a house to be foreclosed."

Again, part of the answer is that someday most of you will have a little Junior to feed and clothe and put through school. But before we even get to that part of the drama of life, look at what having some savings can mean to a young single person.

First, if being single means having a certain degree of freedom and independence that married people do not have, consider that having savings means real independence and freedom. Even if you are single with ten different girlfriends, you are not free if you have a MasterCard bill ten times your monthly wage. Even if you are a single woman who would never consider being tied down to send hubby through med school, would never dream of devoting your life to changing diapers and being chained to the PTA, you are thoroughly and completely enslaved if you have to stay at your job, at your location, in your same apartment, all in the name of reducing your bill at Ohrbach's, Saks, and Neiman-Marcus, not to mention paying your telephone bill down to where Ma Bell won't rip it out of the wall.

To be really free in modern society (maybe in old society, too) means to have some measure of financial independence. Independence and the free spirit are meaningless if you are deeply in debt. They are redoubled in meaning if you have the wolf well back from the door. (We'll get to how far back he should be—how much savings is right for the young and single—in a few pages.)

The flip side is just as true. If being single means occasional sleepless nights wondering if those bills are ever going to be paid, if anyone will ever be around to share the burdens, then insolvency and looming financial catastrophes are a dead weight you do not need.

By this I mean something very basic: For many people, it is frightening to be alone. Even those who spend the evenings at the local hot spot, living it up and drinking Long Island iced teas until daybreak, often wake up at 3 A.M., wondering if there would be anyone to take care of them if "something happened." One of the best sleeping pills is the knowledge that you are taking care of yourself, and that if "something" did happen, you would be even better able to take care of yourself than someone else would. If you, as a swinging twenty-seven-year-old single man or woman know that you are financially prepared, constantly able to save a little bit, month by month, you will be able to pass through those dead-of-night crises far better than if you have a stack of unpaid Sears bills on the night table. If you know that you have kept your consumption of stereos and vacations at a low enough rate so that you would not feel your mouth go dry if you did *not* get that raise, you are way, way, way ahead of the game.

If you take the "power of positive thinking" part of the deal and the "middle of the night blues" part of the deal and put them together, you find that the highs will be higher—and the *lows* will be *higher*—if you have been able to keep your consumption within a limit set by your earnings.

Notches on Your Belt

Now, how do you do that? How do you set yourself apart from the generality of young people and get yourself into a position of strength? First and foremost, by spending less.

There are several areas in which single people tend to overspend. We have already covered "show-off" type expenses, which an economist might call "recreation expenses not otherwise classified," "travel expenses," or "clothing," or "food consumed away from home." Those expenses are so obviously either under control or not under control that they hardly need to be further discussed.

In addition, many young single people spend unwisely on automobiles. Automobile expenses per person tend to be significantly higher for single people as compared with married people in the same age group. Car expenses tend to be additive as well. That means simply that if you spend a lot of money on buying a Jaguar, you are also likely to spend a lot of money repairing your Jaguar. Or, put another way, if you buy a Seville, you are going to find that taking the dings out of the front fender costs too damned much.

Making a hard and fast rule for how much to spend on a car is impossible. A car can mean much more to some people than to others. A rule of "one week's pay for all automobile expenses" is both far too lavish for people who hate cars and a little too modest for people who absolutely love cars. Generally speaking though, if you find yourself spending more than 25 percent of your take-home pay on a car, you should be morally certain that the car is ultraimportant to you. If you find yourself spending more on your car than on your housing, you should eat, drink, and make love with cars only.

To whatever extent you can substitute the peace of mind of having savings for the mad ecstasy and terror of having a Mercedes convertible, you will be miles ahead of the game. To whatever extent you can substitute your own charm and lovable nature for showing up in a gleaming black Mustang 5.0 convertible, you are miles and smiles ahead. The young man or woman who can achieve status within his or her group without having to overspend on a car is dramatically better off than those who rely on major expenditures on steel, chrome, glass, and rubber to make themselves big.

But to go back to an earlier square, the most major area of savings for single people has to be in their most major cost: housing. On a *per person* basis, the average young single person living alone spends almost 40 percent more than the average family of two for his shelter. Obviously, this tends to skew all other expenses.

To some extent, this kind of expense is unavoidable. People who live alone tend to have a strong preference for living alone. Generally speaking, they know that it is much more expensive to live alone than to live with someone else. Many young single people have had roommates or a succession of roommates and now are sick and tired of having to worry about somebody else's unmade beds or unwashed dishes. Young people who live alone have had it with phone calls at midnight from ex-boyfriends or ex-girlfriends, wanting to know just what that last card or letter meant, threatening suicide if your roommate does not return that piece of jewelry or that book of Kahlil Gibran. The modal single man or woman shelling out half her salary or his wages for single living knows all too well the pain of splitting telephone bills, gas bills, and Christmas gifts to the trash collectors. The man or woman living alone has decided that the cost of living solo is worth every penny.

All well and good, but then the one-man one-apartment kind of young person should realize that every other expense must be scrutinized with a fine microscope to get over the financial shock of that apartment rental bill. It is completely understandable that human beings should want peace and quiet where they live. It is also understandable that if they do not make serious adjustments in other costs, they will go broke in a hurry.

That means even more careful attention to clothing, meals away from home, travel, gifts (for some reason a huge expense item for singles), "miscellaneous recreation durables" (read stereos), and utilities (read long-distance telephone bills).

It also means that the single person would be doing himself or herself a huge financial favor if he or she could possibly find a roommate who would be compatible and not a cross to bear. The cost per person of two people sharing a two-bedroom apartment is often (though not always) lower than the cost of even a one-room apartment (efficiency, studio, single) per person. Having a roommate reduces the cost of utilities per person, greatly cuts down on meals eaten away from home as a general rule, and can also lower recreation costs. After all, it is sometimes more fun to watch "The Jeffersons" with your roomie than to go out to a movie in the bitter cold.

If you can bear to live with a roommate, you can proudly go into your bank more often knowing that you are not overdrawn, can afford to buy that set of headphones, can have that heady feeling that your expenses are under some kind of control.

Sooo . . . if you are one of those swinging singles who cannot bear even to think about a roommate, you must go back to shaving expenses elsewhere. There is basically only one other way to acquire savings: Earn more money.

Navigating Around the Averages

In the chapter above, we talked about how there is no commandment that says that men and women are not allowed to work at more than one job or take classes that raise their earnings. If this is true for married couples—and it is—it is true in No Trump for the single.

The lessons of the past fifteen years for Americans are meaningful indeed for the ordinary citizen without a spouse. From 1967 to the present, the real income of all American families rose fairly dramatically. The real income of single people hardly rose at all by comparison (although this does not mean that an *individual's* income did not rise as he or she grew older). The reason was that more family members went to work, pure and simple.

There is no reason that the single man or woman cannot do the same. He cannot send a clone of himself to work, of course. But he or she can get another job. There are many people in all different lines of work who are not dead tired when they come home from work. They have the time and the strength to work again at night or else on weekends. In fact, there are many young people who are so bored by their nine-to-five jobs that they are dying to get out and do something different in the evening. If they can get paid for it, more power to them.

If your expenses tend to outstrip your income, you can cut your expenses—or you can seek to raise your income (or both). It may well turn out that you get more pleasure—as well as income—out of teaching a night school class than you would out of eating home more often. You, a single man or woman, may meet more of the friends you want working at the electronics counter of Sears than staying at home talking to your mother on the telephone.

Working a second job is by no means a litmus test of the worthy personality. But it is often a fairly painless way to make ends meet and even go a little farther than meeting.

The mathematics of even a fairly small addition to income from part-time work are astonishingly encouraging. If you can work four hours each week at $8.75 per hour, and if you can bank that sum at the relatively modest rate of 10.5 percent, at the end of the fifth year, you will have $11,222.47 in savings that you would not have had.

Another avenue more open to the single than the married person is to raise his or her productivity and hence his or her pay. The married man or woman by definition has something to do each evening and on weekends. The single person by definition does not have such hard-and-fast rules of companionship. He or she is free to take courses in computer sciences or library science or interior decoration or automatic transmission repair or new developments in trusts and estates. Those courses can and do often lead to higher levels of skill at the current job of the student. They can and do lead to new jobs and promotions. Part-time schooling is one of the all-time best ways for a single person to raise his income function.

(It is crucial for the single man or woman in the early phases of his work career to realize that while there are averages and generalities about income in his group, his own income or her own income are largely determined by his or her own exertions.

(For example, the average man or woman in his or her twenties may see his or her income double in the decade. But beyond that, there are those who will see their incomes triple because they learned more, worked harder, made better connections. Others will only see income rise by much less because they did not work, did not learn, did not make connections. The general condition of the economy dictates averages. Luck and connections and work and brains can affect the individual in little or large circles around the mean. Average and predictable crises are still valuable as road maps, but you are driving the car, and you can drive around the detours.

(The alert reader will notice that there is no chart here laying out expenditures for singles by category. Nor will there be for any singles age category. This is for several statistical reasons.

(First, statistics are kept by head of household's age, sex, education, location, and even by religion. But detailed statistics are not kept for single persons by age, alas. For reasons best known to the government, detailed data are kept on what families spend by age, but not on what single people spend by age. That is, there are categories for all families by income, and even categories for families and single persons lumped together by income or by education or race or decile of national income. But I have no good data besides anecdotal data and what can be separated by examination from the family data on exactly what singles spend on which categories by age.

(Second, what data on singles as a large mass does exist tends to confuse single young persons with single elderly persons. Needless to say, when you put people who spend every dime on jogging shoes with people who spend every dime on walkers, you do not come out with a meaningful average.

(Third, I was able to get some data from insurance companies on categories of expenditure by age and whether single or married, but this data tended to stop before the great inflation of 1967, which distorted all other spending in favor of home buying.

(The data are not complete and neat like the family spending categories. But every single usable piece of data goes in the same direction: Young singles spend less on shelter as a "family" but more *per person* than real families. Likewise for transportation. Young people tend also to spend more on clothing per person and also more on health care.

(This difference lasted past middle age. If you imagine as the typical single person a librarian who has decided to live alone in her own apartment and drives her own car to work but does not spend much on meals away from home or meals at home, you are heading in the right direction. If you further imagine that this same single person has far more discretionary income when young and middle-aged but no more when elderly, you are also right.

(Sadly, if you postulate that he or she is not paying as much attention to savings or the future as he or she should, you are also correct.)

By dint of restraining spending on automobiles, housing rental, travel, meals away from home, and recreation, and perhaps by dint of a second job, the ordinary citizen may well find that he or she, in his or her twenties, can start to accumulate savings. Now comes the hard part: What should he or she do with those savings?

To Own or Not to Own

Basically, there are two broad choices. The savings can be put into the form of down payment on a house or they can be put into some more liquid form, such as savings accounts, stocks, money market funds, or the like. This boils down to an even more fundamental question which came up some pages ago: Should the young single man or woman buy a home if he has the savings for a down payment?

In many articles lately, there have been statistics about unmarried young people buying homes. These statistics tend to wander all over the lot, as if the statistics had been gathered by someone who had taken them on the moon and Saturn as well as on the earth. But the basic trend of more and more young single people buying their own dwellings is indisputable. During the housing boom of the late seventies, Americans of all ages and all social conditions got the idea that they were fools for not buying their own homes. Home or condo ownership was considered the sure way to a prosperous, if not rich, future.

In fact, homeownership is an extraordinarily good deal, as detailed in the preceding chapter. But two major factors add up to a negative answer to the question of whether young singles should buy homes. One of the factors is demographic, and one is economic.

The demographic factor is that the great majority of single Americans between the ages of twenty and twenty-nine will not be single by the time they are thirty-nine. Between 60 and 70 percent of all Americans who have never been married by age twenty-nine are married by age thirty-nine. Although that percentage will probably fall in the future as single living becomes more socially acceptable, it is unlikely that the single man or woman in his or her twenties will remain single for ten more years.

When the swinging single hangs up his disco shoes for Harry Homeowner coveralls and do-it-yourself kits, he may well find that he wants to live in an entirely different area from where he lived as a single. He may want to move from Greenwich Village to Riverdale, from Old Town to Oak Park, from city to suburb. In that case, he may find himself with a home which is utterly unsuitable for a married couple and even more unsuitable for a married couple with a baby.

By itself, that is not a problem. In a perfect world with a perfect free market, he or she could just sell that old dwelling to some new swinging single and then take the profit and move to suburbia. The problem is that the market is a long way from perfect. In real life, even in a lively housing market, houses take a long time to sell. In a weak resale market, such as we had for three recent years and which could continue for a few years more (New York City is the exception), houses can take an eternity to sell. One of the most aggravating things in all life is to have a house on the market for month after month, year after year, and see hordes of lookie-loos and not one buyer. Another of the most maddening things in life is to have almost all of your assets tied up in bricks and mortar and landscaping and chandeliers that you absolutely cannot turn into cash.

This illiquidity (the inability to turn a real asset into cash) can be much more of a problem for a single person than for a family. After all, a family's housing arrangements are presumably set for some time to come. A single can expect to get married and want a different home. That bachelor condo, that bachelorette cottage, may have a lot of paper profit in it, but turning it into cash may turn out to be nearly impossible, or at least nearly impossible in the short run.

The confluence of these two factors (likelihood of getting married plus difficulty in selling quickly because of the lingering poor real-estate market) can make buying a house or condo a nightmare for a single man or woman.

On the Other Hand . . .

Of course, as the saying goes, there are horses for courses. There are some single people who, for reasons of utter devotion to their work, can feel quite certain that they will never marry or at least not for a number of years. They may also have unshakable faith in their future in a certain part of town or even in a certain office or plant. For those people, buying a home makes sense. They will get the tax benefits, the buildup of equity, and the security of owning their own dwelling without the heartache of suddenly having to move and being unable to sell. Similarly, there are men and women who, because of their personality or sexual orientation, can be quite certain that they will never need to find a home for a spouse and children. If those people feel certain that they will stay in the same town or neighborhood, they too may well decide that they should have a home which they own. While the argument about having more space for baby will not apply, the arguments about compulsory saving apply even more forcefully to the single man or woman than to the married couple. By definition, by statistical fact, by psychological necessity, single people tend to spend more and save less than married people. If buying a house is a way of enforced saving— and if that may well be the only kind of saving that can be managed—

the single man or woman with a high unlikelihood of marrying, high job commitment, and love of place should and must consider buying a home. Again, all of the pro-buying arguments *do* apply, and the demographic arguments and economic reasons for not buying do *not* apply.

How Much of a Cushion?

But if you are the happier single in your twenties, able to keep your income function above your consumption function (able to save, in other words), how much should you save in some liquid, nonreal estate form? And, what should you do with it? (Now the marrieds should tune back in—this advice is for them as well.)

Primarily, be careful with it. Imagine two twenty-seven-year-old men. Allen Gray and Michael Greene. Both of them are sound engineers for a major recording company in Nashville, Tennessee. They are pals. By dint of hard work and continuous attention to learning new techniques in recording, both men have raised their wages considerably since they both started five years ago.

Allen Gray and Michael Greene are each earning about $475 each week, after taxes. On an annualized basis, each one takes home $24,700 per year. By dint of careful economies such as not going to the Grand Ole Opry except when they got free passes, not flying to New York City except when close friends were appearing and the company, Good Old Boy Records, picked up the tab, and not going whole hog into the cowboy fashion look which died after twenty-four months, Allen and Michael have been able to save about $12,000 each.

At first, they were unable to save a penny. They lived in new apartments, which needed furniture. They had no cars, so they each had to get a pickup truck, standard for their work environment. They also needed nice neat clothing, so that no one would think they were rock stars. Finally, they absolutely had to have good stereos so that when they brought home their handiwork, they would be able to hear what they had done right and done wrong.

But they first started saving $20 out of each paycheck, then $30 out of each paycheck, then $50, and pretty soon they were passing by the Rebel National Bank every day at lunchtime feeling as if they had a future. The savings were in certificates of deposit, which earned a better sum than passbook. So by the time that Allen and Michael had been at work for five years, they had savings equal to six months' salary, after taxes, or about $12,000. Not only was this exactly the sum generally recommended as the desirable amount of savings, but it gave Allen and Michael considerable peace of mind. The music business had fallen into the doldrums with a vengeance that no one had ever predicted in his worst nightmares. While their fellow recording engineers went around with a roll of Tums, Allen and Michael were able to concentrate on perfecting their work, thus making them ever less likely to be fired or laid off.

So far, so good, but after that, things took a bad turn for Michael Greene. He happened to see an advertisement for a local stockbroker who told him that for $10,000, he could get a share in a tax shelter in genuine Santa Gertrudis cattle, right there in Tennessee. For every dollar invested, there would be a $2.50 write-off against taxes. There would also be the prospect of a stream of earnings from the prize bull semen that the tax-sheltered enterprise would generate. Counting the tax shelter aspects and the anticipated (but not guaranteed) flow of funds, the tax-sheltered investment in Santa Gertrudis cattle looked as if it would pay about 22 percent per year. That had a mighty sweet smell to Michael Greene. He was concerned about whether he would be able to get his money out in an emergency, but the stockbroker *promised* him that while the investment was itself illiquid, any bank would be proud to lend against his share of Santa Gertrudis bull semen.

Michael Greene still had some lingering doubts, but he loved the sound of 22 percent per year, so down went $10,000 of his $12,000 into the black hole of the Santa Gertrudis tax shelter.

Things started to go wrong from the very first instant. "First instant" in this case meant that the stockbroker immediately took 8 percent off the top for his fee. That meant the investment would have to do unusually well for Michael to get back his investment. The second problem was that because of the extraordinary 2.5:1 write-off of the shelter, which allowed Michael to pay almost no tax in the year he made the investment, the Internal Revenue Service called Michael in for an audit. The audit took six solid weeks of preparations by Michael. In those weeks, he could not go out of the house with his girlfriend, Lou Ann. He had to spend every moment finding receipts and trying to reconstruct with whom he had had lunch on a certain day and why there was a legitimate business purpose. He also had to track down every medical bill, every credit card interest expense, and every gasoline bill.

The whole affair made Lou Ann so angry at being neglected that she walked out of Michael's life and wound up in Miami Beach with a major contractor of condominiums for the elderly.

The third problem was that Johnny Snowbird, the last best-selling, platinum recording artist for Good Old Boy records, abandoned music and turned to God. He went to New Guinea to convert the natives and GOB records went into Chapter XI within six months.

When Michael went to the broker to get his money out to pay his bills, there was no sign of the broker. When Michael took all his paperwork on the tax shelter to the Rebel National Bank, the bankers just stared at him.

"How on earth could we possibly take bull semen as collateral for a loan?" the banker asked. "These papers don't even tell us where the bull is."

By then, Michael Greene in fact had a good idea of where the bull was. He still had his $2,000 in savings that he had not plunked down, plus an additional $2,000 he had been able to save since. His life was therefore not rendered hopeless. But he had been through an experience he did not care to relive. His nights became sleepless as he looked for a job. Even as he found a job with Jefferson Davis Rat, the punk group that had taken Nashville by storm, he worried about what would happen when Levon Squash, lead singer of the Rat, decided to kill himself with an overdose of Seconal. It took two years of very careful savings and economies to get Michael Greene up to the place in his consciousness where he had some optimism and confidence in the future. In the meantime, his life had taken on the weary, bleary, definitely anxious coloration that creeps over those who are worried about money all the time.

Allen Gray had taken a different course. He had not liked the looks of the broker of bull tax shelters. More to the point, he had felt himself quiver with anxiety when he learned that his money would be tied up for years to come at the whim of the manager of the tax shelter, who might or might not give a damn about ever paying off the investors. Despite the magical allure of getting 22 percent on his money, promised by the broker with the Tennessee accent, Allen Gray left the office with his checkbook zipped up. He kept his money in boring certificates of deposit, which offered between 8 and 12 percent per year and never sheltered his income from taxation.

In the first year, all signs were that Michael had a winner and Allen had a loser. After all, Michael was getting by without having to pay any taxes, which increased his income by about $4,000 in that one year alone. He received a check from the tax shelter for his first annual $500, fully tax-sheltered. In the same period Allen had only received about $1,000 in interest, all of it fully taxable.

It was when Good Old Boy records folded its tents and drifted off to Hillbilly Heaven that the big difference showed up. Both Michael and Allen urgently needed money. Only Allen knew for sure that he would be able to lay hands on his in a hurry. That huge need, the first real working life shock that Michael or Allen had ever had, was a stunner. On a mathematical basis, Michael was far ahead of Allen (because he had saved so much on his taxes), but he felt a powerful psychological imperative to have his money at his beck and call. He could not get it. That upset him terribly and more than offset any gains he would ever have from his bull semen tax shelter. (It turned out to be a fraud. He was eventually required to pay all his tax "savings" back to the IRS plus interest.) Michael kept thinking about how hard he had scrimped and saved for that money. It was a bitter pill indeed that it had somehow slipped from his grasp, even if it had yielded an excellent tax shelter for one deceptive year. Moreover, at the tender age of twenty-seven, Michael felt as if the savings of an entire lifetime were now chewing on grass somewhere in Never-Never Land utterly oblivious to his needs.

Allen, the grasshopper in this tale, felt a great deal of comfort from his little CD in an envelope in his top desk drawer. He knew that if need be, he could look for a job in a leisurely, careful fashion, without having to worry about where his next meal was coming from. He felt as if he had, in a sense, taken care of himself for five years and now it was all warm and snug there in his top desk drawer, in a tangible form.

The lesson of all this is not complex. At the early stages of work, savings require a lot of hard work and self-discipline. Every dollar is precious. Once saved, every dollar should be put into a form in which the saver knows for damned sure that the money will be available when he needs it. That means, first of all, that the savings should be in a liquid form—i.e., convertible into cash without much hassle. It means that the savings should be in a form which cannot ever be touched by unscrupulous people.

Later in one's work life, when one has several chunks of $12,000 each lying around, one can do what he will about tax shelters or growth stocks. At the beginning, play it safe. Not only does each dollar of savings in one's twenties carry with it heavy emotional content from self-deprivation, but the twenties are, by definition, a time when large changes can and do take place with some regularity. The single man or woman may not need money to put little Joshua through college, but he certainly could need money for moving to a new town if he loses his job. He almost certainly will need money in the foreseeable future for setting up housekeeping as a married guy. The same applies to single women.

Both of these factors—the hard struggle attached to each savings dollar and the likelihood of sudden changes in daily life—require liquidity and security.

This means that extreme caution should be taken in terms of investing in any asset whose value can fluctuate by large amounts, and that means stocks and bonds. Obviously, there are some stocks that represent ownership in some very large and successful, carefully managed, intelligently protected companies. The IBMs, Exxons, and Citicorps of this world are unlikely to disappear suddenly unless we all disappear suddenly. But while the Citicorp Center will be there year after year, along with the Exxon Building and the IBM Selectric III, the value of their stocks and bonds can and does fluctuate wildly. Even the largest industrial company in the world, Exxon, can and does see its stock fluctuate 3 or 5 percent in a single hectic day of trading. Even a titan like IBM can lose 25 percent of its value in a sliding market. This does not mean that the young single man or woman should avoid the stock or bond markets. It does mean that the young man or woman on his or her own should be flexible, ready to sell if things go sour, should be prepared for risks—and should limit his or her exposure in stocks and bonds.

To put all of your assets into something that can go down dramatically through no fault of your own, through events beyond your control, is foolhardy. There is some sense in testing the waters, investing in stocks or bonds to get some familiarity with investment alternatives. But that kind of experiment should never involve as much as half, and probably less than one quarter, of the young single's savings.

For the bulk of savings, an asset which is highly liquid, whose value will not fluctuate, and which is guaranteed or virtually guaranteed, is a must, at least at the beginning. Leave the wild speculations to the experts and to the people who have money they can afford to lose. For the young man or woman who is beginning in the race of economic life, care must be the watchword. Bank CDs, well-tested money market funds, bank money market accounts, all of these assets will pay a good interest rate, will be there when you need them, and will give you that nice warm feeling we all crave. They are your best bets.

The bank CD will not make for good conversation, will never double in two weeks, will never make you look like a hero to your girlfriend. On the other hand, it will never leave you walking down the street with your tongue hanging out, wondering why you were ever born. The money market fund is the tortoise next to the high tech stock's hare, but it will never make you feel as if you were the biggest fool on earth not to have been more careful. The bank money market account will bore the hell out of your office mate, but it will never leave you dry-mouthed at 7 A.M., wishing that all of your savings from five years' iron self-discipline had not disappeared in the flash of two weeks' trading on a market in a city you have never even been to.

Add It Up

Ahem, ahem. In summary:

- The young single man or woman has the chance to take advantage of a steep upward curve in his income function, a period when he or she will be earning more year by year at a rapid clip.
- To come out of the decade with the savings necessary to prepare for career change or marriage (six months of earnings is about the right amount), you have to break out of inertia.
- You must and should greatly restrain your consumption of certain show-off items like travel, restaurant meals, clothing, and entertainment—but most especially automobiles.
- You must try to get some handle on your housing expenses, which tend to be far higher per person than for married people.
- If you do not get a handle on housing costs, you must and should adjust your other expenses correspondingly.
- When you do get some savings, you should not automatically plunk them down for a house. There are many reasons, personal and "macro," that militate against buying a home until you have a good idea of your future plans.
- Since your savings represent such sweaty investment of toil and trouble, you should and must show extreme care in investing them.

- At the age of twenty-to-twenty-nine, savings should not go into illiquid investments in any more than trivial amounts.
- Savings should also not go into investments which are likely to fluctuate wildly except in small quantities. Those savings were earned by a lot of meals in front of the TV that your friends spent at the Pizza Oven. Treat them with the care they deserve.

In one word, the singles' decade of the twenties offers a great opportunity to fortify your economic position because of high earnings growth and low real need for basic expenses; *don't blow it.*

NEXT: How to Be a Conformist.

FIVE

The Laws of Economics
and How to Break Them

Before we leave the glamorous world of the twenty-to-twenty-nine-year-olds, we should go back to basics for a quick assurance that we have the ground rules straight.

The most fundamental plan of this book is that there is a basic relationship between the income function over a lifetime and the consumption function over a lifetime. In the case of most people, that relationship can and does lead to heartbreak and frustration because it so often is a relationship out of control. As the reader will have noticed, this book aims to establish a more pleasant relationship between income and expenditure over a lifetime by predicting what the likely curve of income will be, then relating it to the likely curve of expenditure, then—most important—changing and governing that relationship so that it is under control.

So far, most of the suggestions herein have been about controlling the consumption expenditure so that it does not leap ahead of the income function and put the young couple into the red at a stage when their incomes are rising rapidly. The goal has been to establish a program of savings as a cushion for getting adequate shelter, providing for space for children, and giving young people a sense of safety in their financial lives. All of this comes under the heading of assuring a margin of comfort for changes in life that will come later on.

Put more mathematically, it is all part of making certain that the consumption equation does not yield a larger result than the income equation *over a lifetime*, even though consumption will inevitably exceed income for almost everyone at some stage of his or her life.

Put more colloquially, the goal of the previous three chapters has been to keep young Americans from getting so hopelessly in the soup in their twenties that they have to spend the rest of their youth bailing themselves out.

In the service of that effort, one major fact of life—and response to it —has been barely mentioned. Back when we were talking about Jane Q. Colgrad and her employer, the Pygmy Athletic Shoe Company, we talked about why the incomes of young Americans tend to rise so dramatically. It had to do with learning one's job more thoroughly, with gaining expertise in doing the job better, and with generally becoming more productive so that you produce more value for your employer— and for yourself. In turn, this has to do with your employer's need to pay you more to keep you from taking your expertise and charm and increased productivity elsewhere, as you may recall.

So far, so good. In fact, the income of most twenty-to-twenty-nine-year-olds is destined to rise meteorically over that exciting time. *But,* alas and alack, the fact that the *average* rises does not necessarily mean that *your* income will rise comparably. It is sad but true that just as some persons' incomes will rise far more rapidly than the average, some persons' incomes will rise far less rapidly. This is not a good situation for those persons falling below the trend line of income. No one wants to earn less than his peers, and certainly no one wants to be short of money all the time. The question then is what on earth can the one individual whose income is only rising by 1 percent per year do about it? That is, how do you get yourself back up onto that trend line?

The first way to understand the whole concept is to realize that the reason your income is not rising as rapidly as you would like is that there is not sufficient competition for your labor. This sounds cold and impersonal, and it may also sound personally insulting, but it is neither. Almost no employed person's wage rises substantially unless persons in a position of authority believe that the employee may be hired away by someone else. This is even true in the government. A government employee will get a small raise if he simply puts in his time. The big raises come from a boss's fear that the employee—even in the government— will get lured away. Even if that is a highly contingent and far-removed threat, even if it is operating mostly on a theoretical level, it still has powerful application in every job.

There can be two basic reasons why there is inadequate danger of being hired away in your job. Either there is a problem about your personal work, or there is a lack of competition in the field. Since no one who would trouble to buy and read a book of this kind would be likely to perform his or her work poorly, we can focus on a lack of competition for labor in your field generally.

When I say that there is a lack of competition for persons in your field, that can mean several different things are going on. First, there can be government-required lack of competition for people in your field. For example, if you are a census taker and the government has just cut back funding for the Bureau of the Census, there may well be a hiring freeze within the Census Bureau. That means you cannot be hired out of your department and placed somewhere else within the Bureau, because no other department would have any money for a new employee, either. The whole dismal train of events would mean that your bosses would know that they not only *could* keep you in your current job at the same pay, but perhaps were *compelled* to do so. That is an example of the clearest possible kind of government-enforced ban on competition for your labor.

A slightly more familiar kind of situation is that of teachers in states undergoing budgetary shortfalls. As a matter of state policy, there may be restrictions on how much a teacher can be paid and then restrictions upon how much raise a teacher can get. Even the most startlingly accomplished teachers may not be able to defeat this kind of policy, may not be able to get themselves up onto the trend line laid out by the averages for members of that age group. Moreover, in the teaching field, there is little financial competition from private schools, which generally pay far less than even poorly paid public schools. Again, this is a form of government-mandated control over the competition in your field. The government has basically made it impossible for any other part of the school system to hire you away from your school, and considerations that have nothing to do with your abilities have conspired to lower your pay artificially.

Then there are conditions of work in declining industries. If you work as a designer of ashtrays, for example, there is likely to be only small demand for any additional designers of ashtrays. Smoking is a habit that is (mercifully) becoming more and more rare. There are already many ashtrays in existence. The vogue of forty years ago for artistically designed ashtrays has virtually disappeared. You may be an excellent designer of ashtrays that look like Space Shuttles or like kittens, but you may still find only small demand for the services of a really top-drawer ashtray designer. Probably there are only a small number of artistic ashtray manufacturers in your area. You may find that your boss can keep your pay extremely low and still keep you under his roof because there is no danger of anyone hiring you away.

Or you may be in a declining part of America. If you are a secretary/receptionist in Dallas three months after the price of oil has dropped by $5 per barrel, your pay is likely to remain fixed for some time to come. After all, everyone in Dallas will be on hard times—or think he is on hard times—and the demand for secretary/receptionists is likely to be considerably lower than the demand for referees in bankruptcy.

In any of these cases, you may well be kept at your job at the same— or lower—pay. Your present employer will know that he does not need to keep giving you raises despite your increased productivity because you are just not going to be hired away. (There will be some rare employers who will continue to give raises because they have good hearts or because they like you or because they want to store up good-will against the day of some future catastrophe or good fortune. Like anything rare, they cannot be counted on as a regular part of life.)

The forces that restrain one's pay are impersonal, but the effects on you will be extremely personal. One might usefully compare the phenomenon with getting struck by lightning. The complex interaction of heat, moisture, changes in temperature, and motion that go into making a powerful charge of electricity are quite independent of the human being who gets struck by that bolt of lightning. But the effect is still decidedly personal.

If you are one of those persons who reads with envy and amazement that your income should rise at 8 percent after inflation throughout your twenties, and wonders what went wrong, you have a number of choices. Some of those choices involve reconciling yourself to your fate. Some of them involve finding the ladder up to your desired curve of rising income. Some of them involve a combination of reconciliation and action.

The first thing to realize is this: When you think of how to concoct a lifetime financial strategy for harmonizing the earnings and consumption function, *neither side of the equation is engraved in granite.* We have just examined a number of ways to alter your life so that you do not make the same mistakes in spending made by the average man or woman. *By the same token,* there are a number of routes to taking yourself out of the dreary statistics about teachers' pay, declining industries, stagnant geographic regions, and below-expected earnings, and all of them can change the income side.

The first step in bridging the gap between the real and the ideal is to consider whether you are working at the kind of job you love regardless of its pay. That is, do you love your career so much that you would prefer to stay in it, more or less independent of the pay? Do you find yourself champing at the bit each morning, absolutely dying to get to the shop, forgetting when payday comes? Do you wake up in the middle of the night thanking the lucky star of your birth that you get to work teaching young minds or guiding tours at an art museum or teaching stroke victims to walk? In a word, do you feel as if that huge percentage of the day devoted to work is the best time you could possibly spend with your clothes on?

If you answer yes to these questions, you are probably going to have to reconcile yourself to not getting raises quite as fast as persons who have jobs that they may perhaps not love as much as yours. The plain fact is that some of the most wonderful, interesting, exciting jobs do not pay as well as the average job. If we are talking about your job, you must prepare yourself to live under far more straitened circumstances than will the average man or woman described in this book. You will be in essence getting paid with enjoyment more than with money. That is perfectly fine, but you will just have to remember that you cannot spend what you are not paid. You can spend your knowledge of art and music derived—with great happiness—from that low-paid job at the gallery. You can spend it in conversation or letters or thought. You cannot spend it on a suit or a trip to Nassau. Bear it in mind. We all make choices in this world. If you choose to enter and stay in a low-paying field, that has big consequences in terms of pay, and if you ignore them, you *beg* for trouble.

To harmonize earning with spending you have to know whether your income will rise at the levels attributed to the average worker. If you know for certain or almost for certain that your income will lag well below that level, you must live with according frugality. It is great to enjoy your work and noble to live with low pay for your love of your career. But you have to live far more carefully than the people who are not making such sacrifices. That is the meaning of sacrifice.

But for most young Americans, the quality of work is not so overwhelmingly positive that it outweighs every other consideration, including pay. Statistics tell us that the majority of young workers like their jobs, but would definitely be ready to change jobs in order to improve their incomes. In fact, in the first decade of work, the average young American changes jobs no fewer than five times. The reason most often given for leaving jobs is because the new job offered better pay.

All of this makes fairly elementary sense. For most people, work is a means to pay the bills. If a given job does not pay the bills, it makes perfect logical sense to look for a job that does. Anyone would understand that. The key points to remember are these:

1. Do not feel certain that the law of averages will lift your income. It probably will, "but here on earth, God's work is truly our own," as John F. Kennedy said. If we want to get up to the modal income level, we may often have to go out and hustle up some decently paid work. It will not inevitably happen by itself as much as we would like for it to do so.

2. The same dynamics that make for low-paying jobs—absence of competition for your labor—suggest where high-paying jobs are to be found: in markets where there is high competition for your labor.

This means that you can and should do all you can to get an income which will rise at least as fast as the average. The extraordinary volume of job changes in this country shows that the labor market is highly fluid. People can and do change jobs for the better every minute of every day. If you are able to get yourself into a job which allows your income to rise by at least the national average increase year by year, you will find that the harmonizing of income and expenditure becomes correspondingly easier. Again, this is a basic concept. But it is a basic concept that has action consequences in your life.

If you are a schoolteacher in a school district teetering on the edge of bankruptcy, you can and should realize that you are free to leave the field, leave the area, change your occupation, and generally do any number of things which would make your life easier. The mathematics teacher in junior high can become a computer programmer. The unemployed mechanic in Hamtramck can become the owner of a Jaguar repair shop in Beverly Hills. By shifting from work and from neighborhoods where there is no competition to areas of high competition, you can and will shift your income function to a more acute upward slope.

It will not be easy. For almost any thinking human being, there is a natural reluctance to step off the career path upon which you find yourself at any given moment. Inertia, after all, is just as much a human quality as it is a quality of stones or missiles. To the teacher, the obstacles involved in becoming an engineer look immense. To the engineer, the obstacles involved in becoming a manager look immense. But there is almost nothing more expected and more frequently done in this country than changing careers, locations, employers. This is a society in which workers, especially young workers, are *expected* to change careers to make more money. The whole capitalist system is based upon flows of labor into and out of jobs that pay more or less as society wants more or less of what the jobs produce. Do we want more home computers? San Jose booms. Do we want less natural gas? Young people leave Bartlesville. Are adults reading less? Editors become professors. Are fewer children becoming college students? College professors become accountants. This kind of change is, of course, far more difficult and painful on a personal level than on a national level. The point is simply this: To move yourself into a better position on the income side is something society not only tolerates but encourages. Where you stand relative to the income of your age group is determined not only by huge aggregate movements, but partly by your own energy, flexibility, and imagination. Look to it.

NEXT: The Best Years of Our Lives.

SIX

The Thrilling Thirties

How to Ruin Your Life—A Case Study

The apogee of most persons' lives—as measured by psychometric testing—is in their thirties. Social scientists and psychiatrists have asked a great many people in old age at what time they believe they were the happiest. The answer given by the most people, men and women, is "In my thirties." Apparently, that is the time at which many people lose the pimples and the stuttering of youth, without quite getting the tremors of eternity of middle age and the illnesses of the golden years. Perhaps there are other hormonal or glandular reasons why men and women from thirty to thirty-nine years old consider that time the best of their lives. Perhaps, like Jean Brodie, they are simply in their prime in some biological sense. Possibly, because of the way work and income are structured in America, young Americans in their thirties are able to reap more of the good things of life than at any other time—at least in terms of their expectations. *It may be that the thirties are one of those magical periods of human life in which achievements outpace expectations.*

Whatever the reasons are, we know by now that the thirties should be a time of happiness even beyond the twenties. But there are severe risks awaiting men and women who sail blithely into that age bracket without realizing what they can and cannot do.

For variety's sake, we can and will look at the problems first in terms of an example rather than in terms of statistics. Take, as an example of what can go wrong, the case of Sergio and Juliette Capretta, a thirty-three-year-old couple in the outskirts of Dallas. They live in a fine three-bedroom apartment on Lemmon Boulevard, hard upon Love Field. They were careful and prudent in their twenties, and they happen to own that apartment as a condominium.

Sergio has the unusual but interesting job of airplane salesman. He works for a huge enterprise—Aviall Flight Services—and he has been ringing up solid wage increases, plus bonuses, year by year. His income, at age thirty-three, is almost three times what it was in the first year of his work, when he began at the tender age of twenty-two. His income then was a mere $10,000 per year. Now it is $29,000 per year. His income has been rising at almost exactly 10 percent per year compounded. He is doing better even than his age group in terms of yearly wage increases (which are about 9 percent in real terms).

His wife, Juliette, works as the chief of housekeeping at an elegant hotel, the Mansion on Turtle Creek. She has been in and out of the labor force because of the two children they have had, lovely boys named Steven and Barron. She originally started as a clerk at a clothing store near downtown Dallas, but now she wants to work closer to home. In fact, because of a conference she recently had with Steve's teacher in second grade, she is seriously contemplating leaving the labor force altogether. The teacher, Miss Moore, said that Steve had a tendency to sit in the corner and stare during recesses. Juliette, as a good mother, sees that she might need to spend more time with him.

Juliette's income as chief of housekeeping is $20,000 per year. She also gets a free lunch every day in the employees' cafeteria.

Because the Caprettas thought and planned, their interest payments plus principal reduction on their home are no more than $950 per month. That puts them within the ambit of sensible home expenses, at 28.5 percent of after-tax income.

The Caprettas have been frugal in their spending and have managed to save $25,000, including interest. They took a flyer on an airplane manufacturing stock and did very poorly. They then took another flyer on a boat manufacturer and did extremely well, so they also have $6,000 in stock.

Now their problems are about to start. First, Juliette arrived home one day to find the baby-sitter sitting in front of "Days of Our Lives" with a jelly jar filled with Wild Turkey Bourbon. Steve was sitting in the corner staring at the wall, tears running down his face. Barron was eating Cheerios from the box, getting them all over the floor.

The baby-sitter was fired immediately. The resignation was handed in at the Mansion Hotel the next morning. The family income was cut by 41 percent in one week's time.

A psychiatrist was called in to see little Steve. The doctor said that Steve was a great kid, but that he would probably do well to have more personal attention than he could possibly get at the Lemmon Park Elementary School, which had been the subject of mandatory busing and where there had been serious discipline problems even before the busing.

Because Steve was a precocious little thing, he was admitted to the University Park Center for Elementary Learning. His attitude immediately improved. The bill for tuition was $1,800 per semester.

Once Juliette was home from work every day, she noticed that there was a great deal of traffic on Lemmon Boulevard. She was trying to study at home to learn accountancy to become an auditor eventually and add to their earnings. But the noise of the tractor-trailers going back and forth on Lemmon drove her crazy. Besides, for little Steve and Barron, there was only a small grass and concrete park for playing. She badly wanted her children to be able to play in a shady, sprawling park. Each school day, she drove past the quiet streets and meandering parks of the University Park area. It sure looked like a nice place to raise kids.

One day, Juliette saw a house for sale on a dead-end street. Amazingly, it was only $199,000. It did need a lot of work, but both she and Sergio were good with their hands. They were able to sell the condo on Lemmon and walk away with $49,000 in cash after paying off the mortgage. They were able to talk the price of the house in University Park down to the unheard of price of $189,000, which was *nothing* for a house in that part of Dallas.

By fudging just a little on their mortgage application and pretending that Juliette still worked at the Mansion (her best friend was head of personnel and would answer the call from the bank), Sergio and Juliette were able to get a mortgage for $140,000 at an even 12 percent, fixed for the first five years.

Payments each month were about $1,440. Since the family income had fallen by 41 percent to $29,000, the mortgage payment now represented an even 60 percent of their gross income, and an amazing 72 percent of their after-tax income, although that would fall as their enormous interest costs reduced their taxable income to almost nothing.

Of course, Sergio's instincts told him that when he was spending such a huge amount on his mortgage that he should cut back drastically elsewhere. He knew that was even more true because he now had a son in private school. But he was now in one of the prestige neighborhoods of Dallas. He did not want to look like the neighborhood beggar, and he certainly did not want his children to be the objects of ridicule. So, he went to Roche Bobois and bought new furniture for the house. Because he had impeccable credit, he was able to carry $13,000 worth of furniture at no money down, all payments spread over three years at 14 percent. In fact, as the salesman at Roche Bobois said, the payments would not even start for three months, during which time anything could happen. Sergio could sell a new plane. He could get a giant increase in pay. The extra payments of $444 per month would hardly even be noticed!

Sergio further talked himself into trouble by telling himself that he was going to be able to exchange one kind of savings for another. After all, he would have less money in his savings (he was planning to pay off the first few months or years of his furniture bill from savings). But he would have all that beautiful furniture, which was "an investment in the future" in and of itself.

And, truth to tell, Sergio, Juliette, Steve, and Barron did take in their belts in a few small ways. They ate more meals at home. They did not even think about going on a vacation that year. Mommy replaced the baby-sitter, and they gritted their teeth and kept the same old cars—a Pinto and a battered Volvo.

But even so, the cost of the furniture, the forgone income from Juliette's job, the enormous mortgage payments, the private school, meant that Sergio and Juliette had to draw down their savings by almost $3,000 per month.

One day, as Sergio added up his liquid assets on his calculator, his heart went into his mouth. He saw, quite simply, that he would be out of money in almost exactly six months, which was not at all far in the future. He became hysterical and started to hyperventilate. In the next few days and weeks, he became increasingly upset. Sadly, he took out his anxiety on his wife. When she learned that they were heading toward using up all of their savings, she became extremely upset as well. After all, she had quit her job and stayed home mostly for the love of little Steve, not out of a desire to lie in bed and eat bonbons. And, truth to tell, Steve had gotten much better since his mommy had been home with him. He no longer stared, and he liked his playmates at the University Park Center for Early Learning far, far better than his old classmates at the Lemmon Park school.

Juliette very much resented the sudden intrusion of this financial worry upon her peace of mind. She had, after all, trusted in Sergio's ability to plan their financial future, and if he screwed up—as he apparently had—he certainly should not take it out on her and the kids. Arguments led to sulking, which led to more arguments. Soon, there were harsh words exchanged. Next thing Sergio knew, he had moved out and into the Lemmon Boulevard Holiday Inn.

Soon divorce lawyers were being called in at $100 per hour. The stock was sold to pay legal fees in a flash, and the sale, alas, took place on the day that the boat manufacturer announced lower earnings forecast for the next three years. In a word, things were in an almost unbelievable mess. We leave Sergio so worried about his finances that he cannot even remember his prospects' names. We leave Juliette applying for a job as a real estate saleswoman. And we leave little Steve staring at the wall because he misses his father.

This has been a horror story of our time. In the sad tragedy of the Capretta family, we have learned that a steadily rising curve of income in one's thirties does not spell nirvana. The Caprettas made almost every mistake a family can make as they enter that wonderful decade, and they did not really ever get the chance to have the happiness they longed for.

The Caprettas saw that their incomes were rising—and they saw right. For the average American worker from age thirty to age thirty-four, income rises at the fastest rate of any time of life—a blistering 9 percent, which will double real income in eight years, if sustained. They also saw that this rise in real income (we will leave the effects of inflation out for simplicity) had afforded them the chance to save. They saw their standard of living rising—seemingly inexorably.

Avoiding Detours by Reading the Map

What they did not see—because they had stars of rising expectations in their eyes and because they did not have access to the mass of data that I have—were some of the giant pitfalls that lay waiting for them in their thirties:

- Dramatically rising education costs for children in modern-day urban America and the ever-surprising cost of child-rearing.
- The movement in and out of the labor force of mothers of young children.
- The powerful urge to move up to a new generation of life-style as one leaves one's student days behind.
- The astronomically rising incidence of divorce in one's early thirties.

Taking these one by one will show us how the expenditure side of life can be predicted more carefully than Sergio and Juliette and millions of others were able or willing to do.

Education

First, there is a genuine national crisis in education. Twenty-five years ago, few American families even considered sending their children, especially elementary school age children, to private schools. The public schools were far from perfect, but they performed an adequate job of socializing youngsters and teaching them the basics of learning. Except for wealthy families, families with distinct religious beliefs which they wished to see taught in school, and families with problem children, public schools were the norm.

Then came a variety of extremely basic changes in the demographics of big-city life, a drastic loss of discipline in the classroom, and a rapidly unraveling educational process. Teachers were often unable to keep order in the schools. Students became necessarily preoccupied with survival rather than with Horace. Getting home in one piece took the place of calculus. Class syllabuses changed. Students were not taught to add, but they were taught about "life adjustment." The net of it all was that by the early 1980s, in large cities and in many suburbs, public education had become not only unresponsive to their children's legitimate needs, but actually dangerous. For a plethora of reasons that may never be fully known, the entire national public education system could no longer provide a mass education.

This is a national problem, of course, of which politicians make hay, as they tend to do about all problems. It is also a personal problem for the young American family. The mommy and daddy who once paid their property taxes and sent off Junior and Sis with their lunch pails to public school often are not willing to do so any longer. The percentage of middle-class children going to private schools has leaped startlingly in the last ten years, especially in large cities.

In other words, the young couple with children would be smart to plan to send their children to private schools and might just count themselves lucky if they did not have to. Of course, if there is a neighborhood in your town in which the public schools are far better than in other areas, you might want to consider living there. To send a child to a private day school at a cost of $3,500 per year will cost $42,000 over the course of a twelve-year precollege education. Many schools cost more. If you have two or more children, you can see that the total cost can radically affect your total expenses over the time of your child's schooling. To forgo spending that money by living in an area with better public schools is a consummation devoutly to be wished. Alas, the free market, ever efficient, always puts a higher price on residences in a "good schools" area. That is, a house which saves its owners from having to send Junior and Sis to St. Mark's is going to cost much more than a house next to the Blackboard Jungle. But the difference might be extremely worthwhile if you have more than one child in school. You will have to calculate the savings and the costs yourself. The main concern is to be aware that in today's America, you will almost certainly have to pay *in some way* for a decent education for your children. If you plan for that expense in advance, you will be miles ahead of the game.

To bring in mathematics again, if you can save money and earmark it for Junior's education before you actually have to start sending it to an anonymous bursar somewhere at a private school, you will be ahead of the game. That way, the money will start to earn interest and will, in a primitive sense, work alongside you to pay for Junior's old school tie.

For example, if you can save about $21,640 before Junior starts the first form, and if you put that money at interest at 12 percent, it will yield the $3,500 tuition all by itself, paid out as an annuity. You will not even have to think about it. Even if you can save only about $5,000 before a child starts school, you will find that the savings, paid out as an annuity, will pay for almost one fourth of Junior's tuition (at the same price of tuition), taking enough load off your back to save plenty of sleepless nights.

But what if you cannot save, and what if you simply cannot afford to pay for Junior's private schooling out of your current income? Is precollegiate nonpublic school tuition a worthy subject for borrowing? Of course, the answer to that question depends on how you feel about your children. But if you believe, as most Americans do, that they owe a duty to their children to send them out into the world as well-prepared for the struggle as they can possibly do, then good education is a must. It is one of the most clearly proved ways of improving a child's life chances in terms of income, emotional maturity, and health.

Private or parochial schooling should first be paid for by spending less on entertainment, housing, transportation, meals away from home, telephone, or anywhere else that fat lingers in the family budget. A father who buys himself a Mercedes while Sis walks cowering down the hallways of the local public school is not really a caring human being— or a smart one. A mother who buys herself facials while Junior is *not* being taught the multiplication tables should never have been a mother in the first place.

But if drastic economies in spending on Chez Louis, manicures, trips to St. Lucie, and cable-ready Sony TV's do not make up enough to pay for school where Junior can learn about science and Sis can learn confidence in mathematics, then borrowing is definitely in order. But how should one borrow? Obviously, you cannot pay for private school on your MasterCard. Just as obviously, most banks do not have a usual category for nonpublic school loans, and even if they did, the rate would probably be the same as the rate on a loan for a trip to Yellowstone. In other words, the interest rate would be unconscionably high.

Lenders who happen to work within banks or finance companies are very much like you and me. They want to lend on the best possible security. If at all possible, they want to lend against *both* collateral and income, and they will charge less interest if they can. That means that for most young families, the best kind of loan would be a loan against a residence, if at all possible. Generally speaking, second mortgages or refinancings of existing mortgages will cost far, far less than personal loans. If you can get a "refi" for enough money to pay for some or all of the kiddies' private or parochial education, you will usually be miles ahead.

Of course, there are precautions that must be taken. If you have a first mortgage at a low rate, do not even think of refinancing the whole mortgage at a new, higher rate. If you have only got a small deficit to make up in payments for Junior's school, do not go to the trouble and expense of refinancing your whole house. Often, refinancing a house costs "points" or percentages of the total loan in advance of the repayments. There is no point in paying these points unless you are going to need at least $10,000.

That brings us to the urgent requirement that you not plan to pay for *all* of the children's schooling through borrowing. That would impose a staggering burden on most families. More important, it should not be necessary. As your income rises over time, you should absolutely plan to control your expenditures enough so that, at some time *in the near future,* you will be able to pay for school, loan repayments, and all your other expenses out of current income. (This does not mean all the loans have to be repaid completely by a time in the near future, only that you no longer need to take out fresh loans.)

Many private and parochial schools offer tuition assistance in the form of scholarship grants and loans out of their own funds. This should be a basic resource for the young couple trying to make their way financially and also to educate their children.

The most important points to remember are these:

1. You are likely to have to pay in some way for the education of young children.

2. The family who makes advance preparation for this possibly large and increasing expense in advance will be far ahead in terms of lightening their burden.

3. Borrowing for education is a legitimate and even noble reason for borrowing, but do it sensibly.

4. Make a plan for controlling expenses over time which allows you to pay for education and loan repayments out of current income.

It is a national disgrace that our public school system is so weak that middle-class people not only have to pay property taxes but sometimes must sacrifice drastically to pay for a private education for their children. But, alas, this is life, and realistic people make plans for life as it is today, not as it was yesterday. The Caprettas did not do it. You must do better.

In Toddler-Land and Beyond

There is a semi-facetious basic rule about paying for the costs of children as they grow up:

• However much you think it will cost, it will cost more.

Within that rule, there are a number of subrules:

• Whatever controls you try to put on your children's costs, they will not work.
• However much your neighbors can save on raising their kids, you can't do it.
• Whatever you remember as the expenses of growing up yourself, forget them.

One entire branch of the Department of Agriculture works on statistics about how much money it costs to raise a child in many different environments in the United States. There is a high budget for the Far West, a low budget for the Northeast, a moderate budget for the Midwest, a large-family, high budget for the Plains States, and on and on. These figures are updated with great frequency. They yield a continuing graph of how much it costs to raise a child according to the standards laid down by the Department of Agriculture.

Just to take a figure that lies about in the midpoint of all the data, the 1982 estimated cost for raising a child in the Northeast from the time he comes home with Mom from the hospital until he is eighteen was approximately $93,000.

High budget for the Far West was several thousand more. Low budget for the South was several thousand less. The basic idea was that $90,000 is the ballpark figure.

The problem is that this figure changes rapidly over time. It also is an average number, based upon preferences for shelter, food, recreation, and transportation which you may or may not share. However, the figure is by no means useless. Statisticians have found a more personal, more individual way of using all that data. They wanted to take it from a musty building at Fourteenth Street and Independence Avenue, S.W., Washington, D.C., to Anytown, U.S.A., and set it down right in front of you while you were eating your meat and potatoes. What they found is that while the relation of one year's costs to the next year's costs varies dramatically, there is a *fairly stable* relationship between the costs per child and the *family income*.

That means that while you often cannot predict how much the absolute cost will be of raising a first child or a second child or a third child, you can almost certainly predict at least roughly how much of your total income *and total expenses* will go toward child raising at the precollege level. (We will get to the dreaded college years in the section on passages through the forties.)

Over the last ten years, the relationship between family income and child rearing has been about as follows:

The cost of raising a child from just after birth to the beginning of higher education has been approximately four times one year's income *for the first child.* For each additional child, the cost of rearing from postbirth to precollege has been only about two times one year's income. In other words, the costs of having children diminish extremely rapidly after the first child.

Before you faint dead away, remember that you will be spreading that cost over about eighteen years per child. In addition, the "one year's income" that we are talking about is one year's income *at the time the child is born.* If current income rates of rise continue from the early thirties to the late forties, the total cost of raising a child to age eighteen would represent only about *one and a half years' income* at the time Junior was trundling off to Princeton or State. For example, if your income is $35,000 in 1985 when Junior is born, you can expect his upbringing to age eighteen to cost about $140,000 (in 1985 dollars). For Sis, born in 1987 when your income is $40,000, you can expect the additional cost to age eighteen to be $80,000 in 1987 income.

Another, even more helpful way of examining the likely relation between the cost of raising a child and the cost of all other purchases is by studying the *long-term* relationship between the family expenses of families who have different numbers of children *but are otherwise similar.* Through almost unbelievably thorough research by the world's premier research-gathering apparatus in economics, the Bureau of Labor Statistics of the U.S. Department of Labor, we humans have learned that as families expand, their expenditures expand much like the following, per year.

Man and Woman	Plus First Child	Second Child	Third Child
1.00	1.24	1.43	1.53

(This takes 1.00 as the total of all expenses—but does not include savings or taxes—at the time just prior to the appearance of the first child.)

One immediately striking fact is that when the first child comes along, consumption expenses rise—over time—by almost one quarter. But when the third child comes down the pike, expenses rise by only about 7 percent, or about one fourth of that original fourth. Again, two cannot live as cheaply as one, but they can live as cheaply as 1.7, and five can live as cheaply as four plus 7 percent. *Rapidly diminishing costs greet each additional child as a general rule, which is good news.*

There are many important caveats about these statistics: First, that one-fourth increase in expenditures *does not come all at once.*

You need not fear getting home from the hospital to find that each of your VISA bills is 24 percent larger. The increases come gradually, and, in fact, if you have followed the path of common sense, you have already provided for one of the major costs—the expense of larger living quarters. Further, the increases are by no means invisible. Because growing children outgrow their clothes rapidly, there will be a much larger item for clothing. Because little babies, unlike cats or parakeets, cannot be left at home alone, there will be a whole new item for baby-sitters. This means that you can see the money going out, so that you do not suddenly feel an overwhelming, powerful *jerk,* as the money is mysteriously sucked out of your savings account.

Second, as the increase in your living expenses occurs, your income will rise, and your taxes will fall. As we have learned, income rises at about 9 percent per annum in real, inflation-adjusted terms from age thirty through age thirty-four. This means that for every dollar of real income on your thirtieth birthday, you can—on the average with all the cautions that implies—expect that on your thirty-fifth birthday, you will earn $1.54. By adding inflation to that, the gain becomes even greater in nominal terms. That tells you that as you and your spouse see those rising bills from the pediatrician, the finger painting class, the Pampers store, the baby-sitter, and the baby photographer, you will also generally see larger paychecks. Moreover, under present law, there is an exemption, or a standard deduction, for each dependent, and since child care costs are now deductible on a sliding scale inversely related to income, tax payments will fall proportionally.

Far more important, for both good and ill, your tax will fall, at least for a while, if Mom leaves the workplace to concentrate on bringing up baby. After all, under our progressive income-tax system, the less income we earn, the less tax we pay.

Mommy's Missing Paycheck

Now, about that little problem of Mother leaving the work force: It can be a killer. By the early 1980s, almost 62 percent of mothers with husbands present and children from ages six to seventeen worked full- or part-time. This represented an increase of over 50 percent in twenty years. For mothers with husbands present who had children under six at home, almost 45 percent worked full- or part-time. The increase from 1960 in the participation of this group in the labor force was a staggering 150 percent.

Those working wives contributed plenty to the family's take-home pay. For white families where the wife worked full-time, her contributions to the total family income were almost one third of the total sum. For black families, the figure was close to 40 percent. Even for wives who worked part-time, the contribution to income was about 15 percent for whites and 22 percent for blacks. (All figures for 1981.)

That means any family with any sense (unlike the Caprettas) has to understand that there will be a very large jolt downward when the wife leaves the labor force to bring up baby. If families prepare for that jolt —by accumulating savings and drawing up a new spending plan for when Mom quits work—they will be miles ahead. If families expect that by trimming a little around the edges they can adjust to a one-third drop in income, they are dead wrong. Losing one third of total family income is a shock that cannot be dealt with by small changes. It must be made up by major controls on spending, the husband's adding to his income in some way, by large drawdowns of savings, or by borrowing. It cannot—repeat, *cannot*—be done by having the cheeseburger instead of the Big Mac or by brown-bagging it for lunch.

Even if the husband gets a 9 percent real increase in wages each year after the wife leaves the labor force, it will still take him four years and ten months to get up to the total income he and his wife (if she had average contributions to income) had before she left the labor force.

The net of it all, in plain English, is that if the wife quits work to have a baby and stays home to raise baby, as more and more wives are doing, it will take drastic surgery to make up the difference. Expect to spend less on amusements, autos, vacations, telephone, and your own clothing. Expect to withdraw from savings.

Know this in advance: If you have already gotten a big enough home and if you have already gotten sufficient savings to get you over the rough spots in the road while you become a one-paycheck family, you will smile a lot more at the baby.

The Sex-Class System and You

One other painful note regarding mothers who leave the work force: Once they return, they will be shocked at how much they will have to give up in the way of accumulated pay increases. Because they have been at home raising baby, they have not added to their productivity or seniority. Women and men who stayed in the labor force received pay increases year after year as their skill and productivity rose. The mommy who was at home teaching Junior to read will not get those raises. She will be lucky to get the same salary she got when she left work to go to the obstetrics ward.

This may seem to be wildly unfair. After all, raising children is a crucial, integral part of the work of the nation. Why should women who have been doing that work be "penalized" for it by not getting wage increases that workers who did not leave the labor force got? Alas, however unfair it is, that is the way things work. It is no secret that women generally earn less than men in this country—as in all countries which have statistics. The reason for this is that women leave the labor force far more frequently and for far more prolonged periods than men do. They do not get all the accumulated momentum of raises that persons who do not leave the labor force get.

Whether or not you believe that this is an injustice, your anger will not get the family through the financial narrows when baby comes. Make realistic provision for the world as it is. Then you can do something about the injustice if you believe it to be that, *and* you can also avoid those sleepless nights.

Madison Avenue's Snares and Delusions

Next, and closely allied with all of this, there is a great temptation to move up to a whole new generation of life-style when a family gets into their thirties. Why not? They see other thirty-year-olds who have a

Mercedes and a cottage for the summer in the Hamptons. They see thirty-year-old people in advertisements and in movies and in TV shows. They look like they are having a great time with fancy cars and travel and large houses. The young family in their thirties might well assume—as many do—that it is their god-given right to live as well as the people in the General Foods International Coffees advertisements.

That belief is a trap. Human beings like you and the Caprettas can only afford to live as well as they can afford. The appearance of another family living in a certain way in a commercial or an advertisement is simply irrelevant to the way real people can and do live their lives. There is no reason at all for real live people to imitate video or newsprint people unless they can afford to and unless they have nothing better to spend their money on. If you let it happen to you—if you let yourselves get captured by a Madison Avenue-inspired way of life—you are just shooting yourself in the foot.

One loan officer after another at banks and finance companies will say that what gets families into financial disaster in their thirties is that they try to reach a life-style that is simply not accessible to people with their income. The family sees the boats and the cars and the RVs and the travel, and they simply believe that it is their right as young Americans to have these goodies. The fact is that it is not their right, and if they try to fantasy about it, they get in trouble. If they try to dream their way to affluence, they wake up with powerful real-life nightmares.

Just because you are sick of that old couch, that does not mean you can afford a new living room suite from Knoll. Life does not work like that. Just because you see neighbors who have a new Seville, that does not mean you can afford one. You can afford one when you have enough money to pay for one after you have paid for all of the major, necessary expenses, such as the education of your children.

In the early thirties, when income is shooting upward, there is great temptation to spend like a sailor. If you do it, you are not facing reality. You will—as we discussed above—inevitably have large expenses for raising your children. You will inevitably lose some income while the mother is out of the labor force. Do not ignore these real world limits on how much you can upgrade your life-style. Yes, we all want to live in a nice house with nice things in it. Yes, we all want to have a nice car and a maid. No, just because we want those things it does not mean we can have them.

Upgrading of life-style can and must be intimately linked with the more pressing needs of raising children and buying a home. There are no general guidelines about this except the obvious: Do not ignore your real world income and your real world spending needs when you set about reaching that fantasy life-style.

This is a country in which everyone from coal miners to sharecroppers is encouraged by advertisements to live like Rockefellers. The misguided of this world do it. The smart ones live on what they can afford. Which are you?

Divorce—American Style

Now for a few sobering thoughts about divorce. In a word, there is an awful lot of it going around. The financial implications of divorce are enormous. People of a certain age can not only fear divorce but positively expect it.

Take it step by step. In this country, by 1981, the number of divorces was exactly, precisely half the number of marriages. That might seem to mean that a new marriage had a 50 percent chance of ending in divorce. Alas, that umbrella figure conceals some bad news for young marrieds. While the rate of divorce per 1000 persons was indeed half of the rate of marriages per 1000 persons, that incidence of divorces was not scattered all over the age curve. Marriages were spread all the way from those under twenty-one to nonagenarians and above. But divorces were very highly concentrated around the mid-twenties-to-early-thirties. In fact, young Americans who are married *are more likely to get divorced by the time they are thirty-five than to stay married.*

Of course, we all think and hope it won't happen to us. But it happens to persons across every kind of income and educational and even religious background. It sounds macabre to suggest planning for divorce, and indeed it may be. But to ignore the possibility of divorce is like ignoring the possibility of catching the flu. It is a bad thing, but it happens to innocent people. If they are prepared, it can be less painful.

To be prepared does not mean to have signed depositions and demands for visitation in your cupboard. It means to realize that if you, as a family, are about to undertake huge financial responsibilities, you might just give some thought to two questions:

1. Will these responsibilities cause so much strain in our marriage that they raise the risk of divorce in an already divorce-prone age group?

2. Will these responsibilities be so weighty that in the event of a divorce they make life impossible afterward?

The first is a less macabre question, but one which even intelligent persons rarely ask themselves. There is a mass of data that shows us that financial arguments are either the first or second proximate cause of divorce (competing with sexual arguments). It is a fact that human beings can only absorb so much stress without collapsing under the weight. This includes human relationships, and it includes stress about money.

Men and women should pause before buying a Porsche or a new set of Henredon living room furniture to ask themselves if they can really spend that money without raising the level of anxiety within the family. If the new purchase will really lead to stress, the family should carefully weigh whether or not that purchase is so important that it outweighs the dangers of damage to the personality and to the marriage. There are a lot of beautiful cars and beautiful living room suites that have wrought ugly havoc on marriages. The real cost of any purchase is not just cash and forgone interest. *It is the stress brought on by having to pay for it.* Everyone should bear that cost in mind, but men and women in the high-risk age group for divorce should pay particularly close attention. The most sleek Thunderbird is hardly worth divorce court, and the most elegant living room furniture is not worth loneliness.

Second, divorces rarely happen out of the clear blue sky. Persons who are having trouble in their marriages usually know it. For those persons to enter upon large purchases is extremely risky. Expensive buys by husbands and wives that precede divorces or separations are emotional arsenic. At the least, they use up savings. At another level of horror, they impose future payments upon divorced individuals, who often will be financially strapped. At the worst, they add bitterness to an already painful situation in that ex-husbands and ex-wives blame each other for making their new single lives far more stringent than they need have been. That Sony TV or trip to Europe looks very different one year after a divorce when its ghost keeps showing up on an impoverished ex-wife's MasterCard or a strapped ex-husband's bank statement. Purchases made by a couple or a family contemplating divorce or having emotional problems should meet tests of *extremely* clear need.

Juliette and Sergio Capretta made every mistake in the book. They did not even start to think out the increased risk of divorce that their wild spending led them to. If they had thought about the potential wreckage of their lives that their new home and their new way of life would cause, they might have been more careful. Was the house in University Park worth ruining their marriage? Was the expensive school worth a life alone? In the event, they now have neither the home nor the school nor the expensive furniture (it was sold to pay legal costs of the divorce), so that the real question might better be "Was a very brief enjoyment of a life-style that could not be afforded worth wrecking a promising family life?" To that kind of question there can only be one answer. The tragedy is that few young families pause to ask the question, or to ask other questions about the costs of education, houses, lifestyle, and how they affect a marriage.

Once informed of the dangers, anyone in his right mind will take sensible precautions to avoid horrible diseases. The statistics of divorce tell us of the dangers. So do the data on the contribution of financial worries to divorce situations. You have been warned!

Conclusions to Live With

The net of all the existing data about financially passing into one's thirties in America is that

- Your income will rise very fast for the first half of the decade. This *should* provide the wherewithal for having children, educating children, and a *gradual* increase to a new level of comfort in your life.
- There are crucial dangers involved in the large expense of child raising and educating, which can best be avoided by setting aside money for those needs as early as possible.
- It is perfectly understandable and even desirable to borrow for providing a good education to your child, but do it sensibly.
- Bear in mind that divorce is a major threat to young Americans in their early thirties and take steps to make certain that your spending habits do not aggravate the problem.

The thirties are the period in which families can expect to move to a position of financial stability if they do not go crazy thinking they can afford everything all at once. If families can realize that their ability to pay is not infinite just because their incomes are rising rapidly, and keep their expenses under control, they will soon get to a warm and comfortable feeling deep down inside.

Just to give you some idea of whether you have things under control, the following table tells you *approximately* what percentage of your income you should be spending on the major categories of your life in your mid-thirties. The second chart tells you the result of your income rising by 9 percent in real terms from age thirty-one to age thirty-five, starting at $30,000. The chart also shows what the result would be of having your expenditures rise by only 7 percent per year, while you bank the difference at 11 percent interest.

For Families in Their Mid-Thirties—
Percentage of Total Consumption Expenses After Taxes
(not including savings except for pension and insurance)

Food—total	16
Food at home	9
Food away from home	7
Alcohol and tobacco	2
Housing (rented or owned)—total	35
Utilities	3
Telephone and other household operations	5
Home furnishings and appliances	4
Rent or mortgage and taxes	23
Clothing	5
Transportation (including auto purchase)	17
Health care	5
Recreation	5
Education	7
Insurance and pension contributions	9

(Total may not add to 100 percent because of rounding.)

The Big Time . . . Fat City in Your Early Thirties

Age	Real Income rising 9% per year	Real Expenses rising 7% per year	Savings per year	Cumulative Savings at 11% interest
31	$30,000	$30,000	———	———
32	$32,700	$32,100	$600	$600
33	$35,643	$34,347	$1,296	$1,962
34	$38,851	$36,751	$2,100	$4,278
35	$42,347	$39,323.88	$3,023	$7,771.38

(And this is not counting any savings you were able to make in your twenties.)

NEXT: Housekeeping . . . About Life, Death, and Cars.

SEVEN

Savings, Insurance, and Other Real-Life Aggravations

For the average family in its early thirties, there are not only children and promotions at work and divorces among friends, but also a startling increase in savings. While the average family has only saved about fifteen weeks' worth of earnings by the time the head of the household reaches twenty-nine, the average family with a head of the household in his or her mid-thirties has been able to save about ten months' income and in addition has equity in their house equal to about one *year's* income. In other words, there has been a major improvement of the net worth position of the family.

This has implications for what should be done with savings. It means, basically, that you can and should feel able to invest more aggressively as you acquire more gray hairs and more capital. Only a fool will take that as a license to begin speculating in commodities or buying stock on margin. But where the twenty-five-year-old might well have stuck exclusively to money market funds and CDs, the thirty-five-year-old can try a flyer in stocks on occasion, always bearing in mind that, even in the most exuberant bull markets, prices both rise and fall.

For the thirty-five-year-old family with an eye on investments, the key word should always be "liquidity." "Liquidity" is the ability to turn an investment into cash on short notice, preferably instantly. That means stocks on major exchanges, bonds on major exchanges, money market funds, CDs, and other instruments like mutual funds for which a ready and highly fluid market exists. It does not include real estate, no matter what your broker says. It does not include shares in limited partnerships, which are among the most illiquid assets one can own. It does not include sailboats or antique cars. Liquid assets are those which can be turned into currency within a few days, and they are determined by the availability of markets, not by the promises of salesmen.

The reason that thirty-to-thirty-nine-year-olds need liquid assets is that they are likely to have sudden needs for cash. A child can need private schools. A family can need a new home. A husband can lose his job. A wife can need advanced education. The thirties are a period of flux, albeit generally of *good* flux. Money is the magic that makes the flux happen the way you want it to happen. Or, to put it another way, if Junior suddenly needs a private school, you are going to feel fairly sick if you have all your money in an oil and gas partnership that you cannot get out of to save your life. You will feel much better if you can just write out a check from your money market fund.

Life Insurance

There is a burden that comes along with the pleasure of making more money and having children. The burden is that if Mom or Pop passes from this earthly vale, there will be a giant economic hole in the picture. Not only will there be a catch in the throat when Sis says grace at Thanksgiving Dinner, but there will be a big, giant catch when the family opens their bills each month and looks longingly at the spot on the desk where Mom or Dad used to put the old paycheck.

That is why America has a $200 billion (at least!) insurance industry: to make certain that absent Moms and Dads would be able to help their kiddies and spouses maintain a decent standard of living. The question about insurance is never whether to have it or not. The question is almost always what kind to have.

There are four basic kinds of insurance for life and death now available:

1. Whole life, the favorite of agents, which provides a prescribed death benefit and which also has a residual and growing cash value as premiums are paid over time.

2. Term life, which has a prescribed death benefit, but which has no cash value at any time if there is no death. It might be thought of as a

simple bet about whether or not the insured will die within the term of the policy.

3. Universal life, which is a supposed combination of term and whole life. It provides a cash value and a prescribed benefit, but the cash value is much lower than in whole life while the payoff upon death is much higher than the same amount of premiums would buy with whole life. The universal life policy takes some of your premiums and invests them in a term policy and takes the rest of your premiums and invests them in a whole life policy, which is to say, some of them build up a cash value at a rate of interest prescribed by the insurance company.

4. Variable life, which is really a variant of universal life. It takes some of your premiums and puts them in a term policy, then takes others of your premiums and puts them into stock or bond mutual funds. The policy pays out a prescribed amount upon death. It acquires a cash value determined by the performance of the stocks or bonds in the whole life component of the policy. In a rising market, such policies are popular and pay off handsomely. In a long-term bull market, they are disappointing, at best.

Which one should the young family in their thirties have? There is fairly general consensus, even among insurance agents, that if a family can save on their own, whole life is not for them. The rate of return paid by insurance companies on premiums paid under whole life tends to be inferior to many other safe returns. At one time it was scandalously inferior, and now it is less scandalous, but it is still not exciting or even competitive.

If whole life is no bargain, that fact casts a shadow across universal life as well. After all, why buy even a partial whole life policy if whole life is not a bargain? Unless you absolutely cannot make yourself save and you need the compulsion of paying those bills for premiums to make yourself put money aside.

How about variable life? If you feel certain that you are buying into a long-term bull market and if you feel even more confident about the ability of the people who will be investing your hard-earned money, you might very well try variable life. The problem, of course, is that *no one* can know with any confidence at all what the future holds for any particular market. Alas, money managers who were superhot and picked every winner there ever was in one decade sometimes lose their touch in other markets. The gunslingers of the sixties were often wildly wrong in the seventies, and the hotshots of the early eighties were afraid to show their heads by the mid-eighties. Variable life tends to tie up money in the hands of persons and forces which are not necessarily sensitive to your needs and to your relation to larger economic trends, and for that reason it rates a big caution light.

In fact, that big caution light glows over any insurance plan that ostensibly provides for goals other than insuring your life. After all, your goal in buying life insurance is to provide money after your death. To the extent that insurance companies try to piggyback their goals upon your goal, their effort may blur your real goals and needs. If you maintain the focus of your need—to insure your life—and concentrate on how to do that most economically, you will almost certainly choose term life. Per dollar of benefit, it is by far the cheapest of any method of insurance. There are intelligent persons who have spent their entire lives trying to figure out what is the most efficient way to buy insurance. Their advice has been so consistent that it has become a cliché of adult life: "Buy term and invest the savings above whole life in your own investments."

That means *safe, conservative investments,* not the two-dollar window at Del Mar. But it does mean that even a relatively innocent man or woman who places his or her bets on a well-known or well-respected mutual fund or money market fund is likely to have far better results than those persons who trust their money to insurance companies. The data on this is so conclusive and so exhaustive that it is hardly bearable to contemplate it all, but the bottom line is "Buy term and invest the difference." It is a moral certainty that any insurance agent that you talk to will have very different advice. Insurance agents want to sell whole life, universal life, and variable life policies. The reason is simple: They get much larger commissions from whole life and its sisters. In fact, there is virtually no demonstration of statistics so fascinating or so misleading as the bag of tricks an insurance agent has to sell whole life insurance policies. You can go to the most remote township on the Alaskan tundra, and there will be an insurance agent there with state-of-the-art statistical work showing—with data so complex that an MIT professor cannot follow it—that you will be better off with whole life. The fact remains that men and women who study these things without an ax to grind, without any commission to earn, tend to say the same thing decade after decade: "Buy term and invest the difference."

Keeping the Car off Your Back

Now for a few words about transportation. As we saw in the chapter about life in the long-ago twenties, car costs can be a killer. The family or individual that gets its act together will rarely spend more than one in five after-tax dollars on a car. The family or individual that is looking for trouble will often spend more than 40 percent of its after-tax income on a car. Those who can restrain themselves from *needing* a car that costs more than they can afford will be miles ahead of the game. Those who can get some satisfaction from their work and their family instead of from a Porsche 928 or a new Corvette will buy themselves a lot of peace of mind.

Department of Labor statistics show that families that are able to save significantly in their thirties are generally spending less than 16 percent of their after-tax dollars on transportation. Families that get into trouble and add to their indebtedness during their thirties (except for mortgage debt, which is often *good* debt) usually spend one fourth of their after-tax income on transportation. In other words, the lid must still be kept on about Jaguars and Cadillac Sevilles, unless your income has grown so much that you can afford those baubles while still spending only about $1.00 out of every $6.50 on your car.

However, this is not as grim as it sounds. If you were earning, let us say, $20,000 (after taxes) when you were the breadwinner and you were twenty-six, you should have been spending about a maximum of $316 per month on transportation, including car payments, gasoline, insurance, repairs, and parking.

But if normal trends hold, by the time you are in your mid-thirties, your after-tax income should have more than doubled. By now, if you spend only 15 percent of your after-tax income on transportation, you will be able to spend about $518 per month on transportation. This may have to be spread over two cars, alas, so that there is still hardly space there for a Ferrari. But you can and should be able to afford substantially more elegant transportation by your mid-thirties, even if you are not yet in the Mercedes class. (All figures here are inflation-adjusted, by the way, so that your nominal income and your actual costs for transport will be higher. In inflation-adjusted dollars, you should be able to spend about two thirds more on transportation—usually cars—in your mid-thirties than in your mid-twenties.)

Odds and Ends

A basically identical analysis holds for housing expenditures. Families in their twenties were expected to spend about 25 to 34 percent of their income after taxes on shelter. But by the time of a couple's mid-thirties, they were generally spending only about 26 percent of their after-tax net on housing. In other words, shelter costs fell from one third of net income to one fourth of after-tax net. Once again, since the base number had just about doubled (base number = after-tax income, inflation adjusted) that smaller percentage yielded many more dollars.

For example, the twenty-five-year-old husband and wife earning $20,000 after taxes could figure on spending $580 dollars per month on shelter, taking up about one third of all their after-tax income. (As we saw, more restrained families spent less and saved more.) But the same family earning twice as much inflation-adjusted income by their mid-thirties could spend only about one fourth of their after-tax income on shelter and still spend almost $890 per month. In real terms, controlling for inflation, the mid-thirties family could spend 41 percent more on shelter per month than the mid-twenties family and still have money available for saving.

In case you wondered, as you should, where the money went that is being saved on transportation and housing as their relative shares of income fell (even though their absolute amounts rose), there were substantial increases in the thirties in education expenses, all child care expenses, health care expenses, charitable contributions, contributions to pension and health plans, and also, as mentioned above, to savings. (See charts above.)

Summing Up

The net of all of these odds and ends is that if the family can avoid extravagance, can avoid pretending that they are Rockefellers just because their income is rising rapidly in their early thirties, they can have more dollars for the kiddies, for slightly better cars, and for a generally superior life-style, while at the same time saving and providing for their untimely disappearance in an orderly and economical way.

Again, the thirties should be a time of unparalleled achievement of emotional and material goals. If families can measure their reach by their grasp, at least financially, they will avoid a great deal of heartbreak, and, more wonderfully, the stage will be set for a joyous decade that you can look back upon happily for the rest of your life.

EIGHT

Thirtyish Singles—
Agony and Ecstasy

Facts of Loneliness and Cheer

Not everyone in his or her thirties is married. In fact, millions are unmarried either because they were never married or because they are divorced. Out of all men in their thirties, 12 percent have never married and another 8 percent are divorced. Among women in their thirties, about 9 percent have never been married, and another 11 percent are divorced. To put it mildly, the circumstances of the single thirties differ wildly from the circumstances of the married thirties.

To point out the most obvious difference among certain thirties generation singles and marrieds, more than half of all single women in their thirties are divorced with one or more children under sixteen living at home with them. Another 25 percent have never been married and have children living at home with them. The enormous majority of such persons do not receive regular child support. Although the numbers are hard to pin down on a nationwide basis, *it may be that 80 percent of women living without a spouse and with children do not receive regular child support from their ex-spouses or cohabitators.* This fact means that their earning, spending, and savings decisions will be, for the most part, limited, painful, and unglamorous. Thomas Hobbes described the human condition, indeed human life, as "solitary, poor, nasty, brutish, and short." For single mothers he was painfully close to the mark.

At the other end of the spectrum are single men with no dependents, rapidly rising income, and the fine financial problem of how to spend their money fast enough.

In between those two extremes is a huge mass of single women without children, single men with children, and single men and women who may well not be single for long. Their situations can and do vary so much that a few general guidelines about the situation of the thirties singles are far more useful than a hopeless attempt to cover every case specifically.

A Non-Wedding Surprise

First of all, those who are in their middle-to-late-thirties and have never been married have probably revealed a preference to remain unmarried, *and they are unlikely to be married.* That is, of all the men and women in their late twenties who are never married, most of them will be married within the next ten years. But of all the men and women who are thirty-five and unmarried, most will remain unmarried for the next ten years.

This is not true of the divorced. Interestingly enough, women who have been divorced are far more likely to remarry than women who have never been married are to marry. The same is true for men. This, again, is merely the working out of a revealed preference by men or women to be married at all. This has important implications, as we shall see.

Mother as Losers—A Note of Warning

Next, as to the most basic part of this book, the likely curve of income for single thirty-year-olds: For men, the curve of rising income is likely to be steep indeed. Just as for the married couple in the previous chapter, a single man can expect his income to rise by close to 9 percent per year in real terms for the first five years of the decade of the thirties. This is the highest rate of most persons' lifetimes. For the single woman without children, she can expect about the same astronomical rise in income. Again, the growth of productivity, expertise, and contacts will make the thirty-to-thirty-four-year-old man or woman a very good and intelligent hiring bet. That will lead to the demand either to lure that man or woman away or to keep him or her happy in his or her job. Either will keep income and raises high.

Alas, the woman with children can expect such high pay only if she stays in the labor force. As we discussed above, one cause of lower pay for women is that women tend to leave the labor force and miss the steady accretion of seniority and experience and connections that men acquire. (It seems to me to be outrageous that the economy thus penalizes women who are doing the most important work in the society—preparing the future—but it does.) Women leave the labor force to have children and take care of them, and their seniority vanishes. As it does, so do presumed productivity and connections within the given industry, and so does rapidly rising pay.

With that in mind, just for variety's sake, we might try addressing the questions of the single thirties through a series of questions and answers:

Savings Options

Q. Should a single woman have a certain amount of savings when she is in her thirties?

A. Everyone should have savings. Life at its best is filled with challenges and opportunities. If the boss comes in and puts his hand on your knee and says that he wants to talk about a raise, you want to have the option of flipping him the bird and walking out the door (to your sexual harassment lawyer). The single woman with savings has what are politely called F—— You Options that the woman living from paycheck to paycheck simply does not have. The desirable amount of savings varies, depending upon how certain and settled your job is. But the general rule for families is that they should have six months' savings. Since a single woman without dependents can obviously cut back far more than a family of four, a single woman should not need that much savings. But a few months' worth of savings (by which we mean a few months' *income)* is a minimum amount to give peace of mind and the opportunity to make career jumps without passing out from hunger. It should also allow for taking advantage of investment and bargain-purchase opportunities best left to the imagination of the individual.

Certainly, the single woman in her thirties without dependents should have been able to put aside three months' worth of savings. If she has not been able to do that, something is definitely wrong on either the savings or spending side.

The single woman with children should have an even simpler rule about savings: She should save all she can. Frankly, considering the disgraceful way that society refuses to support single mothers and the even more disgraceful way that ex-husbands refuse to support their own children, it is a miracle that women with children can save anything at all in most cases. But for those who can save, they can be sure that the savings will come in very, very handy. Having small children is like having machines for generating unforeseen and expensive contingencies. If you have savings to cushion the blows, you are miles ahead of the game. Again, there is no maximum amount, within reason, for the single mother to save. If she can save several months' worth of income, she will be happy at some future day when the doctor tells her that her son needs an ear operation and her insurance will not cover it. Savings, for the single mother, are the solvent that makes a smooth passage through life possible. Lack of savings, while perfectly understandable, are the ground glass under the bare feet of life's pilgrimage.

Men's Savings—A Lucky Break

Q. How much savings should a single man have in his thirties?

A. Luckily for single men in their thirties, there is almost no other group in the society which is so readily employed as single men in their thirties. In the minds of employers, single men in their thirties are finished with their restlessness but still have youth and energy, and are filling themselves with the kind of knowledge that will lead to major productivity gains in the future.

That means a man in his thirties will have an easier time finding a job than will almost any other age/sex combination. This obviously has implications for how long a man in his thirties should expect to be between jobs if he is fired, as well as for how much savings he needs to have.

While everyone should have savings to cover contingencies and changes of mind, everyone should also realize that some people need savings far more than others. If a family of four should have six months' income saved and if a single woman should try to save three months' income, a single man could probably get by with two months' income. *Ironically, this is exactly the person who can probably save one year's income without much trouble.* To him that hath shall be given, says the Bible, and that certainly applies to single men in their thirties as far as money is concerned. Such men are able to have large savings, do not need large savings, and generally remind me of the banks that will only lend to customers who do not need a loan.

Investments for Families and for Individuals

Q. Should single people in their thirties have different kinds of investments from families in their thirties?

A. The usual role of investments as related to the life-cycle theory of earnings and spending is simple: For money that was hard to earn and hard to replace, invest carefully and prudently. For money that comes easily and would not be much missed even if it were gone, feel free to invest more daringly.

That means the single man without dependents, in his thirties, should feel free to invest in high-flying stocks, real-estate tax shelters, and even that trickiest of all flyers, long-term bonds. The single mother with three children and two months' of savings which have taken years to accumulate should stick to bank CDs and money market funds.

No one, at any age or of any sex, with any family responsibilities or with none, should ever invest more in risky investments than he or she can lose without missing more than fifteen minutes' sleep—the so-called sleeping point rule.

Everyone in his or her early-to-mid-thirties should bear in mind what this book has said ten times already—that the early-to-mid-thirties are for most people the high point of their earnings curve, *not in terms of total salary,* but in terms of the *rate of increase* of earnings. The usual working man or woman will see his wages increase in both real and nominal terms until the end of his or her working life. But he or she will never see them increase *as fast* as they did from age thirty to age thirty-four.

(An interesting and worrisome exception: men or women who frequently leave the labor force and then return to it without getting any new training. These people can wind up late in life with far lower earnings than they had earlier in their working lives. The worker who loses his or her seniority, fails to accrue perceived knowledge or improved skills and contacts, and in addition can no longer command a premium for youth, energy, and an implicit option on a long and loyal attach-

ment to his or her employer, can wind up with the worst of all worlds—
low pay and little time or opportunity for improvement.

(This is an argument for spending time out of the labor force in
improving skills and in learning, two acts which can definitely be done
by men and women in almost all circumstances. Employers will often
pay more of a premium—i.e., make your income curve rise faster—for
employees with *x* years of education than with *x* years of experience,
even if the education is not formally acquired.)

Houses for Singles—Time to Reconsider

Q. Should a single man in his thirties have a house of his own?

A. Generally speaking, anyone who can afford to own a home should
do so by the time he is in his mid-thirties. The advantages to the home
buyer in terms of reduced taxes (mortgage interest and real estate taxes
are tax-deductible—rent is not), certainly of future obligations (a fixed
rate mortgage has fixed payments—rent can and does change at the
whim of the landlord), the likelihood of price appreciation (residential
real estate has drastically outperformed the Dow-Jones Industrial Average since 1967 in terms of price appreciation), the ability to use borrowed money to make money (most mortgages involve the borrowers'
putting up only 20 percent of a home's price—the balance is borrowed
money which makes money for the buyer just as if it were his own hard-
earned money), and finally in terms of freedom from the insanity of
landlords.

Alas, "generally speaking" can and does sometimes mean something
very different from "exactly right for you." There have been times in
the past ten years when home prices were so wildly inflated that they
would have made a chump out of anyone who bought in at that particular moment. Even though buying a home is a good idea for most people
at most times, there are definitely moments when buying a house is
similar to buying a stock on October 20, 1929. Of course, no one can
possibly know for certain when such times are. The only caution that
must be borne in mind is that when the real estate agent tells you that,
"Yes, prices are high, but in five years all of this will seem like a bargain,
and I guarantee you'll make money," that is often a very good time to
run like hell. The only *other* caution is that a home buyer, whether
single or married, should never load himself up with house payments so

large that they make life miserable. There is an old-fashioned rule about buying houses which has some relevance in this day and age:

- The monthly cost of paying for a house that you buy should not be much higher than would be the cost of renting that house *including* the tax savings from the mortgage interest. Real estate agents sneer at this homely adage and say that the reason you should be *happy* to pay four times as much in monthly mortgage payments as you would to rent is *that you are going to make so much money from owning that house when you sell it.*

That can be true—or false. When you buy a house and pay for it over thirty years, month by month, any excess you pay over the monthly rental cost of the house is in fact a wager that your house will rise in value faster than the interest rate on that money would raise its value. In other words, if you pay a high price for a house, that price includes something for living in the house and something as a bet that the house will rise in value.

The man in his thirties—or at any other age and of any other sex— should always be wary about the premium he will pay for that bet on future appreciation. If the price is grotesquely above the rental price of the house, caution is in order.

But again, as a general rule, a single man in his thirties may not *need* a house, may not need three bedrooms and two bathrooms and a recreation room, but he should probably buy one if he can afford it. Residential real estate is almost always a good bet for singles and for marrieds. The decade of the thirties—when a young man should be and often is getting established at the office or the factory and should have more change jingling in his pocket—is the ideal time to start putting down a residential root which can bear lush financial fruit.

Women, Too . . . If They Can Afford It

Q. Should a single woman in her thirties own a home?

A. All of the same imperatives that argue for a home for the single man in his thirties apply as well to women. In particular, the single woman who is not living with dependent children really should be able to afford her own dwelling if her income has kept pace with the income of other thirty-year-olds.

Unfortunately, there are many thirty-year-old women, many thirty-four-year-old women, and many women in their thirties generally, who have left work to get married, have lost their seniority, have gotten a new job, have left it because (rightly) it looked like a dead end, and therefore their incomes have not risen as rapidly as might have been hoped. Likewise, there are many women (and men) who are in jobs which simply do not pay enough to allow for the purchase of a home or condo even though the individual's pay has been rising steadily.

Also, there are many single women with dependent children who simply cannot afford to buy a house or condo, through no fault of their own.

The real question is whether a single woman in her thirties should buy a house *now,* knowing that paying for it will be a big struggle, in the hope and expectation that income will rise enough in the future to make those payments manageable. This is a good and important question.

A woman whose pay is $400 per week on her thirtieth birthday can confidently expect that her pay, in real terms, will be approximately twice that by her forty-second birthday. For every dollar she is earning at the age of thirty-two, she can expect to be earning $1.19 by the time she is thirty-four.

For every dollar she is earning when she is thirty-five, she can expect to earn about $1.25 by the time she is thirty-nine.

All of this means that income definitely rises steadily and rapidly for those who stay in the labor force. *But* it does not rise miraculously. It still bears some relation to what it was a few years before.

If you are contemplating buying a home, you should certainly expect to be able to grow into the payments if they are somewhat out of reach at the date of closing. *But* the drill press operator should not expect that the natural course of events will make him or her into a millionaire. The stenographer should not expect that the usual growth of her paycheck will make her a Saudi princess. Yes, you should expect that your rising income will allow you to afford far more house five years from now than you can now. Yes, you perhaps should buy a little more than you can afford right now. But, no, barring some extraordinary event in your life or the nation's life, you should not buy a house costing ten times what you can afford now. It will still be five times what you can afford ten years down the road—and that spells a lot of sleepless nights. It is great to have a house, great to have a little plot of land or bricks and mortar that you can call your own. *But*—of all the self-inflicted traumas of this world, few are more completely unnecessary and more readily avoided than making yourself house-poor.

The single woman in her thirties should *not* assume that owning a house is so important a goal that it supersedes all other goals. In particular, owning a home is not so important that it legitimizes poverty and fear about every other area of your financial life.

In one sentence: The single man or woman in his or her thirties should definitely buy a dwelling if it can be afforded now or grown into with the income *foreseeably* coming down the pike. Owning a home is not so important that it should make you impoverish yourself or your family to do it. Nor should a home ever be bought with phantom money that will come mostly in dreams and wishes and not in paychecks.

There are other questions that would apply to individuals in the thirty-year-old-and-single category. But the questions just preceding illustrate the basic facts for thirty-year-olds-to-thirty-five-year-olds:

Take Notes

- They can count on rapidly rising incomes unless they leave the work force sporadically and fail to improve their education. They need not expect any sudden financial shocks such as divorce or private schools for the kids. They should have more daring investments as they acquire more savings. If they can pull together the money, they should try to buy a home.
- Owning a home is not the be-all and end-all of life. If the square peg will not fit into the round hole, there are other consolations in life. There are also other needs far more important than holding title to a house.

Singles in their thirties can enjoy the ecstasy of rising income, no financial surprises, and the opportunity to feel safe and secure about money if they have no dependents. They should not throw that away trying to buy something they cannot afford and do not need.

Single mothers in their thirties should not expect to get their heads far above water. To the extent that they can, they should not risk tragedy by taking on daring investments that can evaporate. Nor should they tackle house payments that will put a strain on their finances—and will eliminate their ability to deal from strength about any unforeseen events. Having a cushion for emergencies is far more meaningful than telling your friends that you just bought a house. *Do not expect that the natural progression of the income curve will allow the single mother to pay for a house with money she does not have now or cannot see coming in soon.* There is nothing worse than having no money when you need it for any reason, and the growth of your productivity and your seniority over a decade are no substitute for money in the bank.

Now for the bad news about what happens after you hit thirty-five. . . .

NINE

The Late Thirties—
The Income Apogee Passes

The Age of Limits

Trees do not grow to the sky. Income does not keep rising at ever faster rates for young and middle-aged Americans. The steadily growing rate of increase of income of Americans from the age of twenty to the mid-thirties simply cannot be and is not sustained for most people.

As a general proposition, income growth begins to slow down drastically after thirty-five. While income had risen at the blistering pace of 9 percent per year in real terms for the first 5 years of the thirties decade, it slows down to about *6 percent for married men* and for women who have never been married for the rest of the decade of the thirties. For women who have been married, the rate is only about half that fast, around 3 percent. For men who have never been married, the rate is about in the middle of those rates, at about 4½ percent.

By understanding a little bit about why this slowdown happens and in particular why it happens to married men, single men, and married women at different rates, we can get a better understanding of how the income curve works.

The income growth happened at those superrapid rates from age twenty to age thirty-four largely because of

• Growing expertise on the job.
• Rising productivity because of skill and knowledge in the field.
• Some premium for youth and energy.
• Some implicit bonus for presumed loyalty and growth of ability.

When Americans start to hit their mid-thirties, several things happen.

1. The most important parts of their jobs have probably already been learned. The additional bits of knowledge usually are part of what might be called the diminishing returns knowledge, possibly costing more to acquire than they are worth in terms of what they produce.

2. New employees have been hired who may have come straight from school with the knowledge they can use and which their employers need already in them, at no extra cost, so to speak.

3. Some of what the thirty-five-year-old employee knows may have been rendered obsolete by time and circumstance and the appearance of new techniques, new players, and new rules within the field.

4. Most heartrending, some of what was once an implicit premium for youth is now gone, as youth itself is going.

5. The implicit bonus for performance and for longevity within the firm is often gone as employees show that they will move around and that they may not be quite as much of an asset to a firm as they once thought they would be—and more importantly, as their employers once thought they would be.

All of these events conspire to reduce the rate of pay increases for married men and for single women who have never left the labor force. The increases are still good—a 6 percent annual increase will double real income in twelve years—but they are not the stupendous gains which were made back in one's salad days.

The Changing Center of Gravity

To see how and why all this happens, look at our friend Jane Q. Colgrad back at the Pygmy Athletic Shoe Company. She has been doing just great, learning who the buyers were, who the cheapest suppliers were, who the best distributors were. She has learned how to invest any spare cash that was lying around at the office. She has learned how to get along well with the out-of-town buyers for Macy's and for Carter-

Hawley-Hale. In a word, she is doing well for herself and for her employers, the wonderful Pygmy people.

However, over in far Manila, a startling development has taken place. A small Filipino manufacturer of athletic shoes has built a factory with Swiss financing. That factory builds athletic shoes out of woven palm fronds entirely with robots. There is not one single human being on the factory floor. The manufacturer can undercut any American, Japanese, or Korean manufacturer with a high-quality product.

Not only that, but at the same time, the Congress of the United States passes new legislation about the importation of shoes made from palm fronds. The regulations are extremely complex, and it takes a lawyer to understand them.

In addition, as it happens, the new buyer from the May Company is a young kid from Harvard who likes to associate only with other young kids from Harvard.

All of a sudden, the center of gravity of the athletic shoe business has shifted. Jane Q. Colgrad still knows lots of important facts, but much of what she knows is now out-of-date. She could learn about it, but she is set in her ways by now, and she feels, with some justice, that she should not have to run as hard as a young kid to keep in place. There is a new M.B.A. from USC in the office. Jane Q. Colgrad delegates to him the important task of finding out about how to make shoes with robot labor. The kid is a hustler. He learns everything there is to learn and soon is out making deals to build robot plants in New Guinea. Meanwhile, Jane Q. Colgrad is still working on the old-fashioned human-worker plants in Bethpage and in Osaka.

The new M.B.A. has a friend who is a lawyer at Hale & Dorr. The new lawyer happens to know a great deal about the latest legislation bearing on importation of palm-woven athletic shoes. As it happens, he also boarded at Choate with the new buyer from the May Company. Pretty soon, the new M.B.A. has an impregnable web of connections dealing with and about the latest developments in the athletic shoe business. He is taking that old ball and running with it while Jane Q. Colgrad makes dinner for her lover, Lenny Liquid, and whines about how much more successful the new guy is than he deserves to be.

When the raises are passed out, Jane's is still good, but it is no longer anywhere near as good as the new boy's. As far as the boss can tell, the new boy has everything to recommend him: brains, rapidly growing knowledge, youth, that certain *edge*. His productivity is rising almost as the boss watches. In a word, he gets—and probably deserves—the biggest raise. The boss demands that he stay and will bid up his salary to the point at which it is almost impossible for him to leave. The boss loves and admires Jane Q. Colgrad, but it is a different situation. Jane is a settled company lady now. She is not really up on the latest technology. Of course, she will get a raise. But she is not such a hot item any longer. She need not be given a huge raise to stay, and she will not be.

(Note well that this sad turn of events for Jane Q. Colgrad did not have to happen. She could have said, "Well, whatever there is to learn about the new field, I'll learn it." But she did not do that. Instead, she rested on her laurels and her seniority and let someone else build up his seniority and his productivity through his knowledge of the state of the art in the field. There is no shame in that. After all, in our cautionary tale, Jane is thirty-five. She has been working hard for Pygmy for fifteen years. She assumed that her future was assured without having to continue to hump those new subjects the way she had humped the old ones. Indeed, her future was assured, but there are futures and there are futures. The natural wish of the slightly older employee to take it easy, the natural belief that some rest period is deserved, kept her from staying at the battle front. Again, this is how people's income curves stop rising so fast, but it is by no means shameful or disgraceful.)

Jane Q. Colgrad in this tale is a proxy both for unmarried women who have never left the labor force and for married men. These two groups have similar income curve prognoses, for the simple and compelling reason that they leave the labor force rarely if at all. Therefore they get all the benefit that can be gotten out of a long term of unbroken service in the field.

The married woman gets the bad effects of age—obsolescence of knowledge, lack of the best contacts, failure to acquire new expertise, loss of premium for youth. In addition, she almost always gets the negative effects of leaving the labor force for a time. That means she misses the seniority payoffs which are a large part of the benefit of continuous service.

Even the most career-minded mother is required by the laws of nature and medicine to take some time off when baby arrives. As the modern era has worn on, there has been a growing trend for mothers to take off large blocks of time as their babies are born. Where the average mother once thought that she was doing plenty by Junior if she took off a few months after he was born, now the modal model mother often considers taking off a few years while Junior is still in swaddling clothes. This may well make sense in terms of the psychological and physical well-being of the child. However, it will without any question at all impact negatively the income function of the mother.

Look at it from the standpoint of the employer. He pays the bills, and his views definitely have to be taken into account. He sees Jean Q. Valleywife, who has been a good employee of his company for ten years. She is, let us say, a sales representative for cable TV decoders. She has always been "one of the boys." She has always gotten at least as big a raise as any of the boys, and the employer has prided himself on this fact.

Now, at the age of thirty, Jean Q. Valleywife decided to have a baby. She took off two years from her work to have that baby. When Jean returned to work after two years, a lot of things had happened in the cable TV decoding business. She hardly recognized the field. She had to study night and day to learn all of the new developments in electronics. That studying was not easy because she had to stay up large parts of the night with Jason, doing things which were not compatible with examining the inside of an Oak fifty-channel box.

Jean tried gamely, but when the big buyers came to her showroom, they were a little disappointed that Jean did not seem to understand the new laser technologies as well as the men in the office. They did not want to be male chauvinists, but they found themselves going for their big orders to the men who were a little more up-to-date in the field.

Not only that, but while Jean had been out with the baby (again, a highly important and necessary act for her and for the society), the personnel at some of the major players changed. Oak threw out all of its old management. Warner-Amex burst upon the scene like a rhombic nebula. The two darling old guys who had pioneered the field in their garage retired to the Lyford Cay Club in Nassau, the Bahamas.

The major players who came along now were new to Jean. They were not particularly impressed with her knowledge, even though they could see she was a quick study, intelligent and eager to please. They had no experience of going out and drinking with Jean, no idea that they could treat her like "one of the boys." To them, she was a married woman who was really out of her depth in discussing the new infrared technologies for channel selection.

All of this meant that Jean was at a distinct disadvantage in terms of selling cable TV decoding boxes. She was still a little pistol in terms of selling effort, and she had a friendly, cheerful way about her. But she had too many disadvantages from her long absence from the labor force to sell at top speed. When it came time for the raises or bonuses to arrive, Jean saw with sorrow that hers was far smaller than the one she had expected—or the ones that her male colleagues rudely boasted about.

This disappointment, compounded over two years by yet another small pay increase, led Jean Q. Valleywife to decide that maybe she should have another baby. She and her husband in fact had a lovely girl, and they were extremely happy with the little darling. However, in the meantime, Jean's husband's business, seamed hose for the punk market, had gone completely to hell. Although they had once planned that Jean would stay home for the rest of her married life, they now saw the need for two paychecks.

Jean's old employer was genuinely fond of her. However, the field had become poisonously competitive. There was simply no easy way that he could fit a new saleswoman in laterally with his sales force. Most of them were engineers by now, and they would resent a woman with the dew of diapers and formula coming in to the office to compete with them day by day. The problem was compounded by the enormous changes in cable in the two years while Jean was at home taking care of the new girl. The old employer knew that if Jean came back to work, she would require a good long time to learn about the business all over again. The other salesmen would have to take time out of their earning hours to teach her, and this was definitely something they did not want to do. With real sorrow, the old employer told Jean he could not take her back.

Within a few months, she had a new job at a chain of retail stores that sold decoding boxes. Alas, as everyone knows, pay in retailing is miserable except at the very top. Jean was not at the very top. She had to start at her new job at about one third less than the draw in her old job—without counting the old job's bonus. Besides, at the new job there were no bonuses at all. Counting the effects of inflation and the lack of a bonus, Jean's new job paid only about 50 percent of what the first job had paid.

Jean was a hard worker and an intelligent human being. Moreover, she still had her excellent personality. But even after three years of raises, she was still only up to about 75 percent of what she had been making before she found her need to have a second child. Now, she is back in the labor force for good because she has found an excellent au pair girl and because she is eager to stay out in the world of adults for a while. But she is also on the slow track for a good long while. Her new employer likes her, but he can never tell when she might just decide to pick up and go home to take care of the kids. Her new employer knows she has a husband with a business and has the option to leave at any moment she chooses. He also knows that she is a fine and devoted mother. He is not eager to put her into a position of high responsibility from which she just might back out some day, leaving him in the lurch.

The net of all of it is that while everyone at work likes Jean Q. Valleywife, she is not going to get up onto that fast track of pay and promotions any time soon.

(In a perverse but nevertheless real way, the very fact that Jean had the option to leave the labor force—and did so on two occasions— threw fear into her employer and encouraged him to keep her in a position in which her leaving could not do major harm. Alas, that was also a poorly paid position.)

Although the situation of Jean Q. Valleywife is unusually stark, the basic facts are unarguable: Married women who leave the labor force even sporadically have drastically lower rates of income increase than men or than women who never leave the labor force. Usually, the effect is a lower rate of *pay increase,* rather than an actual fall in income, but that in itself is a shock in a society accustomed to constantly rising real incomes.

(And Men, Too? And Men, Too)

Now for a curiosity, like a man with two heads: In this country, there are a great many single men who have never married. Their rate of pay increases after the age of thirty-five is *also* much lower than that of married men or women who have never left the labor force.

(It is not exactly clear why this should be so, and far less government investigation has gone into this than into the questions of why women's pay is less than men's. The apparent reason for the lower wages for unmarried men is that they too leave the labor force frequently, although not to have babies. Apparently the same options of leaving work that are available to married women are felt to be available to single men: They have no dependents, and they can leave the labor force any time they feel like a trip to Greece or to the Florida Keys. Their longevity of labor force participation is decidedly less than that of married men as a matter of observed fact.

(There is some thought that single men generally have lower educational levels than married men by the time they are in their mid-thirties —although obviously we all know cases of very educated single men and very ignorant married men.)

At any event, there is no doubt that married women who have ever left the labor force are dramatically less able to get the pay increases they would like to have than they were before they left the labor force. To give some idea of just how drastic the change is, look at it with numbers:

If a woman were earning $20,000 per year and if her income rose by 6 percent per year for fifteen years, at the end of the fifteenth year, her income would be $47,931.16.

If the same woman, earning the same $20,000, had 3 percent pay increases for fifteen years, her income would only be $31,159.35—a big, 34 percent difference—by the end of her fifteenth year on the job.

All of this comes under the heading of cautionary advice. Songs say that life, in the end, is just the wink of an eye. The Bible says that we are all "dust" in the wind. Every one of us knows that the good moments of life are as evanescent as a perfect summer evening in the backyard, under a maple tree, gone into history despite its seeming cricket-filled eternity.

Summary and Conclusion

Unfortunately for Jean Q. Valleywife and Jane Q. Colgrad and all the rest of us, the peak years of earnings growth are like that, too. They go on and on, and then, quite suddenly, they are gone. It is helpful to know that this point comes, for most of us, in our late and mid-thirties. The fact is that earnings will grow, but

- Either they will grow much more slowly than they did in the five previous years, or
- it will take an enormous effort to maintain the same level of earnings growth as when you were younger. These facts should motivate us to make the adjustments that will keep income, spending, and saving in the harmony that is the goal of any man or woman who craves security and peace of mind.

The tools of adjustment are at hand for men and women as they leave the thirties and enter their forties. They need only have some idea of how to use them. They often will get their first opportunity to cope with a falling rate of income increase and a rising need for money in a familiar context: sending Junior and Sis off to college.

(To give you some idea of what you can expect if you save even a small amount, even with your income no longer rising at peak speed, see the chart on the next page. It shows how much your family or individual income will grow at an annual rate of increase of 6 percent starting at $40,000 at age thirty-six. It also shows how much you will save in the years from thirty-six to forty if your spending only rises by 4 percent per year and if you bank the difference at 11 percent interest per year.

Just for variety's sake, it also shows how much in debt you will get if your spending is exactly equal to your income at age thirty-six, but grows by 9 percent per year. We assume you will pay 15 percent interest on your debts. Read it and weep.)

Still Hot . . . But Not Like Before . . .
Income, Spending, and Saving in Your Late Thirties

Age	Real Income rising 6% per year	Real Expenses rising 4% per year	Savings per year	Cumulative Savings at 11% interest	Expenses rising 9% per year	Debt each year	Cumulative Indebtedness at 15% interest
36	$40,000	$40,000	—	—	$40,000	$ −1,200	$ −1,200
37	$42,400	$41,600	$800	$800	$43,600	$ −1,200	$ −3,960
38	$44,944	$43,264	$1,680	$2,568	$47,524	$ −2,580	$ −8,714
39	$47,641	$44,995	$2,646	$5,496	$51,801	$ −4,160	$ −8,714
40	$53,529	$48,666	$4,863	$10,964	$61,545	$ −8,016	$ −18,037*

* A debt of $18,037 would cost $225.46 monthly in *interest* alone, without any reduction of principall

NOTE: If savings on pp. 16 and 92 are added to the totals in column 5, the total savings by age forty would be $138,652. That is actually *less* than the real savings would be if the ratio of earnings to spending proposed in the decade of the twenties were continued. It does give some idea of the value of persistent savings.

TEN

The Married Forties: Self-Help in a Time of Deceleration and Transition

School Daze

Human life is so charged with events that any decade can and should be considered a time of transition. But the decade of the forties for most families marks a time of such heavily freighted transition in terms of youth and age and money growth and decline that it is a particularly acute time of transition.

For most American married couples with children, the forties are the time in which they send their children off to college if they are going to send them to college at all. This means a genuine shock to all but the most gilded pocketbooks. Learning how to cope with that shock in a straightforward way, learning why sometimes clear answers are the only answers that make sense in the real world of men and women in their forties, and learning the facts of financial life for children and parents will go a long way toward harmonizing the discordant melodies of sharply lower income growth in the forties and the clear economic value of a college education.

To understand that harmony, we have to know just how much of a jolt college can and will be financially, just how a sensible person should look at a college education, who owns that education, what that education is worth, and why the economic necessities of the decade of the forties make it virtually imperative to place the burden of that cost where the benefits also go.

Then we can get to some more pleasant subjects. . . .

College Is Expensive

Americans love to go to college. In this country, almost one third of all high school graduates now enter college. Among middle-class persons, families with incomes of $25,000 and above, more than 50 percent of all eighteen-to-twenty-four-year-old children enter college. This is a love affair—Americans in love with higher education—that has blossomed like a weed since 1960. Where only about one in ten American high school grads attended college in the late 1950s, the proportion has now tripled. The absolute number of eighteen-to-twenty-four-year-olds attending college has now risen to nearly 8 million. (There are about three million additional students in higher education who are older than twenty-four, attending institutions of higher education either by day or by night.) While there has been a slight dip in the proportion of Americans attending college since 1979 (a very slight dip), the long-term projections are that by 1988, close to half of *all* American high school grads will attend some college and more than 80 percent of all middle-class children will attend college.

In other words, if you are a young person starting out in the world of married folk, and if you are a middle-class couple or become one, and if your kiddies are at all bright, you will almost certainly have to send them to college.

The average *public* four-year college costs of a twenty-year-old are now close to $5,000 per year. For many private colleges, the total costs are now (1983) in excess of $15,000 a year per student, including tuition, board, fees, books, travel, clothing, telephone, automobile, and so forth. It is *easily* possible to spend even more.

Moreover, as high as these costs are, they are rising rapidly. While the consumer price index had slowed to less than a 5 percent annual increase in 1983, educational costs for both private and public higher education were still rising at above 9 percent per annum.

Before you go into shock, bear in mind that most young Americans—close to 90 percent—attend public colleges and universities. That $15,000 per year is not the number that the average family will have to cope with. Still, if you have a ten-year-old child in 1983, you can confidently expect that his first year of college will cost you close to $10,000 even at State. If Junior sets his heart on going to Stanford, you can pretty clearly expect that 8 years from now it will cost you $30,000 per year *at a minimum.* This is serious money by almost any standard.

College Costs Come at a Bad Time (Is There Ever a Good Time?)

To understand about numbers of this magnitude, they must be set against the backdrop of all the other likely expenses of a married couple with children. The expenditures of a typical middle-class family on education *for one child in a public school of higher education* would generally exceed total expenditures on food and transportation plus recreation for the entire family. They would come close to equaling total expenditures for shelter. They would be very nearly as large as all state and federal tax costs. In other words, they are a tremendous cost.

Unfortunately, they come at a time of slow growth in real incomes, which makes them even more of a burden.

All of the reasons that slowed down earnings growth in the late thirties begin to bite even more in the forties. The premium for youth has by now gone almost completely, along with invitations to the prom and running shoes. The increments of knowledge that used to be so valuable for every day on the job are now of trivial importance. Indeed, imagine in a typical job just how much you learn about doing that job on the fifth day as compared with the fifteen hundredth day. On the fifth day, you learn crucial data about how to work. On the fifteen hundredth day, it's mostly more of the same.

Not only that, but some of that old "same" is by now highly obsolete and not particularly useful, as we saw in the example of Jane Q. Colgrad. Technology changes. The rules of the game change. Pretty soon, there are new players. Then there are whole new products, whole new approaches to the field. What you once knew is now worth much less. You *could* learn the new tricks, but do you really want to go to all that trouble?

All of this changes the lifetime earning's curve position on which you now find yourself. Instead of the glorious place where you were headed upward at a dizzying angle, now you are lucky indeed if you can head upward at a decently acute angle.

Back there in the early thirties, income was rising annually by 9 percent in real terms. Now, in the early and late forties, income rises by only about *3 1/2 percent* per year. To get some idea of the difference: Real income will double in *eight* years at a 9 percent increase per year. At 3 1/2 percent, income will actually take *twenty* years to double.

The sad fact is that by the time most workers are in their forties, they are no longer such hot items in the job market. They may be perfectly wonderful workers, good parents, loyal friends, devoted members of the Kiwanis—but they are just not in the kind of demand that thirty-year-old hotshots are in. This is not an indictment of age, but rather a simple fact about the coloration of the job market circa the last twenty years of the twentieth century. Employers want the young and the hustlers. They are less thrilled about the forty-year-old solid workers.

Social scientists and human resource economists have a great many theories and explanations for this depressing phenomenon, but they all go back to what we have discussed above and in the preceding chapter: There is a pervasive feeling, based upon some evidence, that you can't teach an old dog new tricks. In a phrase, that summarizes real life problems about lack of the youth premium, obsolescence of knowledge base, and competition of newer labor inputs. You can't teach an old dog new tricks.

(Of course, the numbers and the facts behind them are average numbers and average facts. There are plenty of people who constantly teach themselves new tricks, who are way out there in the real world keeping themselves ten jumps ahead of the new boys. That is why there are doctors whose incomes keep rising rapidly for as long as they practice. That is why there are lawyers at law firms whose incomes rise *more* rapidly rather than less rapidly as they enter their forties. They are adding constantly to their *human capital* by keeping up with the latest developments in their fields, by making sure they know the new players, by keeping up with state-of-the-art work in theory and practice in their areas.

(For persons in their forties who will demonstrably keep adding to their human capital, the income curve will rise far more steeply than for the average person. The truth is, however, that most human beings simply do not have the inclination and the energy to keep constantly running faster and faster even as they grow old. There is nothing disgraceful in this, as this book has said before. It is nothing more or less than the nature of human life for persons to believe that they should be able to relax a little more as they grow older. That is a fine and understandable thought. Unfortunately, the labor market understands it and then passes out lower wages as a penalty for it.

(Even in highly unionized jobs which pay according to seniority, the pay is usually also by hour and according to overtime, so that the people with the highest hourly rate often do not make the highest wage. This is even more true in the majority of fields where there is not strict unionization and strict pay by seniority. Considerably less than one fifth of all American workers are in unions, and for most of them, pay strictly by seniority is unknown.)

While pay increases slow down drastically in the forties, most people also have far less real need for cash to come pouring in as fast. The home has usually been bought several years before the fortieth birthday of the breadwinner. Inflation and the growth of earnings have made the monthly payments perfectly manageable. Husband and wife have adjusted to whatever kind of cars they really want—*in the sense that they know now that everything they buy costs something.* They have the kind of cars they can afford to buy and are willing to pay for.

True, the kiddies cost more year by year as they go through public or private high school. They need new shoes, perhaps a used car, a stereo, his or her own telephone, a video game, a summer at camp, a bicycle. But these expenses tend to be fairly small in terms of the growing family income, especially compared with what they were in the early thirties. That is, while the absolute amount of spending on the children rises slowly and steadily, it does not tend to rise as fast as family income. (Remember that family income had those big jumps in the twenties and early thirties.)

The forties become a time when the mommy and daddy and the kids can stretch out and enjoy life a little. There are some savings, some security in the job, some feeling that life is going to work out after all. In particular, for most middle-class families, savings grow rapidly in the late thirties and early forties, even as the rate of earnings growth is slowing down. By the time the average middle-class family is in their forties, they have savings equal to about six months' earnings, not counting their on-the-job retirement plans or IRA or Keogh plans, or the equity in their homes.

In a word, everything is going swimmingly until college comes along, causing a dramatic, spectacularly painful spike in the spending curve of the ordinary family. It is as if the family were cruising along the highway of life in the Olds Vistacruiser when they suddenly came to a pothole about twenty feet deep and fifty feet in diameter. It is a big problem, and solving it requires reconceptualizing the whole idea of college.

What Is a College Education?

Imagine that your son or daughter wants to buy a piece of rental property. The kid is a shrewd little hustler. He or she figures that owning that piece of income property will make his or her life a lot easier in years to come. After all, that property will come in handy, pouring in rents, rising in value year by year as the neighborhood becomes more valuable. The kid figures that whatever he or she can add to the pot by working will be nice, but that piece of income property will really do wonders for the old family budget.

Or imagine that the kid wants to have, as a birthday present for his or her eighteenth birthday, a handsome new diesel tractor-trailer rig, cost, about $60,000. The child figures that he can rent out that rig to a driver, collect a portion of the haulage fees, and make a good addition to his living doing it. He knows that the income from that haulage will make a good large addition to his earnings from whatever job he undertakes.

Would you, as a parent, feel comfortable giving your child a piece of investment machinery, a capital good, that cost you as much as a couple of years of your income? Would you feel that it was your duty as a parent to give your child a piece of income-earning property that sets you back from $60,000 to $120,000?

Probably that idea strikes you as astonishing and more than that, *as something you would never do.* You probably could not imagine that it would be your bounden duty to give a huge capital asset to your child, whose income would flow exclusively to the child, at a time in your life when buying such a gift would wreak havoc upon your own financial life.

Yet, that is what a huge number of parents do by paying for their children's college education at very considerable sacrifice to themselves. A college education at its very most useful is an earning asset for the kids, much like a piece of real estate or a bond. To see just how major a capital asset it will probably turn out to be for your kids—and to think further about who should pay for it—we should look at the history of lifetime payoff from a college education.

How Much Is a College Education Worth?

Once upon a time, a college education represented a truly immense difference for its owner compared with a man or woman with only a high school education. Before World War II, a man with a college education might confidently expect to earn three times what a man without a college education would earn over a lifetime. Of course, there were all kinds of tricks involved in that calculation, such as the much smaller pool of college graduates, the fact that many college graduates were already rich, and the fact that right after World War II there was a period of almost unprecedented economic growth and therefore a shortage of well-trained college graduates. But even as late as 1965, a college graduate could expect to earn approximately twice as much as a noncollege graduate. But by 1983, a college graduate could reasonably only expect to earn about one third more than a high school grad.

Again, there are all kinds of flaws in the comparison of 1983 and 1941, such as the vastly larger pool of college graduates, necessarily meaning a lowering of average ability within that pool, the increased demand in recent years for persons with skill at manual trades, raising the pay of high school grads, and the flat performance of the economy for most of the last fifteen years, which led to a weak demand for college graduates in many sectors of the economy, lowering their wages.

However, despite all of these factors, the pay of a college graduate is still far higher than the pay of a high school graduate over the course of a lifetime. At present, the difference is a minimum of one third of lifetime earnings, as projected, on average. That means that if the typical high school grad can expect to earn about $1.5 million over his lifetime, the college graduate can expect to earn about $2 million over the course of a lifetime.

In plain English, that college education is going to be worth a huge amount of money to your child or children. It is like starting them out with a cushy inheritance or trust fund purchased with the blood, toil, tears, and sweat of Mom and Dad. Tell the truth now: Is that fair or decent or even sensible, for the old and tired to bleed for the young and vigorous?

Certainly not. Now that we know that Mom and Dad's earnings' increases will be far smaller in years to come, making Mom and Dad shell out for the kids' college is not fair or decent or sensible.

Make the Kids Pay

It is only sensible and only decent that the *owner* of that college-generated stream of income pay for it. Unless Mom and Dad are so well-to-do that they will not miss $15,000 a year for the college costs per child, unless Mom and Dad are so guilt-ridden that they feel that they owe a lot of suffering to themselves in return for Junior's love and kisses, they should let Junior pay for college himself. Unless Mom and Dad feel that they are war criminals unless they pick up the tab for college themselves, they should definitely let Sis pay for that piece of investment property—that college education—herself.

There are a million ways that kids can pay for their college education. There are scholarships, loans, work-study plans, deferred tuition plans. There are loans handed out by the federal government, loans offered by state governments, grants of a hundred different descriptions offered by the federal government, scholarships of every conceivable kind, and jobs checking out library books that allow the students to study while they earn a small living.

All of these are resources for allowing a child to acquire his or her college education with the active help and subsidization of the state and its citizens. Frank Knight, one of the great geniuses of all times in the field of economics, said that the key to success for young people was "Take advantage of all subsidies." After the huge subsidy the government gives for housing, its next largest subsidy is for education. The government takes tens of billions of dollars away from bricklayers and field hands and assembly line workers and dentists and doctors each year to create gifts for young men and women who want to go to college. The gifts are in the form of outright grants, subsidized low-interest rate loans, subsidized jobs, and gifts and loans to the higher education institutions. There is absolutely no reason why you and your children should not take advantage of them.

Beyond that, even if your child cannot qualify for a government gift, there are other ways for him or her to pay for college. There are non-subsidized jobs. There are scholarships based upon merit or upon the specialization of the student (scholarships for studying telescopes in Texas, scholarships for studying marriage in Maryland, scholarships for studying topology in Tennessee, literally hundreds of thousands of specialized scholarships for young Americans).

There are loans from financial institutions which are specially geared for the unique circumstances of the college student, allowing the student a long period before he or she must repay any of the loan and then stretching out the payments over a number of years. There are loans from potential employers which are automatically repaid by the graduate's working for the employer. First and most well-known of such employers is the Department of Defense, but there are others as well, generally large corporations with an urgent need for a certain kind of specialist employee.

If worst comes to worst, there are loans from well-to-do family members, which should always be entered into in the *solemn spirit that they will really and truly be repaid.*

However these loans and scholarships and work income are combined, the bottom line is that the student should pay for his education. Yes, if Mom and Dad are millionaires, Mom and Dad can pay without missing a beat. But for most parents who see their income rising far less rapidly than it once did, there is nothing compelling which argues that a student should do anything but pay for his own education. What the family accomplishes by doing this—or by doing it at least in large measure—is to make the owner of the asset pay for it.

Just as compelling, the student will then be repaying his loans out of an income stream which is *rising dramatically,* instead of compelling his poor old Ma and Pa to pay for that education from an income which is rising distinctly *less* than spectacularly. Of course, Mom and Pop will have an income stream far larger than Junior's when Junior gets out of school. But they will also have far greater expenses and possibly other dependents still in secondary school. Mom and Pop will also be in the distinctly depressing situation of paying with their leisure and well-earned security for the luxury and unique college indolence of big strong boys and girls—*unless* they make Junior pony up. Mother and Father have scarce dollars in the future. Junior has plentiful dollars ahead. Make him pay.

Will making Junior and Sis pay for their own capital goods (college education) keep them from getting good grades in school? No. There is simply no evidence available from the financial aid officers at ten major colleges and universities with whom I inquired to suggest that the marks of students receiving financial aid are lower than those of students not receiving financial aid. More interesting, several financial aid officers told me that students who work part-time through college tend to be more studious and get better grades than those receiving all of their support from home.

This is not really surprising, since we would expect a student who knows what education costs in terms of sweat to value it more highly than a student would who signs a series of checks each semester from Mom and Dad. The essence of the human condition is to value things more highly the more difficult they are to acquire.

But what about the idea that Junior and Sis are not only getting knowledge at college but are also having fun and living it up in a way that their poor old parents were not able to in their poverty-stricken youth? Shouldn't parents feel good about giving their kids a four-year party when they, the parents, had to work at the dry-cleaning shop all week long when they were in their twenties?

The answer to that is that such a line of argument has nothing to do with economics. If there are compelling psychological reasons for parents to stretch themselves thin financially so that Junior and Sis can live it up, that has nothing to do with the lifetime earnings function and the lifetime spending function. "Each to his own poison," said someone, probably not for the first time. If Mom and Dad really believe that they are doing something noble by depriving themselves so that their son and daughter can stay out all night drinking on Nassau Beach at spring vacation, that has little to do with rational thought.

(Suffice it to say that those dollars which Mom and Dad are sending to Junior and Sis so profusely will grow steadily more difficult to earn, especially as other needs begin to collide with the need for educating the children.)

The net of it all about college education is that college is a fine thing, that it civilizes young men and women and prepares them to be adults. However, it also is primarily a capital expenditure: money spent to produce income. Unless the parents can spend the money without missing it at all, they should make Junior and Sis pay for as much of that capital good as they can.

Not only is this the most rational way to look at the process. It is also the way that will help to develop the best appreciation of college and of education generally in the minds of college students.

For most parents in their mid-forties or in their forties at all, the palmy days of huge increases in income year by year are gone. Every dollar you send to the bursar will be progressively harder to replace out of future earnings. Junior and Sis will soon have those spectacular skyrocketing earnings. Be smart about this: Make them pay.

A Word About Investments:
A Time for (Small) Risks

As the life of the forty-to-forty-nine-year-old breadwinner and his wife and kiddies (or husband and kiddies) falls into place, with expenditures now carefully paced to earnings, there is a time and a place for some serious thinking about investments. By the mid-forties, the family who have been harmonizing their spending and their earnings should have more than one year's worth of income saved. This amount should be in addition to the money put aside for retirement—IRA's, Keoghs, or employer-sponsored plans.

While it was perfectly sensible to put this money into CDs, blue chip stocks, money market funds, and other fairly secure investments, the decade of the forties may be the moment for taking a few shots at high-risk, high-reward speculations.

You can feel free to do this *only* if you have already bought your home and your cars and have a safe reserve for loss of job, prolonged illness, or other misfortunes. You should only do this if you play with a small fraction of your savings. Most crucial of all, you should only do it *if* you will not be distraught if you lose your stake.

But into every life comes the need to try to get rich quick. A friend starts a software company. You want to know if you should put up a few thousand to get in on the deal. You see a vacant lot next to your bakery and you think it is a good property. Should you buy it? You read about a new invention for cooking fish over a grill without letting any of it fall into the flames (a particular problem of mine). Should you buy stock in the safety fish-grilling company?

The answer to questions such as this is that in general you will never again see your dollars pouring in on a steeply ascending curve. But on the other hand, you will never see those horrendously rising bills for buying a new house again, for paying the pediatrician, for taking up the slack when Mom leaves work to have the baby.

In other words, to restate something important, in your forties, you should have achieved some measure of financial control. If you know that your income is rising slowly, if you mesh your expenditures with that income stream, you should be able to take a little slice of dough from the kitty and take a chance with it. But if you take out so much that you wreck your financial structure, you are cutting your own wrists. If you take out so much that you will now have to scrimp and save to replace it, you have probably lost more than you could ever have hoped to gain even if your investment turns out well.

Look at it like this: If your investment or your speculation turns out wildly well, even a small amount originally invested will make you rich. If it turns out lousy, the loss of a small amount should be plenty to ease your mind that at least you *tried,* even if things did not work out perfectly. More important, the loss of only that small amount will allow you to get to sleep at night.

Never, never, never speculate with money that you know you will need. Never, never, never speculate on anything illiquid if there is even a remote chance that you will need to get cash out in a hurry. (For example, do not go into limited partnerships, land deals, tax shelter deals, expecting to be able to get real money out when you need it.) Never, never, never go into deals you do not understand. The IRS will understand them and make your life miserable. The promoter will understand them and soon live in Rio de Janeiro with your money.

We all want to get rich quick. For most people that wish leads only to sorrow. You must know that the money you put up to get rich quick has only a remote likelihood of making you rich, but has a very real possibility of making you poor, if you put up too much of it. Only invest in speculations *what you can afford to lose,* and you will be miles ahead of the game.

Avoiding Future Shock . . . and Having Some Just Deserts

And now for something completely different: As the investigator looks through the data about where household income goes as families move into their middle and late forties, he is struck by the fact that percentagewise, expenditures on almost every major category decline year by year.

For example, the totals spent on food at home and food away from home decline after forty-five. The percentage spent on housing declines slightly. The percentage spent on household operations also declines. There are tiny increases in the amounts spent on clothing and a very tiny increase on the amount of spending on transportation. But over all, household expenditures generally shrink little by little in almost all areas as aging within the forty-year-old decline sets in.

This raises a fairly obvious question. If expenditures are falling in all of those categories, where is the money going? Income is still rising, both in nominal and in real terms. Where is it going?

Not surprisingly, it is going into insurance, retirement, and all of the other preparations for even older age. Also not surprisingly, it is going into a category it should be going into: recreation, which is not strictly classified as a household operation.

To take these in reverse order, look at recreation first. The ordinary family needs and must have recreation. For most families in their thirties, life has been too hectic to enjoy much recreation. There were the pressures of getting ahead at the job, of bringing up babies, of getting divorced and remarried. There were also the sudden needs of replacing a spouse's lost income and of making certain that the children were finding their own ways in the world as young men and women.

It is extremely typical and probably inevitable that young families in their thirties do *not* take much time off for fun and games while they are having their period of greatest income growth. Indeed, the very reason that they can take off so little time is that they are doing the key things that young families do—replacing their generation and improving their standard of living. Neither of those is a part-time job and neither allows much time for travel or other recreation.

You can hardly expect to see Mont St. Michel and Chartres while you are working long hours trying to become vice president for sales. You can hardly expect to take a hiking tour of Provence while you are awaiting word from the pediatrician about whether or not Sis has the measles. You cannot expect to become a ten handicap golfer while you are working every Saturday trying to learn tax accounting.

But in the forties, when career paths and home life have stabilized somewhat, the time for recreation is at hand. You have the advantage of being young enough to enjoy the strenuous pace of athletics and of travel, as you did when you were in your twenties (the best time for travel if you can afford it) and you have the professional and family stability to enjoy it *with some peace of mind.*

Family budgets for recreation generally rise to close to 10 percent of spending in the late forties. This is not at all undesirable or bad. It is well deserved and money well-spent. (Much better spent than in supporting your children in acquiring their degrees in veterinary medicine, the money from which will be theirs, not yours, *even if they are wonderful kids as I am sure they are.)*

Man and woman live by raising children and by doing their daily work. But man also lives by getting to the beach and to the mountains. Man also lives and restores himself or herself by whacking the hell out of a divot or by blasting in a high hard one at forty-all. Man and woman need rest and diversion. They deserve to take in a play or a class about the Flemish masters. Especially in the decade of the forties, when men and women have done the enormous chores of bringing their children through youth and have presumably achieved some small measure of professional and financial security. To give in to those needs on the order of 10 percent of your overall spending is not at all excessive *if you have the money,* and you should not be afraid to do it.

While you are resting on the beach at Kona or watching the smoke rise in the Tetons, you had better start thinking about the second financial change that comes into life in the forties: beginning to prepare for approaching age. The sooner you start providing, the more painless it will be. Most particularly, if you start *early enough,* you can mesh *steadily decelerating income growth* and the need to stash away ever larger sums for the future and beyond. But this subject is so important that it deserves a special chapter by itself. . . .

NEXT: Numbers to Conjure With . . .

ELEVEN

More on the Married Forties—of Numbers, Exponents, and the Future

Why You Don't Want to Think About the Future and Especially About Money

There are occasionally important lessons of life that can be conveyed only with numbers. One of these is that it will take a tremendously greater amount of money to prepare for your retirement than you think. Another of these is that you can slip out of the noose of unpreparedness for retirement by starting with amazingly small sums now, while you are in your forties.

Of course, both of these ideas repel many people. After all, when a man is forty-five years old, he still sees his high school days as just yesterday. If he has been exercising regularly and eating only fish, he may actually feel better and stronger at forty-five than he did at twenty-five. He may have just been to his twenty-fifth high school reunion at the Smallville Holiday Inn and seen that he hardly looks any different from when he was center on the Smallville High basketball squad.

Mom, if she is forty-five, may be doing her aerobics every day. She may eat only macrobiotic foods and feel as if she were going to live forever. She may actually be thinner than she was when she met hubby at that mixer twenty-four years ago. She may have now gotten up to the full-length marathon level in her running program. She may have quit smoking, rubbed in Oil of Olay, and may feel as if she is at the peak of her youthfulness.

Alas, despite every effort, nothing can call back time in its winged flight. Time is passing, and at least on the cold, viciously scientific level of economics, your best years of earnings growth may already be past. For many persons, the peak years of earnings on an absolute level are also past. Of course you are still hale and vigorous, and of course, you still feel like a world-beater. But you are now at the midpoint of your careers, in most cases. However much you may want to avoid thinking about depressing numbers and statistics about age and youth and retirement, however much you may want to avoid thinking about numbers at all, you should and must start to think about them. A small amount of thought now will revolutionize your life in the near future, entirely for the better. So, grit your teeth now, while you are still young, and think about a few numbers in your future.

How to Get Up to Big Numbers Very Fast

First, imagine that you now earn $40,000 per year as your family income. Imagine that you believe that when your kiddies have finally left the nest, you will be able to live comfortably on $30,000 per year *in today's dollars*. That means you will need the purchasing power of $30,000 of this moment's dollars to live the life you comfortably deserve and desire.

Now, imagine that you will retire at the age of sixty-five, twenty years from now. That $30,000 now will have to grow quite a lot in current dollar terms to offer the purchasing power of $30,000. Just to give you food for thought, if inflation tools along at 7 percent per year between now and twenty years from now, you will need *$97,930* in twenty years' time to make up the equivalent of $30,000 right now.

Even if inflation is *only* 5 percent per year, you will still need $75,000 and quite a lot of change to make up what $30,000 made up today in terms of purchasing power. If inflation should, God forbid, go up to 10 percent, it will take slightly over $200,000 per year to buy what $30,000 per year bought in this year. (Both examples assume the inflation lasts for twenty years, at the end of which you need to start spending the money.)

In other words, however much you think you will need to spend on your retirement, you will, in all likelihood, need more. Inflation, compounded mercilessly over twenty years or more, raises prices to unheard of levels. Just ask the man who bought a house when he got out of the Navy in 1945 for $10,000 and just sold it for $200,000.

Of course, not only will you need a huge amount of money per year when you are retired, but you will, by definition, be *retired,* which means you will not be working anymore. In other words, you have to have some lump of cash or insurance or annuity that will pay off *each year* as much money as you need to live on.

Just to give you more figures to conjure with, imagine that inflation is a conservative 5 percent per year. Imagine therefore that when you retire, you need to have about $75,000 per year to live on. Assume further, just to make it easy on yourself, that the inflation stops dead at the age when you retire, so that you do not need to allow for more loss of purchasing power after you retire. You will need a nest egg that throws off $75,000 a year. At current rates of interest, that means you will need about $750,000 invested, earning interest, by the time you hit sixty-five.

If that seems like a lot of money, there is one simple reason: It *is* a lot of money. How on earth are you going to get it? Especially, how on earth are you going to get it now that your income has passed its peak of earnings growth and may even start to slow down in real terms in some workers' cases?

Making Your Own Big Numbers

The short answer to how you are going to manage is simply this: *Start early.*

The exact same mathematical principles that make inflationary dollars grow as fast as we saw just above can be put to work for you. The very forces that make it necessary for you to have big bucks stashed away on that day when you get your gold watch and a hearty handshake can be harnessed—and must be harnessed to get you those big sums.

The principle is, of course, nothing more complex than compounding of payments and interest. It works *against* you each and every day that there is inflation, in that it makes your money worth less and less at a compounded rate for every day that inflation rages. By the simple and necessary act of saving regularly and putting the money at interest, you can and will also make that compounding work for you. Practically every American already knows that there is *some* value in saving money and putting it at interest. What most Americans do not know is how enormously effective that technique is—and how absolutely vital it is.

The Stairway to Heaven

For example, imagine that you have figured that you are going to need a capital sum of about $750,000 when you retire. How are you going to get it?

First, to simplify things, imagine that you are able to earn a consistent 11 percent on your money. To get up to the huge sum of $750,000 at the age of sixty-five, if you started at age fifty-five, you would have to put aside $40,000 each year. To put it mildly, this is not a realistic possibility for most persons. If, by some miscue, you do not start saving until you are sixty years old, you will have to put aside $108,000 per year, which is also impossible for most people.

However, if you start at age forty, aiming for that same $750,000 at that same 11 percent by that same age sixty-five, you would need to save only about $5,900 per year—still a hefty amount, but only about one seventh what you would have to save if you started saving at age fifty-five. If you start at age forty-five, to get up to that $750,000 at age sixty-five, you will have to put aside about *$10,500 each year.*

That is, if you give yourself twice as many years to accumulate your savings, you need only about *one fourth* as much put aside each year. If you give yourself three times as many years, you need save only about *one twelfth* as much as you would to get to the same principal sum at retirement.

If you start early enough and get up to those huge sums gradually, compelling the compounding effect to work for you instead of against you, you can accumulate more money than you would ever have thought possible. By starting early, you can quite literally convert the impossible to the possible. Since there are no reasons *not* to start early, you might just as well do it.

Finally, since the lifetime earnings function tells us that most persons and families "enjoy" still lower growth in real income in their fifties and sixties than in their forties, the person who starts saving in his or her forties, while income is still growing at a fairly good clip, will spare himself or herself the burden of trying to drink more and more out of a steadily smaller cup.

Interest, School, and the Future

In a way, you can tie two important ideas together by thinking about college educations and thinking about preparing for advancing age. Take it by example. Bob and Janet Colquitt have two lovely children, Peter and Brigid. Peter and Brigid are excellent students at the Purchase, New York, Country Day School. Both of them are reaching graduation from secondary school within one twelve-month period. Bob and Janet want nothing but the best for little Peter and Brigid—as we all do for all our children. But because Bob and Janet have some idea that time will pass, and because they have some idea that they will not always be able to work but will always need to spend money, they are being smart. They are requiring that Peter and Brigid pitch in and help pay for their own education in part. College at Princeton and Smith will cost about $20,000 per year per child. Through a combination of loans, scholarships, and part-time jobs, Peter and Brigid each will have to pay for $12,000 per year of the total.

That means each of the two college graduates will have a total indebtedness of—let us say—$20,000, payable back to the government or to the universities or to a bank at 10 percent interest. The cost to Peter and Brigid will be a mere $264.30 per month. By the time they start work (at investment banks in both cases), they will earn about $3,500 per month. They will not even notice the repayments, especially since their incomes will be rising like the sap in Vermont in the first ten years they are out of school.

Meanwhile, Bob and Janet will have been able to bank the $12,000 per year per child for each of the four years of their college. By the time Brigid (the younger child) receives her sheepskin on a warm, clear day in Northampton, Massachusetts, Bob and Janet will have accumulated about $115,000.

If they put that money away at interest (assume it has been earning 11 percent interest while Peter and Brigid have been at school), in twenty years time, at 11 percent interest, they will have almost $1 million—while Peter and Brigid will have been subjected to an almost unnoticeable, character-building burden.

When you think of what a huge difference that will make in the parents' lives, and what a tiny difference it will make in the children's lives, it is almost painful to provide for college any other way than by having the children pay for at least part.

If, on the other hand, you take the example of Ted and Ruth Gold, who insisted on paying for every penny of their children's college education—out of a foolish pride—you come to a far more somber end.

Jessica and Jonas Gold also went to Princeton and Smith. By the end of the kids' college days, Ted and Ruth had gone into debt for $12,000 per year per child, for a total of almost $115,000, including the 11 percent interest. Ted and Ruth were fifty years old when Jessica received her cum laude degree in mathematics (but she decided to become a preschool teacher in Maine anyway). To pay off their debt at the modest rate of 11 percent interest per year by age sixty-five, Ted and Ruth will have to pay $1,307 each month. Unfortunately, since Ted and Ruth are not wealthy, that will mean no vacations for many years, constant worry about money, and drastically little preparation for retirement. The financial complexion of their entire lives will be dramatically weakened by this one grievous act, well-meaning though it was.

Had Ruth and Ted been able to save that $1,307 each month for fifteen years instead of paying it in loan payments, they would have had over $600,000 in savings by age sixty-five (at 11 percent interest).

You have to make every decision for yourself, especially when children are involved. But by putting a healthy, small burden on your offspring, in the long run you will make your life, and theirs, far more secure and happy.

Think about it.

TWELVE

The Single and the Forty— Good News and Bad News

One might think that the man or woman who is single, without dependents, and making a decent living would enjoy the best of all possible financial worlds. You might think that, but you would be wrong.

The truth is that for a variety of excellent reasons, single persons in their forties face depressing prospects. Yes, obviously a single man who earns as much as his married neighbor and has no dependents will have more money to spend on himself. And also, yes, a single woman who makes as much as the combined Mom and Dad across the hall will have far more money to spend on herself than they do.

But in the decade of the forties, income growth for single persons slows startlingly, far more so than for married persons. This decline is so sharp and so sudden that it can cause serious unease in the land of the Swinging Singles.

We saw that in the latter half of the decade of the thirties, income for single women with children rose at only about 3 percent per year, while income for married men rose at about 6 percent per year. We also saw that income for single men and women, never married, rose by only about 4½ percent per year.

If we recall, we can remember that the main reason why the income of single people rose far less rapidly than that of married people was that the former left and reentered the labor force more frequently than the latter. They therefore failed to acquire the seniority the married breadwinner acquired. Or to put it even more starkly, while the married man is at the grindstone year after year, piling up knowledge, connections, and money, the single mother is at home changing diapers and forgetting what she knew about the job, and the never-married man is changing jobs rapidly and frittering away his seniority and his connections.

That may not in fact be exactly what happens, but it is a rough schematic of what happens—and it certainly is what goes on in the minds of many employers when they think about how much to pay single men or women as compared with married ones. The employer also has another consideration. He may feel that because the married man or woman, usually with children, has those mouths to feed at home, he ought to offer more money for him or her than for a single person with only a cat and a Sony and a telephone to come home to. *Bear in mind:* The employer does not do this out of the goodness of his heart. The whole concept of goodness of the heart is foreign to most employers. The employer offers more for a married breadwinner on occasion because he thinks he has to in order to compete with other employers, pure and simple.

Whatever the reasons may be, the income of unmarried men and women virtually stops rising by the time they are in their forties, at least in inflation-adjusted terms. By the most generous of all data, income growth in real terms, disregarding false increases caused by inflation, is only about 1½ percent for unmarried persons, per year, through their forties.

To get an idea of just how big a drop that is:

When the single man or woman's real income was rising by 4½ percent per year in his or her thirties, real income would double in about sixteen years. When real income rises at 1½ percent per year, real income doubles in about *forty-seven* years. Quite a difference.

Divorce, Realistic Style

This difference has a staggering impact upon all working people who are single, but it has the most devastating and most disabling effect upon one particular category of single person: The man or woman who is getting divorced, still bearing responsibilities to the old family, and possibly about to undertake new responsibilities to the new family.

Look at it carefully: If a young man or woman, say around age thirty, has a family with a wife and two small children, then gets divorced and starts a new family, he can expect rapidly rising real income for at least ten years. He can confidently expect to pay the alimony and the child support out of his income, rising at the blistering pace of 9 percent per year for five years, then a still rapid 6 percent per year after that.

But if a man of forty-five gets divorced, he may still have to pay child support and alimony, as a woman may in the same situation. But he cannot count on an ever-growing pot of money to draw from. By the time of the mid-forties, a man or woman's income is rising slowly, if at all, in real, inflation-adjusted terms. The hordes of dollars that once floated in as if by magic are now slowed down to a trickle.

If a forty-five-year-old man leaves his family and starts to live either as a swinging bachelor or with a new family, he cannot and should not expect that the going will be easy. Whether counted as a single person, with the basically stable income of a single man, or counted as a married man, his income is still rising so slowly that he cannot expect automatically to be able to support two families, or even one family and one individual, on the scale he might have expected.

A staple of fiction and of television is the middle-aged man who leaves his middle-aged wife for a young woman. On TV and in books, they live in glamorous oceanside condos with sports cars and trips to Hawaii. In fact, the old husband and the new wife—or girlfriend—can be expected to be on a short tether indeed, at least financially.

This fact, utterly unappreciated and unrealized by most middle-aged divorced men, gradually gets borne in upon them. When it finally hits home that there is not enough money for the old family and the new man or family, you can guess what gets cut out: Not the new wife or girlfriend and not the swinging life-style. Sadly, it is usually the old family, including the children.

The standard way that divorced men cope with the problem of income rising very slowly while expenditures rise at a crisis rate because of a divorce is to stop paying alimony and child support in a responsible way. This has powerful implications for everyone involved in that kind of situation.

The husband contemplating divorce should and must bear in mind that his life after the divorce will not be one long round of Porsches, blond showgirls, and visits home to dazzle the kiddies with lavish gifts while assuaging the ex-wife with Cartier bracelets. He will probably enter a time of severe economic privation, without any foreseeable end point. The myth is the glamorous life. The fact is riding the bus.

For the wife facing a divorce, a good, healthy dose of reality is in order. Despite all the promises, court orders, and contracts, there is every likelihood that the ex-husband will not pay the alimony and child support he has contracted to pay. This means that the wife, for her sake and for the sake of the children, should and must get her hands on tangible property in the here and now, rather than on pieces of paper about the future. The wife should and must get as much of any jointly owned real property, especially income-producing real property, income-producing assets such as stocks or bonds or CDs, as she possibly can. Owning the things she will need in the future—such as a home and a stream of income—will be crucial.

The cast-off wife and children (sometimes the cast-off husband and children) will be far happier and far better off if they have sources of money that are not dependent upon the ex-husband's financial course. Even if the ex-husband is a genuinely wonderful man, a founder of the local PTA, a blood donor every two weeks, a scratch golfer, and a decorated veteran of Vietnam, he will still come under violent pressure to stop sending those support payments as his expenses inevitably rise and his income virtually stops growing.

To be smart about it, the wife who sees her fortyish husband drifting out the door will take the cash and the house and the financial assets right now. She can and should let her husband make those *promises* of support to himself or his new chippie. For her part, the ex-wife should place heavy emphasis on the here and now, on assets she can hold in her hand or walk around or ride in.

Sharing the Burden, Family Style

In this great country, there are over 4 million families with children headed by women with no spouse present (charmingly classified as "householders" by the Department of Labor). Of these, about 1 million are female "householders" (with children present) in their forties. (To put the film *Kramer vs. Kramer* in perspective, the number of families with children present, a forty-year-old male householder, an absent, divorced wife—all the conditions of the *Kramer vs. Kramer* situation with a little age added—*is so small that it is not even counted.*)

There are, in addition, about half a million families with children present, male or female solo householder, forty plus years of age, where this sad condition was caused by death.

There are, in short, a great many single men and women in their forties whose incomes have virtually stopped growing, while their children may well be growing and needing more money than ever before. This is one of the true financial crises of American life. In a sense, the financial condition of unmarried men and women with children is worse in their forties than in their twenties or thirties. In those younger eras, men and women could expect to be bailed out of their torment by rapidly rising real incomes. In their forties, most cannot *realistically* have that hope.

This has several important implications:

Make the Family into a Team (A Cliché but a True One)

First, wherever possible, those very self-same children who might be seen as a liability have to be converted into assets. In this society, there is an enormous and growing number of jobs which require teenage labor. If you have teenagers, they can supply the labor and help defray some of their expenses. There are car parkers, baggers at grocery stores, dog walkers, baby-sitters, messengers, all receiving less than a brain surgeon gets paid, but also all receiving a great deal more than zero. Unless you have so much money that you don't know what to do with it, you should enlist your children's help in keeping the financial ship afloat.

Will this harm children? Absolutely not. I could easily fill a book of this length with articles and lectures by child psychiatrists and psychologists telling about the value and benefits of putting everyone in the family on the same team to make financial matters work out. It stands to reason that a sixteen-year-old who works a few hours after school three days a week bagging groceries so that Mom can keep the wolf from the door will feel a lot better about himself than a kid who is hanging around the 7-Eleven, cadging quarters from Mom to play Frogger. Giving the kids a chance to earn money gives them a chance to earn some self-respect—and gives the parent a chance to catch his or her financial breath.

A Bad Time for Borrowing

Be very wary of borrowing at this stage of your life. There is an axiom about borrowing which very roughly is that you should always try to borrow valuable dollars and repay them with cheap dollars. This means, for example, that you should borrow when you are broke and in medical school. Each dollar you borrow then is worth a lot to you. You repay when you already have three offices, a hospital, and your own CAT scanner, when the money is pouring in, when you have more of it than you know what to do with.

A second meaning is that you should borrow when there is high inflation, because the inflation will shower you with "worthless" dollars down the road, and you can use those "worthless" dollars to repay your loans.

By the exact same token, you should avoid borrowing valuable dollars and paying them back with even more valuable dollars. That means you should not borrow and have to repay with money that is even harder to come by than it was when you borrowed in the first place. Unfortunately, this is precisely the situation in which many forty-year-old borrowers find themselves. Alas, it is even more exactly the situation in which many single people in their forties find themselves: They borrow money with the expectation that they can repay it from their ever-growing stream of income as they experienced it in their twenties and thirties. Instead, they find that those dollars are no longer growing by leaps and bounds—and may not be growing at all.

Bank loan officers report that one of the classic mistakes that borrowers make is to assume that just because their incomes rose rapidly in the past, their incomes will keep rising sufficiently to repay unsound loans. *Do not let it happen to you.*

There are some situations—medical emergencies, housing emergencies, car emergencies—when borrowing may be absolutely necessary. But in general, the single forties man or woman should fight against having to do it as hard as possible. Repaying valuable dollars with dollars that come out of your hide is not a pleasant or smart way to borrow.

Luxury Bracket Creep—Don't Do It

There is a notion in this country and in most countries that families are supposed to live more luxuriously as they grow older. We expect college students to live like slobs. After all, that is where the expression "She still lives like a student" comes from. We expect men and women just out of school, just starting work, to live modestly, with few luxuries. We expect that men and women in their thirties should start to get the VCR, the trips to Europe, the sailboat, the foreign car. We further expect that individuals and families in their forties will start to acquire the leather and chrome furniture, the Kirman rugs, the swimming pools, and the designer tile floors.

The image of older people living more luxuriously is based upon fact and upon media hype. In real life, we generally see that parents live better at forty-five than children do at eighteen. On television, we see couples congratulating each other on having started out poor and now owning fifty gift shops with annual sales in the tens of millions, now giving each other diamond bracelets.

The fact is that middle-class couples in their forties usually do live better than middle-class couples in their twenties. This is not because the older couples are older, but because they usually have more money.

Many perfectly fine people get confused and think that persons and families in their forties automatically accrue luxury goods *because* they are in their forties, and not because they have more wherewithal. This is a dangerous and foolish mistake. No one automatically gets anything from age except fatigue and gray hair. People acquire material goods and services according to what they can *afford,* not according to the number of candles on their birthday cake.

This means something very important: If you are a single man or woman in his or her forties, with children, without a large income, with your income no longer rapidly growing, maybe not even growing at all any longer, you have got to be alert. Do not think that you can suddenly start affording new furniture and a new set of good China and a trip to Carmel just because other forties friends can afford those things. You cannot afford those things because of your age. If you think you can, and if you obligate yourself to spend money you don't have, you will *really* learn about sorrow.

If you are a single parent in your forties, by all right and fairness, you *should* be entitled to a richer life-style. But that does not mean you can pay the bills. Only a complete fool will throw himself and his children into debt to pay for a life-style that fits the stereotype of his age but is far beyond his wallet. Do not let it happen to you. Avoid the temptation to buy as if you were just as well-off as the forty-year-olds on television if, in fact, you are not. Bracket creep with cars and furniture and vacations is fine for those who can afford it. For those who *pretend* they can afford it, who delude themselves into thinking they can afford to upgrade their life-styles drastically because their age peers have, nothing but crisis and disaster lie ahead. And again this goes double for single parents.

It is incomparably more valuable to have some money laid by for emergencies for you and for your children than to have designer furniture. It is far more important to know that you can survive for a few months if you lose your job than to have expired tickets to Zihuatenejo. The forties man or woman with children is likely to have fairly tough sledding in the attempt to maintain his or her own life-style as it was in the last five or ten years. Again, this will be *especially* true as the single man or woman with children sees that his or her income has just about stopped growing in real terms.

Real avoidance of financial crises comes from knowing the matchup between your income curve and your expenditure curve. In its most basic essentials, for most forties singles with children, that matchup does not permit bracket creep in life-style.

A Small Summary

Making a coherent, lifesaving whole out of the income and consumption function at this stage of life requires effort and sacrifice from the children, making them pay their own way in college and before to the extent possible, and avoiding any but emergency borrowing. It does *not* include trying to replicate a life-style which has nothing in common with your income. Getting by with a static income and children is not easy under any circumstances. Trying to do it with blinders on is impossible.

Housing—Lay Down That Burden

If a man or woman is single and twenty-five, he or she can be fairly certain that marriage will come in the next five years. The same can also be said for a single man or woman at thirty or even thirty-three. But when a single man or woman, who has never been married, reaches forty or forty-five, the likelihood becomes greater than two out of three that he or she will not get married. This is a "revealed preference." The forty-five-year-old single may *say* over and over again that he or she wants to be married. But if he or she is still unmarried at the age of forty-five, the likelihood is high that he or she prefers to remain single—at least under the circumstances likely to apply to marriage and singleness in the particular case.

(This means that, of course, any single forty-year-old woman would marry Prince Charles and any single forty-year-old man would marry Morgan Fairchild—if tastes run to members of the opposite sex. But the real world choice is to marry Lemuel Jones, who smells of beer and cigarettes, or to marry Sarah Mozzarella, who wears a size eleven shoe.)

The question that always comes up at every stage of a single person's life is the one we have addressed before: Should he or she buy a home? Frankly, at the age of forty-five, if a single man or woman does not yet have a home, it may be that the optimal time for owning a home has passed. From this stage onward, it may be better to rent.

It takes energy to get out the old Toro and mow the lawn, to rake leaves into the crisp fall evenings, to wait at home for hours for the telephone company repair men, to bail out leaks from the roof all winter long, to supervise the painters to make sure they don't steal the TV aerial. To a large extent, this is a young person's line of work. Also, to be frank, in this day and age, there are plenty of young people who do not care for it either.

If you are single and forty and are still living in rented quarters even though you have no dependents and could have afforded to own your own home, you are almost certainly revealing a preference to rent and not to own. At the age of forty and up, that revealed preference starts to harmonize with the economic future.

At the twenties and thirties stages of life, it made perfect sense for a man or woman to undertake paying off a mortgage. At those times, when real income was rising so rapidly, the heavy burden of a mortgage could fairly readily be lightened by that rapidly rising river of money. That ever broader flow made a home and a car and fancy stereo doo-dads possible. But now, when income growth has crept to a halt, housing mortgage payments will *not* automatically be lifted from your shoulders. The shock of large housing payments will remain unpleasant for a good long while. (Note that the difference between the cost of rental housing and owned housing is still so large that the new mortgage payments are almost *always* a shock.)

To put all of this more starkly, twenty years ago, you could take on large burdens and repay them with ease because the income function was going up like a rocket. Now, in your forties, even as a single man or woman, large payments will still be large into the foreseeable future. Beware.

If you feel left out because you are not getting the tax shelter advantages of owning a home, have no fear. You can get all of them—and much more—by buying real estate tax shelters of all varieties. You can get the advantages of equity appreciation in real estate by the exact same device.

If you do not need to own a house, if you have only slight inclination to be a homeowner, if you are happy living where you are living (and you can almost always afford to rent in a better neighborhood than you can buy into), hey, go with the flow, and don't even ever pick up that housing burden.

There is no Eleventh Commandment that requires people to own homes despite all other considerations in their lives. If you act as if there were such a commandment, you may well command yourself into a financial crisis you do not need.

Now for the Good News

For those in their forties who are single, do not have children, and possibly already have a home, the situation can be heaven. Although income is barely growing, it is growing somewhat. If you have no children and no relatives to support, you may very well find yourself in the enviable position of having to scrounge around for things to buy. Abercrombie & Fitch and The Sharper Image will send you their catalogs, and you can carefully browse through for new ways and means to amuse yourself.

Of course, since you are single and are forty-plus, you will probably find that your life is much easier if you do *not* undertake any dramatic new financial obligations. For example, you should not buy a huge sailboat and expect to be able to pay for it out of your increased earnings. Except in special and personal cases, that is not likely to happen. By the exact same token, you should not try to buy *anything* that requires sharply rising income to pay for it. That income is just not too likely to be forthcoming.

Yes, for small items like personal computers or digital watches, you will probably be able to buy them with a clear conscience. But all of the above warnings about consumer bracket creep, letting your age instead of your income be a false guide to spending, and the urgent need to start putting money aside for your old age should be followed just as clearly by the unmarried singles as by anyone else.

For Everybody on the Boat . . .

The absolutely irreducible facts about life in the forties for men and women, single and married, with or without children, are the same:

Income growth slows startlingly and will not rise again for most persons.

The man or woman who makes advance preparation for advancing age is doing himself or herself a great, huge favor. Early action for retirement is about as big a favor as you can do yourself on this earth. Even if you have a company retirement plan, even if you have faith in Social Security, every dollar you can save at age forty-five toward your retirement is worth at least three dollars at the same interest rate saved at age fifty-five. If you make early provision for retirement, you can make compounding work for you instead of against you—and you can sleep more easily in these autumnal days when your income has stopped rising.

Being single and enjoying the frivolous luxury of having no dependents does not relieve you of the burden of sensing that you are way past the apogee of your curve of rising income and that the future looms ahead. Being single and having dependents, alas, also does not relieve you of the need to face reality.

The forties are a time for thinking about the future by thinking about the present. They are a time when you can make enormous lifetime progress by taking small steps about education, housing, and bracket creep. Why not do it?

Still Enough Time . . .
Income, Spending, and Saving in Your Family's Forties

Age	Real Income rising 3.5% per year	Real Expenses rising 1% per year	Savings per year	Cumulative Savings at 11% interest
41	$54,000	$54,000	—	—
42	$55,890	$54,540	$1,350	$1,350
43	$57,846	$55,085	$2,761	$4,260
44	$59,871	$55,636	$4,235	$8,964
45	$61,966	$56,193	$5,773	$15,723
46	$64,135	$56,755	$7,380	$24,833
47	$66,380	$57,322	$9,058	$36,623
48	$68,703	$57,895	$10,808	$51,460
49	$71,108	$58,474	$12,634	$69,755
50	$73,596	$59,059	$14,593	$92,021*

* Even without any additional savings, $92,021 would amount to $440,282.71 by age sixty-five.

For Families in Their Mid-Forties—
Percentage of Total Consumption Expenses After Taxes
(not including savings except for pension and insurance)

Food—total	15
Food at home	*8*
Food away from home	*7*
Alcohol and Tobacco	1
Housing (rented or owned)—total	28
Utilities	*3*
Telephone and other household operations	*3*
Home furnishings and appliances	*5*
Rent or mortgage and taxes	*17*
Clothing	11
Transportation (including auto purchase)	14
Health care	6
Recreation	6
Education	9
Insurance and pension contributions	10

(Totals may not add to 100 percent because of rounding.)

THIRTEEN

The Fifties and Beyond

Peace of Mind and How to Get It

For a healthy American male, the age of fifty is a milestone in a number of ways. Usually, if he is a family man, he has raised his children and seen them through school, as much as possible under their own steam if he possibly can. He has achieved some measure of success in his work if he is ever going to do so. He has bought at least some sense of security and staying power by virtue of saving and investing carefully. According to the usual statistics, he also has a good long stretch of time left on this earth. A healthy American male of fifty can reasonably anticipate living another twenty-six years. This, of course, is both a problem and an opportunity.

For a healthy American female, there are also joys and feelings of accomplishment at the age of fifty. She might look back upon having raised a family. Perhaps she looks back upon a career filled with unexpected challenges and unanticipated achievements. Perhaps she has seen her horizons as a woman expand far beyond what she believed possible when she was a child. If she is a not unreasonably lucky woman, she has a mental locker filled with happy memories. She also has a great deal to look forward to. If she is in good health, she can anticipate living until very close to eighty. In other words, she has as much of her adult life left to her as she has already lived. Her male counterpart has about 80 percent as much of his life as an adult *ahead* as he does *behind.*

This situation is *the* financial problem for the American man and woman in their fifties and beyond. There are other financial problems, but the problem of providing for a life span which will, in almost every case, outlast the working years is the key problem of later life.

The Pancake Years

All of the factors that made for a gradual flattening of income gains from the late thirties onward intensify in the fifties. This is a depressing development, but nonetheless true.

In the past, workers got pay increases because they gained more expertise, knew the right people, and raised their productivity and value to their employer. As we might remember from the case of Jane Q. Colgrad, she got to know her company inside and out, got to know the key players in the athletic shoe business, and got to know the entire dynamic of the athletic shoe business beyond what she had ever thought she would know.

That made her invaluable to her employers, who showed their fear of losing her (not their gratitude, which is a null concept in business) by raising her pay to a level which made it very difficult for anyone to hire her away or for her to leave.

As we also saw, when Jane grew older and became subject to the competition of younger workers who knew things she did not know, she began to lose her advantage. The younger workers at Pygmy had connections with a whole new echelon of men and women in the athletic shoe biz who were unaware that Jane Q. Colgrad even existed. The younger workers were fully conversant with COBOL and FORTRAN, while she barely knew BASIC. The younger competitors knew things about making athletic shoes from palm fronds which Jane had not bothered to learn. Gradually, Jane's value as a trusted employee of Pygmy shrank to a fraction of its former self.

Of course, she was still kept on. She knew how to do things at the company that no one else knew. She had left the work force briefly to start a family, but even so, she knew plenty of the old-timers who still owned some stores and did not want to see anybody except Jane when they came into town to buy their athletic shoes. But the Pygmy management, which had now fallen into the hands of a huge conglomerate, which mostly transmitted natural gas from Louisiana to North Carolina, was extremely conscious of Jane's value. They knew she was not going to be hired away. They knew her pension had vested and that she was going to stay with them as long as possible. In other words, they knew they did not have to pay her large raises each year to keep her on the job.

In a nutshell, this is the story of men and women over fifty in the labor force. They are usually no longer on the cutting edge of technology, no longer in with the hip young gunslingers of the business, no longer indispensable. The Jane Q. Colgrads, who knew every detail of every overdue account, gradually get replaced with Apple PCs, which know every detail and can spread it on a screen within one second. The Jane Q. Colgrads, who knew the name of every salesman in every territory, are replaced with catalog selling and computerized order fulfillment. The real life Jane Q. Colgrads, who are about to become grandparents for the first time, are no longer on the fast track of business power, connections, knowledge, and pay.

Of course, this is not true of all workers in their fifties. As in their thirties and forties, there will be some men and women who make it their business to stay completely and totally abreast of everything that happens in their fields. If computers are introduced, they will be up all night mastering programming. If the Japanese become a major factor in the market, they will be poring over the Asian Wall Street Journal at all hours of the night and day. If new players come into the business, they will make damn sure that the new players are invited over to the house for dinner, are helped to find an apartment or a date, and generally know who their friends are. But this takes a great deal of exertion, which most persons are not prepared to give. As with Jane Q. Colgrad, most persons in their fifties feel they have done a great deal of work. They should not have to struggle to compete with persons who can get by on half as much sleep.

For the usual man or woman in his or her fifties, the energy to go through the aggravation of endless competition is simply not there. For that excellent reason, most persons see their pay increases falling even more from the decade of their forties to the decade of their fifties.

For the average worker in his or her fifties, income does not fall in real terms. But its rate of increase becomes smaller in real inflation-adjusted terms. For the average *married* wage earner or salaried worker, *real income rises at about 2 percent per year throughout the decade of the fifties.*

To be sure, this average number conceals a great deal of movement around the extremes. There will be some persons who have consistently raised their productivity, who have been able to keep their curve of income rising rapidly through their forties and fifties. For example, a doctor who keeps completely up-to-date in his field and also constantly expands his patient base will see large income gains throughout his fifties. On the other end, there will be men and women in their fifties who have reached the point of rapidly *falling* income. Secretaries get replaced by answering machines. Bookkeepers get replaced by VISI-CALC. Old, leathery salesmen get replaced by thin new salesmen carrying a new, younger smile. For those people, there is the extremely meaningful problem of drastically falling income or no income at all. This should make everyone hark back to the earlier chapters about having savings for a rainy day.

You can get some idea of just how big a drop in the rate of increase comes from the early thirties to the fifties if you realize that at 9 percent gain per year, real income *doubles in less than eight* years, while at 2 percent per year, real income *doubles in thirty-five years.* Even by comparison with income gains in the latter half of the thirties, which were about 6 percent per year in real terms, the income growth in the fifties is a distinct shock. At 6 percent, real income will double in almost twelve years. At 2 percent, it will take almost three times as long.

Slicing Up the Pie

For most intents and purposes, income growth will no longer be a reliable engine for providing new Winnebagoes, condos in Longboat Key, and Pendleton flannel shirts. That is, whatever you feel you need and must have will now have to be paid for out of a static pool of income. This means, for example, that if you are already committing 100 percent of your income for taxes, savings, and consumption, whatever new thing you buy will have to come from eliminating something else.

At the simplest level, this means that if you have been accustomed to buying certain goods and services for the last few years, and if you suddenly are compelled to support an aging relation at a nursing home, you are going to have to cut out the vacation to Hawaii or the once a week meals at Le Trianon Restaurant—at the very least. To get any large *new* purchases, some *old* purchases will have to be forgone. Once you have reached the point of essentially no growth in your personal income, or at any rate very small growth, you are living in what has been called a zero-sum game. This space-age name only means that what you add to one part must be taken away from the other part. Think of two cows feeding in a trough, and you basically have the idea: Whatever one cow takes means less for the other cow.

In real world terms, the zero-sum or almost zero-sum situation means that if you have not been putting aside enough money for your retirement, if you have to set aside new, larger savings, those savings probably cannot come from income growth. They probably will have to come out of giving up some item of consumption.

For example, suppose you get out the old calculator and calculate that in order to have sufficient retirement income, you should start saving another $100 each month. You figure that this additional saving, combined with what you are already saving, combined with your Social Security and your company pension plan will yield sufficient income to live on after you stop working. Well and good, but that hundred bucks additional into the money market fund or wherever must come out of new slipcovers or a new color TV for the study or a camping trip of Parents Without Partners.

This may seem like a particularly obvious conclusion, but in fact it marks a *radical* departure from the preceding three decades of your working life. In those days and years, if you wanted something new, you could generally pay for it out of rising income. This is the simple reason why couples who start out in married students' housing with a ten-year-old VW bus wind up in Grosse Pointe with a five-bedroom house and two late-model Buicks. But when there is no real growth in income, any additional length you tack onto one end of the blanket has to come off the other end.

Yes, you can still have that antique armchair and yes, you can still have that Christmas trip to Ixtapa. But you must remember that any new expenditures will mean less money for the usual old expenditures. This is crucially important to remember, because if you do not remember it, you will soon find yourself taking money out of savings, and this is something *you do not want to do.*

Bare Essentials

Now we know that it is vital to start saving early, vital to adjust your buying in the era of the fifties so that you do not take money out of savings. We also know that it is deadly important to put aside enough so that at retirement you will have a realistically large enough capital to live off. We know that, adjusting for even minimal inflation, this means, in practice, that it will take what seems today like a ridiculous amount of money to reach what will be a highly reasonable amount of money by your sixty-fifth birthday. And we know that you will not have a skyrocketing curve of rising income out of which to take your savings in preparation for retirement.

All of the crucial facts that you now know prepare you for the heart of the matter, for what people used to call the nitty gritty.

The nitty-gritty comes down to this: Where do you invest your money to make sure it grows to a large enough sum to get you ready for real enjoyment of your postworking years?

Where can you put your savings year in and year out so that they will be there when you need them and will grow as much as they need to grow to yield the amount of money you need?

First of all, we are now talking about the money you are going to need to *live* on. This is not the money we discussed in your thirties, which you might have put into a friend's software business or into a neighbor's hot tip on the commodities market. This is not high-risk capital, in other words. Nor is this the money which you have in the checking account to pay the gas bill and the orthodontist. This is the money you have been putting aside as your rock and redemption when you have been given your gold watch and told to get lost in the sun somewhere. It is absolutely a matter of life or death

- That the money be there—that is, that it not have been lost—and
- That the money has grown as needed.

To make certain that these two criteria are met, there are three watchwords, three keys to look out for: safety, safety, and safety.

The assured safety of your savings transcends any and all other considerations. It is the sine qua non of any savings program, of any preparation for retirement.

Investor Beware

This is a great country, by far the greatest in the world by any measure. But, unfortunately, it is also a great magnet for crooks and con men of all kinds. In the twelve months before this book was completed, more major scandals than I could keep track of have broken upon innocent people saving for their retirement. There have been two giant frauds involving the sale of gold bullion and its alleged storage in impregnable mountain fastnesses. In fact and in truth, the promoter took the money, and the pigeons got empty vaults and sticks of wood painted to look like gold. There has been a gigantic, $500 million fraud involving land in the desert of California. There have been several large bank failures. In one of them, the Penn Square Bank bust, depositors with over $100,000 in an account lost that excess.

There have been subtler scandals. Corporate accountants have juggled the books of major companies to make them look more profitable than they were. This has caused the bottom of some stock prices to fall out, ruining investors who happened to be holding the stock when the market realized that it was worth far less than had been thought. There have been complex write-ups and write-downs of foreign operations which looked good on paper, but later soured on closer scrutiny, making the small investor in the fabricating company take the losses after the insiders bailed out.

In a word, there have been a lot of traps for the unwary investor, carefully set by the unscrupulous.

Alas, there are also traps set simply by the uncertain nature of the universe. For example, if an investor had, in 1966, bought all the stocks on the Dow-Jones Industrial Average, he would actually have lost most of his investment between then and 1983—even allowing for the great bull market of 1982 and 1983. In the spring of 1966, the Dow-Jones Industrial Average hit 1,000. If it had kept up with inflation between then and 1983, it would have reached 3,000 by September of 1983. Instead, it reached the neighborhood of 1,250. That means the Dow-Jones Industrial Average, the price of thirty of the most prestigious manufacturing companies in America, did not even *halfway* keep up with inflation.

Of course, the stockholder would have received dividends, which would have somewhat offset his loss. But even counting in dividends and compounding on dividends, the owner of the Dow-Jones Industrials would not have kept up with inflation and earned even the current passbook savings rate of return. Until the great bull market of 1982 and 1983, the holder of the Dow-Jones Industrials would have seen his investment—ex-dividends—selling for only about *one fourth* its value in 1966.

Of course, there have been some stocks which have done spectacularly well. Lucky people who put their life savings in certain stocks have become extremely rich from fairly small investments. Then again, there are those sad people who had stock in Addressograph-Multigraph and saw it disappear from the world of corporations. Just in the last year (pre-1984), many people with investments in computer stocks have seen their money fall through a gaping hole into eternity.

The point is that the stock market is a wonderful vehicle when it is doing well. It is a wonderful line of work for stockbrokers even when it is fluctuating wildly. But it is treacherous for persons who happen to get caught in a long down draft, or who need the money in their stocks before they can wait for a stock market rebound. Stocks are fun things to play with and certainly are great for the very long haul. But for people who have to get their money out at a certain time no matter what the market is doing, the stock market can be a tragedy.

Sadly, the long-term bond market is even worse. At one time, bonds were the absolutely safest investment that could be made. The long-term bonds of major industrial companies or of the United States Treasury were dull and unexciting, but they were rock solid and secure. Alas, that went by the boards along with the tail fin and the crew cut. Bond prices are tied to the rate of interest in the economy generally, moving inversely to the movements of interest rates so as to equalize yields on new and existing instruments. This means that as interest rates have soared, bond prices have plummeted. Not only have the selling prices dropped catastrophically, but the rates of return have been a source of immense sorrow to holders from years ago.

Imagine, if you will, a poor widow who bought United States thirty-year bonds at 6 percent in 1970. Her bond would have fallen by close to half in value within ten years if she needed to sell it right away. Not only that, but she would only be earning 6 percent on her investment when the market rate on thirty-year bonds is now close to 12 percent.

Note well: When the bond matures, it will still be paid off at full face value, but perhaps the retiree is going to need his money in cash before that. He or she may have to sell at a loss, which is something no one *likes* to do and retirees should *hate* to do.

In other words, while stocks and bonds have their points and may be fun to gamble with, they are far from being the sure things that you need to prepare for retirement. Their prices can and do fluctuate far too much in the short and medium and long term to yield that ease of sleeping which is everyone's goal.

Silver Traps and Golden Needles

In the last fifteen years, there has been a renaissance of interest in so-called precious metals. Gold and silver have come out of the closet they were in post-1933 and have become an obsession with otherwise calm people. Supposedly, gold and silver will "automatically" keep pace with inflation and safeguard your savings.

Would that it were true. In fact, gold has risen spectacularly since its price was freed in 1975 and since gold could be owned by private citizens.

From a low of $35 in 1975, gold rose to an astonishing high of about $850 per ounce in 1979. Unfortunately, if you were among the many thousands of persons who bought gold at $850 an ounce in 1979, you would have been virtually ruined by its downward plunge since that time. Gold fell to less than half of its peak price, to a sad low of below $380 in 1982, and even in late 1984, it was trading for under $400 per ounce. This means that if you had put your life savings into gold in 1979, you would have lost half of those savings, not to mention that you would have gotten no interest on the money in the meantime.

Silver has had an even more notorious career. In 1979, it was zooming around the $50 mark. In the four years since then, it has fallen into the $8.50 range more than once and even after four years rarely exceeds $13 an ounce. Had you invested in silver at $50 an ounce, you would have lost more than three fourths of your money. Again, you also would not have received any interest.

Gold and silver investments are wonderful as baubles and conversation pieces. They are also great for gold and silver coin and bullion dealers. But for people in their fifties who cannot afford to gamble, they are simply too dangerous.

As for gold and silver antique coins, so-called precious stones, or antiques generally, they are absolutely discredited as serious investments, as indeed they should be. Poor people who put their money into "sure thing" precious stone scams and "guaranteed appreciation" coin-buying schemes have rarely had anything but sad, long stories to tell as a result. Diamonds, antiques, rare coins, and collectibles of all kinds are great if you collect them for love or for a hobby. But to believe in all seriousness that you will get your money out of them is expecting the impossible. *The market in all of those "sure things" is so rigged by the dealers, so completely stacked against the ordinary citizen, that you would do very well to stay away.*

On the same depressing note, it goes without saying that limited partnerships in land or in building or in restaurants may be great for the man who puts the deals together, but they are usually better suited to his needs than to the investor's. Many limited partnerships in real estate or gas or oil have done well, some extremely well. But there is usually no guaranteed ability to get your money out at any specific time. There is also usually no way of determining how well your investment is doing before it is liquidated.

This means that your money is, in effect, denied to you and that you simply have to wait like a lottery player, hoping for a successful outcome. The difference is that the date of the drawing for the lottery is usually known in advance, while it is almost always unknown when your limited partnership will be liquidated.

Ahem, ahem. One could go on all day and night listing the investments and scams that are *not* suitable for those whose incomes are barely rising, and who have to make sure and certain preparation for the day when you can sleep late.

The real question is, what offers the best hope of a successful outcome, offering safety so that your income will well and truly be there when you need it.

Well—What Is the Right Answer?

Again, the watchwords are safety, safety, and safety. This confines your options to a fairly small number of choices: federally insured instruments, instruments which are not federally insured but have an independently verifiable record of safety that is reassuring, and little else.

For example, money market accounts at federally insured banks offer an unexciting but competitive rate of interest. They are absolutely as safe as can be if they are kept at levels below the federally insured maximum. Money market mutual funds from the large brokerages have never lost a dime and are generally considered safe. Certificates of deposit which are federally insured yield a consistent if not thrilling rate of return and will always be there if you keep their amount within federally insured levels.

United States Treasury bonds, notes, and bills are completely guaranteed by the full faith and credit of the United States government. There is no better guarantee this side of the pearly gates. The alert reader will recall that he or she just read that long-term bonds were treacherous, and this is a fact. But short-term Treasury obligations do not fluctuate wildly in price like long-term instruments. The reason is fairly complicated, but can be explained by a simple analogy. If you buy a glass of wine, neither you nor the seller of the glass of wine cares very much how valuable that vintage will be in the future. After all, your glass of wine will be gone in no time at all, so why worry about what it might be worth in ten years? On the other hand, if you buy the produce of an entire vineyard, you and the seller will be extremely interested in the long-term value of the wine. There is so much wine there that you will still be selling it for years. You are very interested in what the value of that particular vintage will be in ten years, and you will closely follow every detail of price movement about that kind of wine and that vintage. If the value of that vintage rises, your crop will be more valuable. If the value of the crop falls, your stored wine will be less valuable. The price of all other vintners' wine of the same type and vintage will be of great and vital interest to you, and the value of your crop will move accordingly.

By the same token, if you own a Treasury note that matures in one month, you will soon be paid off the face value of the note. You will not hold it long enough for it to be affected by the movement of interest rates. But if you hold a bond which will not mature for ten years, you should be very aware of interest rates. Your bond will still be paying interest for many years to come. If interest rates rise, and you hold a bond with a low coupon, you are out of luck. No one will want to buy your bond except at a very much lower price to equalize your coupon rate with the market rate over the remaining life of the bond. In other words, your bond's market value can and will change, sometimes drastically, day by day and week by week as interest rates change, *if* yours is a long-term instrument. But short-term instruments fluctuate much less, and if they are very short-term, they do not fluctuate at all.

This means that short-term Treasury instruments are probably the very safest kind of interest bearing item you can own. Add them to insured certificates of deposit, major money market funds, and insured bank money market funds as very safe instruments to prepare for your retirement.

Alas, once you get beyond those few, you definitely leave the realm of sure things. There are bond mutual funds that pay excellent rates of return and where your principal is *probably* quite safe. There are also municipal bonds and bond funds in which the interest can be high *and* exempt from state and federal taxation. These are fine for people who have so much capital that a loss of some of it will not be crippling. They are also fine for people who have so much capital that they earn enough interest so that they will never conceivably have to cash in some of the principal for living expenses. But there are several things to watch out for in municipal bonds.

First, their price can and does vary as interest rates move. In recent years, some of those movements have been sharply lower. Second, municipal bonds often trade in extremely thin markets. This means that there is not a readily assured flow of buyers and sellers standing ready at all times to make a market in your bond, as there is, for example, on the New York Stock Exchange. This does not mean that you will not be able to sell your bonds if you have to. It does mean that you may have to wait a short while to sell them. More important, the thin market can *and does* mean that when you sell, you will probably have to sell for substantially less than you think your bond is worth to find a buyer. When there is not an active market in a bond—or anything else—it almost always works to lower the receipts to a seller in a hurry.

(Note well: This does not affect the salability of municipal bond funds, whose promoters usually assure you that they will redeem your portions of the fund instantly. This phenomenon does very definitely affect the *price* at which the promoters will redeem your bond fund shares. That redemption price can be 15 percent less than the price at which the shares are sold to the public, although a more usual spread would be about 8 percent. Still, to have to take an 8 percent haircut when you have to sell is not something that should make you happy. Losing 8 percent of your capital is a big loss.)

But to get to the good part about "munis," they too are extremely safe and immune from fluctuation if they are of very short duration. If you hold "project notes" or another form of tax-free instrument, which will mature in a month or two and will be paid off by a major state or municipal authority, you are holding very safe "paper." This, along with insured CDs, insured or major-issuer money market funds, and short-term federal Treasury instruments, can be a safe and sane part of your portfolio of assets.

If you have calculated how much money you need to put into your fund of savings to reach the desired goal at retirement, you can and must include taxation on any taxable savings you may have—i.e., something other than IRAs, Keogh plans, or Defined Benefit Plans. It may well be that the lower rate of tax-exempt interest on short-term municipal instruments will be absolutely perfect for your savings plan.

Automatic Inflation Hedging

The alert reader will notice at once that we are talking mostly about instruments that pay interest or otherwise about securities that pay off an implicit interest in the form of paying off at maturity a face value when they were bought at a discount from that face value—that is, a $100 bond may have been purchased for $75. Really, both of these kinds of securities are interest-bearing instruments.

But wait a minute. Haven't we all heard that debt instruments are the worst kind of things to have if inflation starts to rear its ugly head again? Aren't we all taught from childhood about the poor people in Weimar Republic Germany who were ruined because they held fixed interest government bonds paying 5 percent when the interest rate ran up to a billion percent, barely keeping pace with wheelbarrow size inflation?

Yes and no. Yes, long-term bonds are a dangerous card to be holding when and if inflation starts again. As we discussed above, they fall in price if inflation and interest rates start to rise. You can lose both principal and interest, which is something you do not want to do.

However, short-term interest bearing instruments are among the *best* securities to own in highly inflationary times. If you have your money in a money market fund at your bank, federally insured to be sure, and if inflation starts to roar out of its cage, the very first thing that will happen is that short-term interest rates will skyrocket. That means your interest rate on your money market mutual fund will skyrocket, and you will be protected.

If you have a short-term municipal note that matures in sixty days, and if interest rates move up rapidly with inflation, don't worry about it. You will only hold that municipal paper for another sixty days, and then you can trade it in for new, much higher interest municipal paper.

If you have a CD for ninety days at your local bank, and if interest rates start to go up rapidly, have no fear. You will be able to cash in that CD in three short months and buy a new, much higher paying CD at that time. In fact, if you are really dying to catch that interest rate wave, you can borrow against your existing CD, usually at a rate considerably lower than the going personal loan rate, usually at a maximum of two points above the rate on your CD, and take that borrowed money and buy a brand new CD at the new higher rate.

In other words, by holding *short-term* interest-bearing instruments, you can get out of whatever you own and buy new short-term instruments to keep up with inflation at virtually a moment's notice. You are *not* locked into securities with a rate that is fixed for years even as inflation roars around you. With short-term debt instruments, you have the safety and the flexibility to make sure you

- Keep your principal safe against market fluctuations, and
- Keep your interest earnings competitive with those of the market, and
- Boost your earnings to the level at which they can and will add to your nest egg if inflation requires that you earn more money for higher than anticipated future living expenses.

Short-term, very carefully selected debt instruments can give you the safety, earnings, and flexibility you need as you wend your way through the decade of the fifties. Remember, you cannot replace losses through rapidly rising real income. You absolutely need to have a systematic savings plan against the day when work stops. Park in the green zone where your money will not get towed away—safety, safety, safety. It is not glamorous, but you will never get cold sweats when you see a newspaper headline about the stock market or scams or gold prices. More important, you will have the money you need to live on.

The alert reader will perhaps by now say to himself or herself, "Hey, wait just a cotton-pickin' minute. All through the book this guy is really, really careful about what he tells us to invest in. He gives us this very general advice about not getting caught in scams and about being careful, but nothing that specific. Then, out of the blue, he's suddenly crossing every T and dotting every I. What happened? This is supposed to be a book about the financial crises of one's life, not about investment advice. What's going on?"

The answer, dear alert reader, is that what we know about the flattening of income gains in your forties and fifties is so clear and so overwhelming in its implications that it dictates more precise concerns. It is necessary at this point to make it clear over and over again that by a certain stage in your life, the stage when you start having the boy carry your groceries out to the car, you can and must invest as if you simply could not afford to lose the money. In fact, in most cases, for most people, you cannot afford to lose the money because to replace it, you would have to give up something or some things that are fairly basic in your life.

This humble author hates to bore you, but you must remember this and write it on the back of your hand: By the time you are in your late forties and early fifties, for most people, your income growth will have basically slowed to a crawl. Your income is now close to being *fixed*. Any dollar you have to add to savings because you *lost* some of your savings will have to come out of money you are spending on your aged parents in their nursing home or on your only hobby, playing golf, or on your twenty-fifth anniversary cruise—or something else you do not want to miss. Losing any part of your savings at this stage *is* a financial crisis—one you want never to know about at firsthand.

For the umpteenth time, the only clear way to avoid the problem is not to lose the money in the first place and therefore not have to replace it. OK? 'Nuff said.

To Annuit or Not to Annuit

A big question lies in store for the family or individual in his or her fifties who is facing *the* major financial concern of the decade. The question is whether to plan your savings so that at retirement you will be able to live off the *interest* or to plan them so that you can live off an annuity, which means that you draw down both *principal and interest*.

Kindly allow me to make the distinction by an example. Imagine that we go back to our pal, Jane Q. Colgrad, now married and entering upon her fiftieth year on this planet with her husband, Nathaniel Blocker. They each have decent jobs, and each has a pension plan at work. Along with Social Security, it will yield them almost exactly half of what they need to live on when they move to Sunset Shores, a retirement community just south of Sarasota, Florida.

They believe that in addition to whatever they will get from their pension plan and from their Social Security, they will also need $1,750 per month for the rest of their lives from their investments. They plan to retire at age sixty-five. To simplify things, let's imagine that Nathaniel and Jane are the same age. Let's also imagine that they are planning to retire on the same date. And further to simplify things, let's imagine that they expect to live for *about* another fifteen years each after they retire.

Now, if they were to have a capital sum in their hot little hands upon retirement that would yield that sum, year after year unto eternity, assuming (a major assumption but there's not too much we can do about it) that the interest rate on their money will be 9.5 percent and that they are not concerned with taxation, they will need to have, belonging to them, $221,052.63. At 9.5 percent, that will pay $1,750 per month for all eternity, payable yearly.

When Jane and Nathaniel enter immortality, still as much in love on that day as on the day they were married, that money will still be there, to be left to their posterity or to the Fund for Animals or for any worthwhile—or even not worthwhile—purpose.

Now, suppose that Jane and Nathaniel decide that they can live on an annuity, which will pay them the same amount out of both interest and a steady drawing down of principal. A principal sum of about $167,588 will yield that very same $1,750 per month for fifteen years.

Obviously, it takes a lot less effort to save $167,588 than to save $221,052. In fact, for those of you who like numbers, if you are saving for fifteen years, to get up to the larger sum takes $558 per month. To get up to the smaller sum takes only $423 per month, both at 9.5 percent interest compounded monthly.

The question is, should we Americans go for the annuity or for the interest only? The drawbacks of living entirely off interest are extremely clear: Doing so requires that you make considerably more sacrifice during your younger working years to come up to a higher principal sum figure. Many people believe that they should spend more money when they are young and presumably able to enjoy it and live in straiter circumstances when they are older and presumably less able to enjoy the money. That is a weighty argument for taking the annuity route.

There are several arguments for taking the interest-only route, and to me they make devastating sense:

The most obvious, most frightening reason for choosing to live off the interest only for as long as possible is that *no one*—repeat, *no one*—wants to get into a situation in which your annuity runs out before your life does. It is wonderful to live to a ripe old age. But it is terrifying to have your money run out when you are eighty and cannot possibly earn any more. The thought of having to lower your standard of living drastically, very possibly including your standard of medical care, when you are old and infirm is not a happy one. Yet, this can and does happen when people buy an annuity for a certain number of years and then outlive the annuity.

The second reason is related to the first: If economic circumstances change, you have far more room to maneuver if you have a larger capital sum—controlled by you—than if you have a smaller capital sum, locked in the bowels of a giant insurance company, inaccessible to you except through your fixed monthly checks.

For example, suppose there were a resurgence of inflation. With an annuity, your payments would be fixed, based on a fixed interest rate which might be far lower than the new inflation-era interest rates. In effect, you would be stuck with a low-rate investment that you could not get out of, while prices and interest rates surged all around you. You would have the ugly twin specters of rapidly rising cost of living, plus the maddening frustration of knowing that you *could* get those higher interest rates if only you could control your money yourself.

It is entirely possible that Jane and Nathaniel, or you or I, could buy an annuity or buy into an annuity requiring annual payments. It is entirely possible that such an annuity would look good compared with any comparable investment we could get today. For example, we might start making payments toward buying an annuity this very day that would yield its payments at retirement as if we were earning 10.5 percent interest when, in fact, the real rate of interest at the moment was only 9 percent. In effect, our annuity would seem to be outperforming the market.

At the time, the purchase of that annuity would seem to make perfect sense. *But,* what if by the third year after retirement, interest rates are 15 percent? What if they are 20 percent? Jane and Nathaniel and you and I could be up that famous creek without a paddle if we allow our interest rate to stay fixed when it could so easily move against us.

Again, locking in an interest rate might have been fine in the nineteenth century, when prices hardly changed at all for almost one hundred years (except for the Civil War). But to allow the annuity company to lock in your money when interest rates could move against you could be devastating.

(To be fair, interest rates could also drop, and you could be the lucky beneficiaries of a suddenly higher rate of interest than the market is paying. Although such judgments are personal, my own feeling is that if you get that lucky break, that is nowhere near as *good* for you as suddenly finding out that you lack the money to live is *bad* for you. Further, there have only been a few times in the last twenty years when interest rates have dropped dramatically and enriched people holding long-term fixed interest securities. What is past is prologue.)

There is yet another serious problem with an annuity: If you turn over your money to a stockbroker or an insurance company who is selling an annuity, the worthy people there may steal or lose your money.

This does not happen very often, but it certainly has happened. There are dozens of small thefts each year. Little hustlers take people's money and brazenly promise an annuity and are never heard from again. There are also occasional giant scandals like the Baldwin-United problems. Baldwin-United, a piano manufacturer, went into the business of selling annuities on a huge scale. Certainly, the managers of Baldwin-United did not intend to do anything wrong. They were not thieves or criminals. Unfortunately, they were also not managers of a large financial services company. They expanded too fast, did not protect their funds wisely, and in 1983, they were forced into bankruptcy. Tens of thousands, possibly hundreds of thousands, of people will not get the annuities they had counted on getting, at least not for several years.

It is certainly true that annuities do not fail often. A failure on the scale of Baldwin-United is rare. But you do not want it *ever* to happen with your hard-earned money. You do not want that risk to exist *at all* for you.

Plain and simple fact: annuities occasionally do fail.

Plain and simple fact: Government-insured savings accounts, government-insured money market funds, CDs, Treasury securities, very large money market funds *never do.*

Remember, this is a chapter about your fifties. In most cases, you will still have enough time to save for a capital sum that will be sufficient for you to live off the interest. The difference is a few meals at a good restaurant each month, a few weeks in a three-star hotel in Hawaii instead of a four-star hotel. If you make that small sacrifice, you will be in a position of far more flexibility when that sixty-fifth birthday rolls around.

Bottom Line Stuff:

In saving for your retirement, bear in mind always and everywhere that you are probably now in a period of almost flat income growth. You cannot afford any speculations with your retirement funds. Keep them in a safe place. Get out the old calculator and make plans to save enough to be able to live off the interest only when you retire. An annuity is good, but interest-only affords far more protection.

Old Folks in Homes

By now, you're probably pretty sick of hearing about preparing for retirement. It is *the* main problem of the fifties, moneywise, but there are others.

Everyone has parents. Many of these parents have been wonderful people and now, through the inevitable processes of life and entropy, they are growing old. Alas, this happens to everyone. When our parents, dear old Mom and Dad who nourished, supported, and counseled us, get old, they often become weak and infirm. This, alas, is perfectly normal. Sometimes it means that Mom and Pop have to go into a nursing home. This is sad, but it happens to many, many old people. As of 1983, there were over 2 million old people in nursing and convalescent homes throughout the nation, not counting Veterans' Administration homes, which had about another 300,000 in both state and federal facilities.

If you have ever seen a nursing home, you know that some of them are lovely, charming places. Some of them are hellholes.

It is no secret that the nursing homes which cost more tend to be the more lovely homes. The nursing homes that are low in price tend to offer depressing, miserable care to our older Americans. It is bad enough to be old, but to be old in a dark, noisy, unclean atmosphere is truly horrible.

If Mom and Dad have to go into a nursing home, we want them to be in a place where they can and will feel as if they are not in torture chambers.

The federal government, through its Medicare program, pays for a large amount of whatever a nursing home may cost. Your parents' insurance pays for some of the rest. But if Mom or Dad is in a genuinely cheerful home, it will often cost more—far more—than your parents' Medicare or insurance will pay for.

This means that Mom or Dad may have to rely on the kiddies—now probably in their fifties or older—to pick up the difference. To be perfectly blunt about it, paying for that stay in Retirement Palms can cost a fortune. If you feel that it is your solemn duty to do all you can for Mom and Dad, you had better make some provision for those huge monthly statements from Retirement Palms.

You can make that provision either by paying for it as you go or by setting aside some kind of reserve for it. Or you can insure against it. You can insure against it either by buying a policy yourself against the possibility of that stay in Retirement Palms, or you can insure against it by helping your parents to buy more insurance themselves.

How you make such a preparation is up to you. It is even up to you whether you make any such preparation at all. But you should be aware that this is a thunderstorm that falls into a great many lives. Many parents are well off enough not to require help. Many are too proud to take help. Many are perfectly happy growing old where they are. But if Mom or Dad does need help, you can and should expect that it will not be cheap. Nursing homes can *easily* cost $200 each day. If you have not prepared, you can be in for a big shock.

Now, for the Good News . . .

Despite all this grim talk about annuities and old age and risky investments, the general news about entering your fifties is good financial tidings.

If you have not done anything strange or self-destructive, and if your work experience has been fairly typical, you will be earning about four to five times as much in real income—adjusted for inflation—as you did when you were twenty-one. This is an enormous, truly wonderful increase. It means that even including the effects of inflation, you will be bringing home about $5 for every one you brought home when you began your career.

In most cases, if you are part of a family, your home will be owned, or virtually owned. You will probably have seen it increase dramatically in value. You will probably have seen your other investments increase substantially in value. You will probably have at least the equivalent of a year and a half's savings in liquid form, not counting your house or any other real estate. In addition, you will have a steadily growing pool of savings in IRA and/or Keogh plans. You will probably also have substantial vested value in your company's pension plan. You may also have stock options or profit sharing which has been accumulating into a considerable plum.

Not only that, but on the consumption side, your days of big surprises are probably over—except for parental care. Your children are presumably now grown and self-supporting. Your house is presumably furnished more or less the way you like. Your chances of getting divorced in your fifties are only about one tenth what they were when you were in your late twenties or early thirties.

If you provide adequately for your retirement, and if you are not caught by surprise if Mom or Dad has to go to Retirement Palms, you should be able to live it up. The fifties are the time to eat out more often, take off a few Fridays and go up to the lake, and generally have a good time. Remember that your income will be fairly flat from now on, but also remember that if you have carefully planned for your nonworking future, much of what you earn is gravy. Go to it!

(To give you some idea of how a budget might look at this stage of your life, you might take this table as a very rough estimate of where your money should be going at about age fifty-five. The categories include provision for retirement but not other savings or taxes. This is going to be your last table of spending categories. From now on you should be able to make your own decisions.)

For Families in Their Mid-Fifties—
Percentage of Total Consumption Expenses After Taxes
(not including savings except for pension and insurance)

Food—total	12
Food at home	6
Food away from home	6
Alcohol and tobacco	1
Housing (rented or owned)—total	23
Utilities	2
Telephone and other household operations	4
Home furnishings and appliances	2
Rent or mortgage and taxes	15
Clothing	7
Transportation (including auto purchase)	13
Health care	11
Recreation	12
Education	5
Insurance and pension contributions	16

(Total may not add to 100 percent because of rounding.)

Notice the astonishing drops in the percentage of income going to housing and transportation as compared with those expenditures in your twenties (34 percent to 23 percent for housing, 24 percent to 13 percent for transportation). By the time of your fifties, your income should have grown so much that those huge housing costs have shrunk relatively speaking—even if you have moved up to a better house than you had at first. Likewise, you should and must have cut back drastically on your car spending. Again, not as an absolute amount, but as a fraction of all spending, car payments and other transportation costs should be no more than one seventh or eighth of your income. If you have not gotten to those points for cars and homes, you will not have the extra money you will need for health care and pension and insurance, which are now falling into the *must* category.

At this phase of life, as at all phases, singles can have more flexibility. But they should certainly not exceed the percentages on housing and transportation that apply to families. Also, since their base incomes will be lower, in all likelihood, they should not expect to be able to spend the same absolute dollar amounts on any categories as married persons. As always, the possibilities for flexibility are not excuses for waste, especially for wasting time that could be spent assuring future financial peace of mind.

FOURTEEN

A Few Notes on Singles at Fifty

If an American man or woman reaches the age of fifty without ever having been married, he or she probably does not *want* to be married and probably will not ever be married. The chances of a never-married fifty-year-old getting married are extremely small, for both men and women. (Interestingly enough, the chances of a man or woman who is divorced or widowed getting married in his or her fifties is several times as great. This almost certainly reflects the greater ability to get along in the married situation of those who have already been married compared with those who have never been married.)

Therefore, it makes excellent sense, at least as a matter of statistical chance, to assume that if you are fifty and never married, you will not get married. It also makes perfect sense to assume that you will remarry if you are fifty and have been married before.

In the decade of the fifties, the real income of single persons tends to coagulate together along a single trend line, and that trend line is flat to gently sloping downward. As a matter of averages, the single man or woman in his or her fifties should not expect that he or she will see *any* growth in real, inflation-adjusted income through the decade of the fifties.

Of course, as always, there will be some singles who manage to keep their real income rising rapidly year after year. But for most persons in their fifties, the real effects will be mostly downward. Absence from the work force, inability to keep current on the latest technological changes, failure to keep in personal contact with the powers in the business, obsolescence of human capital (what you know), all work together to keep wages flat. For many singles in their fifties, wages will not even be flat. The same factors that encourage employers to discharge employees who have high wages but little potential work against single persons in their fifties as well.

The employer looks at his payroll and sees that he is paying Miss Cranapple four times as much as he would have to pay a new employee (or twice as much anyway). He wonders why he should do that, since Miss Cranapple does not even know how to program in BASIC, when he could get a new kid who could program in COBOL for less money. Miss Cranapple is a dedicated and pleasant fixture at the company, but the future is with the kids. Not only that, but she is an old maid, and she has been acting a little bit eccentric lately. . . . If someone has to be laid off, it would probably be better that it were Miss Cranapple than Charlie Brooks anyway, because good old Charlie has a wife and a family to support.

So goes the reasoning that sometimes leads employers to let go those with the most seniority. In late 1983, the nation as a whole saw a dramatic example of that process. Two large airlines abruptly suspended their pay scales, which paid more money to senior employees. The airlines said, in effect, that they simply could not pay huge wage differentials to older employees any longer when younger employees could do just as well. If the older employees did not like it, they could go on strike and be fired and replaced with plenty of younger people who were dying to have the jobs.

The singles in their fifties have the exact same obligations and crises that younger employees have. They must prepare for their retirement. They must realize that their savings cannot be replaced out of steadily growing real income. They must save with great care and bear in mind the three watchwords of saving for retirement:

- safety
- safety and
- safety.

They must also bear in mind that in American life, 2 can live as cheaply as 1.7. That means a couple can realize certain large savings on shared dwelling, shared transportation, shared cooking, and other shared expenses that a single person cannot. That means higher expenses *per person* for a single person, both before and after retirement. If the single man or woman prepares for it, a lot of unpleasant surprises can be eliminated.

The single man or woman must also bear in his or her single thoughts that parents may have to be supported in nursing homes, that Mom and Dad may need expensive care, and that Mom and Dad can and should deserve some preparation in the child's plans even if the child is now fifty years old.

Other than that, the fifties single doesn't have a care in the world—statistically speaking. He or she has no large surprises lurking, on average, has already bought most of the durable goods he or she will need, and now only has to live it up.

NEXT: Golden Days.

FIFTEEN

The Sixties and Seventies—Retirement Without Blinders —and with a Smile

There is only one major financial event for most persons in their sixties—retirement. For the remaining years of work from sixty to sixty-two or sixty-five or sixty-seven, there is little change in earnings patterns from the decade of the fifties: Income growth becomes virtually nil in inflation-adjusted terms, although it approaches zero as a limit, which is to say that it rarely stops growing altogether as an average number, except during periods of national economic slowdown. For individuals, of course, income growth can and will be either large or negative. That is, there will be some hip doctors and lawyers and candlestick makers who figure out a new wrinkle in their line of work and thereby make a great deal of money. There will also be a great many humans of both sexes who will quit or get laid off or take a shorter work week. For them, income growth will be negative. In a word, their incomes will fall. But for the *average* worker, income growth will be close to 2 percent in real terms into the sixties, just before retirement.

The big change in income comes, of course, when income drops radically upon retirement. This will be the most sudden, abrupt financial shock of a lifetime. If it is faced or approached without preparation, it can be devastating. However, the good news is that it is no more necessary to face it without preparation than to play Russian roulette.

Fascinating Facts and Fallacies

The most basic trip wire lurking in the underbrush of the Golden Years concerns how much it will cost to live when you and your spouse retire. There is a charming but lethal misconception about this whole subject. Somehow, at annuity offices, at real estate agencies, in government proposals, in plain old family discussions, the idea has become current that *somehow* you can live more cheaply when you retire. *Somehow,* almost automatically, it will cost you less to live when you stop working, and therefore—by this same charming but deadly hypothesis —you will also need less money to live on when you retire.

THIS IS DANGEROUS NONSENSE.

There is absolutely no necessary reason why your expenditures *on any household or personal item* should necessarily decline on the day you retire.

Think about it: On Friday, you have to get up and take the bus to work and work all day, then come home. On Monday, you are retired and you can sleep late. You save bus fare or car fare. Then what? Where else will your savings come from? You will not spend less on your food and indeed may well spend more because you may not receive meals subsidized by your employer. You will not spend less on your car, because your car expenses are mainly for insurance and depreciation and repairs anyway. They are hardly affected at all by not having to drive or bus to work.

Will you spend less on food eaten away from home in the evenings? Why should you? Indeed, after retirement, you may well want to eat out more often because you have been home all day. Will you spend less on your home? Not unless, by a miracle of coincidence, your mortgage is paid off on the day of your retirement. You will almost certainly want to spend *more* on travel and recreation. Yes, you probably will spend less on education, but since that amounts to only *1* percent of the average fifty-five-year-old's expenses there will be small savings there.

Health care, even with Medicare, will be dramatically higher. The percentage of family income that goes for health care is 50 percent higher for those sixty-five and over than for those fifty-five to sixty-four.

There is one category where there can possibly be savings, and that is savings itself. Presumably, if you were saving primarily for retirement and if you are now in retirement, you need save no longer. *But* this is not usually a life-changing cost cutter for most people, since average savings are only about 12 percent of spending for most families age fifty-five to sixty-four. There are also minor economies to be made in pension and health insurance contributions, which generally stop upon retirement.

But for consumption of the goods and services of everyday life, *no* automatic savings come upon retirement. This has two crucial consequences and perhaps more:

First, when you plan for retirement, do not expect that you will need a single penny less to *live on* the day after your sixty-fifth birthday as compared with the day before.

Second, if there are to be major savings made in your expenditures, you will have to make them yourself.

In a way, this second lesson is the more important of the two: Nothing automatic happens to lower your food bill or your lighting bill or your doctor's bill or your gasoline bill on that sixty-fifth birthday. If you have definitely got less money coming in after retirement than before, you absolutely have to make whatever adjustments are necessary yourself.

Remember: Government statisticians have found out that, in real life, persons and families over sixty-five do *not* necessarily spend a single cent less *on any major category of consumption* after retirement, just as common sense might have told you. For a period of over a decade during which personal expenses were tracked by age of the person or head of the family, there were no major differences in spending *per person* between those ten years *before* retirement and those *after* retirement.

Again, this leads to a major, crucial lesson. If the budget requires belt-tightening after retirement, you have got to do it yourself and not count on its happening by itself.

As to the first lesson, there is a fascinating corollary to it. While it is true that persons over sixty-five basically have the same costs as persons fifty-five to sixty-four, a great many of them also have basically the same income. In other words, many older Americans have so arranged their financial affairs that they have income from Social Security, pensions, and savings equal—or almost equal—to what they were earning before retirement.

Now, before you kill yourself with envy, bear in mind that there is a joker in this comparison: Social Security and other government assistance programs for the older American have risen in generosity far faster than wages and salaries in recent years. The government has been taking large handfuls of money from working Americans and transferring them to nonworking retired Americans. This means that Grandma and Grandpa's larger-than-expected incomes are not solely the result of their own provident foresight. Partly, they are the result of politicians' generosity with other people's money.

Still, even discounting the disproportionate share of retirees' income made up by Social Security, the ability of Americans to plan for their futures with pensions and with annuities and with the earnings from investments is extremely impressive. For year after year in which statistics were kept, the sudden drop in wages and salaries upon retirement is made up by income from pensions, Social Security, investments, and annuities.

What this basically means is, if they can do it, so can you. As one studies the statistics of families over time, measured by age of householder, it becomes richly impressive how income to families from interest, dividends, royalties, and rents rises steadily year by year. As these incomes reach a crescendo, wage and salary income falls to zero or close to zero, but the two balance each other at least to some extent.

Now, again, before we get carried away, let us be realistic. Income after retirement tends to be *close* to income before retirement but by no means *exactly the same.* You should not expect to make up each and every penny lost from no longer working by interest and dividends. It is great if you can, but if you can't, don't feel that the last thousand-dollar gap makes you a loser.

We should also remember that in terms of income pre- and post-retirement, we have been talking about an after-tax number. This has a *huge* built-in bias in favor of the retiree. For one thing, his or her working income was taxable. Social Security is not, at least as of this writing. For another thing, many pensions and annuities are not taxable. (Usually the dividing line has to do with whether or not the pension or annuity were bought with before- or after-tax income.) Also, many retirees have income from tax-free municipal bonds or notes. This means that the larger preretirement earnings are taxable and boil down to a far smaller after-tax net. The retirement figure is smaller to start with, but since most of it is nontaxable, it does not shrink as much and comes out to a far more nearly equal after-tax net.

Also, some of the government data about family income before and after retirement includes in-kind assistance programs like Medicare, which are usually not available to working people. The statistics attempt to put a dollar value on those programs, and that dollar value raises the income of retirees.

None of this is meant to excuse not preparing for retirement. All of it is meant to keep you from thinking you have committed a sin if you are not all the way there in matching retirement and preretirement income dollar for dollar.

And, of course, if you have planned and executed a decent scheme for actually lowering your expenditures drastically after retirement, you do not have to concern yourself at all with equilibrating pre- and postretirement income. (But don't think that scheme will come easy.)

The key, always, is to have your income match your expenses after retirement. If you can lower your expenses, you do not need as much income. If, like most people, you cannot lower them substantially, then you must keep that income up.

The Old Homestead

Before we go another step farther, we have to talk about houses. In particular, what should retirees do about their houses? There is so much confusion and lack of understanding about this that it is difficult to know even where to begin. But since we have to begin somewhere, let's try this: One way that many retirees acquire a pot of money and the interest from it is to sell their house. Should you do it?

We are all familiar with the concept of the empty nest. You and your spouse bought a split-level ranch house in Smallville thirty years ago when Junior and Sis were just starting to need more privacy. You mowed the lawn for thirty years and shoveled snow just as long. On warm summer evenings, you and Junior threw the old pill around while Mom and Sis made apple pie in the kitchen. At night, you all clustered around the Magnavox to watch "Your Show of Shows" or "Have Gun, Will Travel." But, sadly, now those days are history. Junior and Sis are long gone. Junior is a marine biologist in San Diego. Sis married an accountant in Garden City, and while you hate him, you have to agree that he is a good provider. Now, you and the wife (or you and the hubby) just rattle around in those four bedrooms. Frankly, just seeing the yellow tile of the recreation room, remembering when Sis and Junior were learning the jitterbug, makes you want to cry, so you never go in there anymore.

So, you are contemplating leaving your home in Smallville and moving to Eden Isle, Arkansas. The problem is that whenever you mention this to Manny, your barber, he becomes hysterical.

"What?" he says as you are trying to read *Penthouse.* "But you've paid off the mortgage. That house doesn't cost you a dime to live in. Where else could you go that would be so cheap?"

Alas, if you listen to financial advice from a barber, you probably deserve exactly the fate that awaits you. Saying that it is "free" to live in a large house that has been paid off or with a low mortgage is like saying that it is "free" to keep your savings in a tin box in the backyard as compared with keeping them in a money market fund. In fact, it is very far from free.

That old house has a market value. Probably, unless you had very bad luck in choosing a location, your house has appreciated startlingly in value. In thirty years' time, it might well have appreciated by five times, possibly by a great deal more. That means you are living in an asset that is worth a lot more to someone else than it might be to you— and in a house that might actually be foolish for you to stay in.

Just, for example, imagine that you bought a house in 1953 for $40,000. Now, it could be sold for $400,000. You have paid off the mortgage, so it's free to live there, right?

Wrong. The true cost of that house to you is how much interest you could be earning on that house full of money. If you put that house's value at 10 percent interest, you would earn $40,000 *each year,* just from the interest. So the house is *costing* you forty K each year. Now, is it worth forty K per year to you? Remember, that is $3,333.33 each month. That is far from cheap.

Possibly you could find a little retirement-size condo in Eden Isle or Palm Desert for $125,000, which would cost you less than half of what you are now "paying" each month. You could apply the excess (the interest earnings minus the monthly cost of the new home) to buy golf balls and airplane tickets to Rome. In other words, you might be able to add greatly to your financial assets by selling that old "free" house and putting its value at interest. It may well be that your "free" house stands between you and a peaceful, capaciously financed retirement.

The retiree or potential retiree would do well to find out just how much the old homestead is worth. Then figure out your likely earnings from selling the house and putting the proceeds at interest. On the other hand, figure out how much it would cost you to live by purchase or rental in a dwelling you consider perfectly satisfactory. If the forgone interest implicit in owning the old homestead is a lot more than the cost of new digs, maybe you ought to call up the realtor and see what you can work out.

Naturally, if that old house means so much to you that you would rather die than sell it, then don't sell it. But if you are sick of it, if you are eager for a change of scene, don't let that nonsense about your old house costing you little or nothing a month fool you. A valuable house with *no* mortgage payment and virtually *no* taxes can still cost a fortune month by month because of the lost interest. The retiree or potential retiree can possibly make a big step toward a more secure way of life by selling the old homestead.

The real cost of a house is its market value times the interest rate. On that basis, the house you rattle around in could be costing you a fortune.

Caution: Should you find that you own a home which is rising rapidly in value, that would throw a whole new light on your situation. Obviously, if you own a home that is doubling in value every twenty-four months, you should hold on to it. Its yield far outstrips any likely yield that you could get with the proceeds of the house.

On the other hand, you will rarely run into that situation unless your house happens to be in Manhattan or on a piece of land next to IBM in Armonk or on top of a pool of natural gas. For most persons, there is real sense in considering seriously whether that old homestead is worth as much to you and your spouse—or you if you are living alone—as it would be to another buyer.

It is crazy and painful for young people to be house-poor. It is exactly as crazy for older people to be house-poor from not selling a house which they do not want or need and which could buy them a secure future. Again, bear it in mind. The investments that are "free" are often the ones that wind up costing you an arm and a leg.

The (Almost) Inevitability of Catastrophe

The human body is a machine of sorts, albeit an unusual machine possessing centers of love, hate, fear, envy, sensitivity, and artistry. Unfortunately, like all machines, it wears out. This has religious and moral importance, but it also has financial importance. As the machine wears out, you cannot just bring it to Murph at the 76 Station to have your batteries charged. You get sick and go to the hospital. Sometimes, you have to go to the hospital for a very long time. This is known as catastrophic illness, and unfortunately for those sixty-five or older, it happens to them about ten times as often as it happens to persons, say, thirty-five to forty-four. When you are an older American, all of your sins of diet and life-style and heredity catch up with you. When they catch up with you, they cost you a lot of money. Lengthy stays in the hospital are expensive on a scale once contemplated only by maharajahs.

At present, Medicare pays for a large fraction of all such stays. However, after thirty days, Medicare pays for a little less, and eventually even Medicare runs out. Considering the kind of political turbulence that has gathered around the entire Social Security program, it is not written in granite that the benefits of Medicare will stay as good as they are today.

This has one big meaning: You must, as an older American, have some kind of health program that will cover you thoroughly in the event catastrophic illness catches up with you.

Tragically, this field—supplementing Medicare—is a field rife with criminals and fraud artists. They will sell you policies you do not need or policies which simply do not pay off. But the amount of fraud in the business should not deter you from your appointed rounds of finding the supplemental coverage that is right for you. Hospital stays *routinely* cost one thousand dollars each day, including room, board, and medical tests, procedures, and treatments. If you do not have supplemental coverage, you can be a very sad person some day down the road when you get a bill for hospital costs equal to all of your savings.

On the graph of financial crises that can strike after retirement, catastrophic illness is where the line falls off into Lower Slobbovia. If you let it happen to you, you are being foolish. It is bad to have too much insurance. It is far worse to have too little.

Again, this is especially true when you are out of the labor force and simply *cannot* make up the lost savings that could result from catastrophic illness. You should and must match up the income and consumption function by having insurance, and if you turn out to have bought it in vain, count yourself lucky. Those who have catastrophic illness protection that remains locked up unused are the blessed.

Remember Inflation?

During the late sixties and early seventies the United States went through the worst peacetime inflation, the longest inflation of either war or peace, in our history. The value of the Yankee dollar actually was cut in thirds between 1967 and 1983, so that the average market basket of goodies and services that cost $100 in 1967 now costs more than $300.

Then, along came two severe recessions back to back from 1980 to the early part of 1983, and suddenly the inflation rate had been cut drastically. In 1983, it was still about 4 percent, which is high compared with 1955, but low compared with 1979's 14 percent. People began to forget about how inflation could suddenly flare up and devour the value of their money. They took as given that prices would rise slowly, if at all.

Alas, inflations have a nasty habit of coming back when you least expect them, sort of like a summer cold. For working people, those sudden flare-ups can be bad enough. But they can get their wages adjusted or raise their own fees. The retired person, who can no longer go into the labor force, has a more severe problem.

The retirees, single or a couple, who live on a fixed income and suddenly find that the pot roast they had bought every Friday for twenty years suddenly costs $9 per pound, that the long-distance calls to Sis that once cost $1 per minute now cost $1.50, that the dayworker who cleaned one day each week for $40 now demands $80—those people are in trouble. They face the danger of getting along in a world of rapidly rising prices on a fixed income.

There is one simple cure for this financial passage, one sure way to stay out of that particularly widespread trap: I hate to repeat myself but . . . Do not stick yourself with living on a fixed income. Arrange your finances so that you can and will shift around your assets, so that they will not be fixed at all but will keep perfect pace with changing prices. It's not hard at all to do. People far stupider than you and I do it all the time. Here's how they do it:

They put their financial assets into short-term investments. That way, when the yield on investments rises dramatically—as it always does when inflation rages—they can take out their money and reinvest it in other instruments that have kept pace with inflation.

For example, if you have put your life savings into thirty-year bonds of a small township in Indiana, those bonds will have a fixed yield year by year for as long as you own the bonds. If they yielded 9 percent when you bought them, that means that for every $1,000 you put into the bonds when you bought them, you will receive $90 per year in interest. At a time when inflation was 5 or 6 percent per year, that was a fine yield.

But if inflation rises to 12 percent per year—and it can happen—your bonds are suddenly trash. The market will drive down their value ruthlessly as buyers instead buy new bonds with a much higher interest rate. All of a sudden, there will be plenty of bonds paying $120 each year for each thousand that was put in. No one will want your Indiana township bonds until their price falls so low that their payment each year offers the same yield as a new bond. (Just in a rough way, when your bonds, for which you paid $1,000, are selling for $750, then they will be competitive with new bonds yielding a yearly payment, or coupon, of $120.)

Not only will your bonds not offer enough income to keep up with inflation, but their face value will take a nose dive as well. In other words, you got yourself locked into a fixed-income investment that brought you to grief when inflation reared its ugly head.

An annuity paying a fixed sum is even more deadly. If your annuity pays you just enough for you to live on during price stability, you may find yourself pinched if inflation becomes intense. With the long-term bonds discussed above, you could always sell them if things got desperate and buy new, higher-yielding instruments. If you did that just as inflation was starting, you might actually escape with small losses. But most annuities are very hard to sell. Of course, in a way, there is a market for everything. But individual annuities are extremely difficult to sell and, if sold at all, are sold at a huge discount from what was paid for them.

On the other hand, if you kept your savings in sixty-day notes, you would probably find that if inflation moved up, the yield on your notes would go up as well. In a very much oversimplified way, people have concluded that the interest rate on short-term instruments usually (not always) stays about 3 percentage points above the inflation rate. In other words, you can constantly readjust your investments to get the higher yields that will come as inflation comes.

If you have your money in a money market fund at a bank or a large broker, your adjustments are made for you. Your yield changes day by day, month by month as the market rate on your money market fund's short-term assets changes day by day. If inflation gets really ugly, you can be absolutely sure that your yield will rise on top of it, like a cork bobbing on rough seas.

In a word, by keeping your investments at the short end of the market, you take much of the risk out of inflationary price changes.

(Unfortunately, you also will not benefit if interest rates suddenly fall, as you would if you have long-term bonds. If you are a plunger and have extra money to gamble, you might want to take a flyer on long-term instruments as part of your portfolio—a small part. Then if inflation suddenly and abruptly falls off and long-term bond prices soar, you will not feel left out. But on the other hand, if inflation shoots upward again, you will not be badly hurt.)

Inflation is a treacherous and unpredictable snake. The only way to protect yourself is to be able to adjust your income as it rises and falls. That means *stay flexible* in your investments and stay at the short-term end of the market. It is an unglamorous way to go, and it will never make you rich. But far more important, it will never make you poor. Protection, not adventure, should be your goal at age sixty-five and above.

Signing Off

There is one final consideration for seniors which I will make short and sweet. When you are in retirement, carefully measuring your pennies to make sure that you and your spouse—or you, if you live alone—do not go hungry, you may be haunted by a strange concern: How much should I devise and bequeath to my children?

Actually, this is not a strange concern at all. Men and women feel for their children. They want their children to have a happier, easier life than they did. They want to be remembered and appreciated. Many men and women feel that they can make all of these things happen by leaving money to their children. Many retirees who are extremely poor and hard up for money refuse to use up any more of their savings so that they will not despoil the sums they hope to leave to their children. In other words, they starve themselves to keep themselves from having to contemplate leaving nothing to the kiddies.

This is a sensitive and delicate subject. It would be easy, but wrong, for this book to tell you how to handle it. Whether to leave an estate or to spend all of your savings on your own life and that of your spouse is a question best left to your personal discretion. However, it would not be wrong to tell you that a great many extremely well-respected people from Andrew Carnegie (who said, "I would rather leave my children a curse than leave them my wealth") to the present have believed that it was foolish and dangerous to short-change yourself for your children— especially when you are no longer earning an income from work.

Many economists believe that the real contribution that parents make to children is to leave behind a wealthier and more prosperous society generally. This contribution will make them richer if they work for it. Other economists believe that if your bequest is like most, it will quickly be spent on trifles, leaving your children with a distorted sense of values about money, distorting and upsetting their work habits, and making them less self-reliant.

Of course, your gifts can also do your children a great deal of good. The point is only that in the last financial passage of your earthly transit, you may well be faced with some hard choices. You may find yourself staring at the meat counter wishing you could afford some. You may find yourself choosing whether to put your heart's companion, the man or woman with whom you spent fifty years, into a nursing home with cockroaches or a nursing home with sunny windows and a view of the Gulf of Mexico. You may find yourself choosing between poverty and comfort. In making any of those decisions, you may well weigh just how much or how little you want to leave to your children. If you should decide that you will go for the option of spending it all on yourself, of providing for your own comfort and leaving your children to do the same for themselves, you are not making a cruel, selfish, or unusual choice.

Obviously, if you are a conduit through which a large hereditary fortune has passed, your decision may and should differ from the decisions of an ordinary working stiff. But for most people, the option of improving their own financial security after retirement by reducing their likely bequests to zero is a lively and widely used option. Your first responsibility is to take care of yourself once you are retired, and if you think it is someone else's responsibility, try seeking help from that person. It's a tough old world, and when we do for others, expecting their care in return, we are usually asking for trouble. You can keep your life easier and less heartbreaking if you simply emphasize self-care at the outset and do not wreck your older years in anticipation of an illusory or potentially illusory gratitude.

Conclusion

We are all only flesh and blood. We make terrible mistakes. We have great hopes which are violently destroyed. We bring totally unnecessary suffering into our own lives. On the other hand, we have the possibility in our flesh and blood hearts to enjoy great happiness and contentment. We have the chance to travel through life enjoying the day instead of dreading it.

Sadly, much of our sorrow comes from mistakes and worries about money. This book is an attempt to make your life happier by pointing out for you some of the potholes and canceled flights on life's journey, then suggesting where the detours and the superhighways are that will make up for those aggravations.

The advice and counsel of this book are based on statistics gathered over many years. Those statistics are good, valid predictors for most people. They may be off the mark by a little or by a lot in your own particular case. What is good advice for most Americans may be wrong for you, and you should bear it in mind. You should also bear in mind that the advice in this book is meant as just that: advice. It is not Holy Writ. It is just advice to make your life easier and safer and happier. If you cannot follow it for any important and valid reason, that does not make you a criminal. Mistakes with money are mistakes, and they have harmful consequences. They are not the same as wife beating or armed robbery. They are not offenses against the Divinity. Their only effect, usually speaking, is to make your life less enjoyable. But, frankly, that is more than enough harm for most people.

To make certain that you have the greatest possible chance to avoid inflicting that kind of harm on yourself, here are ten commandments for coping with life's predictable financial crises, a brief summary of what you should remember about this book and this life, financially speaking:

1. Do not buy an expensive car or furniture when you are young. Show off by telling funny jokes—not by impoverishing yourself.

2. Buy a home as early as possible, preferably before your children arrive.

3. Be prepared to pay for private elementary and secondary schooling for your children. If you do not have to, you have won the lottery, but wise people do not plan on winning lotteries.

4. When at all possible, raise your own personal productivity by keeping yourself well-informed and well-connected in your line of work.

5. Do not make any financial moves which will either contribute to the likelihood of a divorce or make life unbearably hard after a divorce.

6. Make your children pay for their own college education to the maximum extent possible. They are acquiring a capital asset. They should pay for it.

7. Do not expect that you should be able to live luxuriously as a matter of right as you enter middle age. People can afford to live as well as they can afford to live—not as well as they think they should be able to afford.

8. Your investments at all stages of your life should reflect how hard it was to acquire the money you will invest and how hard it will be to replace it.

9. Single people, especially single mothers with children, have to hew to a much more stringent line than any other large group in the society.

10. Start preparing for the years without work as early as possible. Each year earlier that you start is worth an hour's more peaceful sleep per night at age sixty-four.

And then there is perhaps one more commandment: Life is an adventure. Get your financial life in order, learn what is predictable and deal with it, and then enjoy the adventure so that when you are on the deck of the cruise ship, watching the sun set, golden and warm, into the

Aegean behind a magnificent ruin of an Athenian temple, you can say to your life's companion, "You know, I think we'll stay here another week. I know it's expensive, but money isn't everything," and then get a good night's sleep.

APPENDIX

For those who love and appreciate numbers, here is some solid meat. The first charts tell you how much money, for how long, you need put away at a given rate of interest to get to some savings destinations—and some stops on the way.

The second set of tables tells you what the effects of interest are on different amounts of time and money. The final column on the right is extremely helpful in computing how much you need to put aside to reach a certain future sum. That helps in guiding you toward saving for a home down payment or a car or private school for your children. It is instructive as well to see how small amounts, consistently invested, yield truly amazing returns over time. I have only gone up to an interest rate of 15 percent, but the eager reader can get more frighteningly inflationary compounding tables from his library if he so desires.

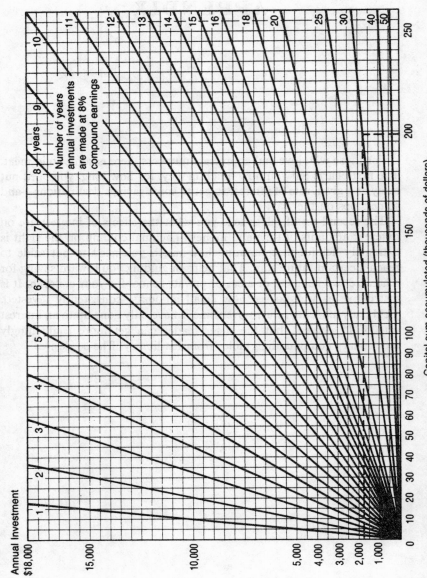

Annual investments to accumulate capital (to $260,000) at 8%

Annual Investments to accumulate capital (to $2,600,000) at 8%

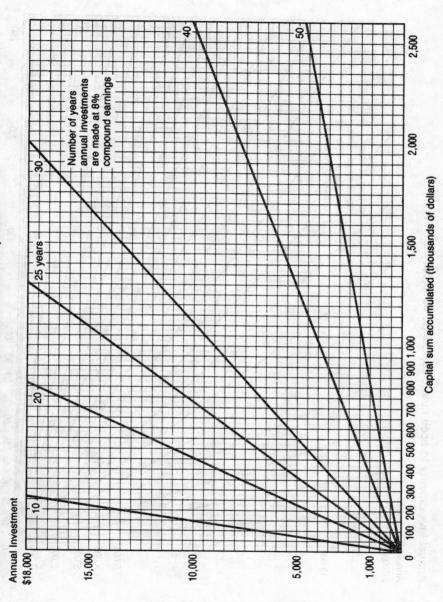

Annual Investment

Number of years annual investments are made at 8% compound earnings

Capital sum accumulated (thousands of dollars)

Annual investments to accumulate capital (to $260,000) at 10%

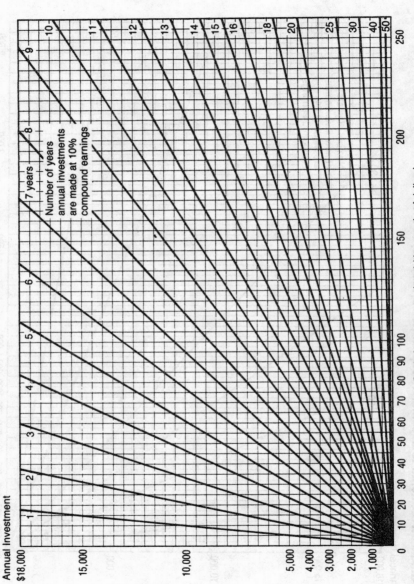

Capital sum accumulated (thousands of dollars)

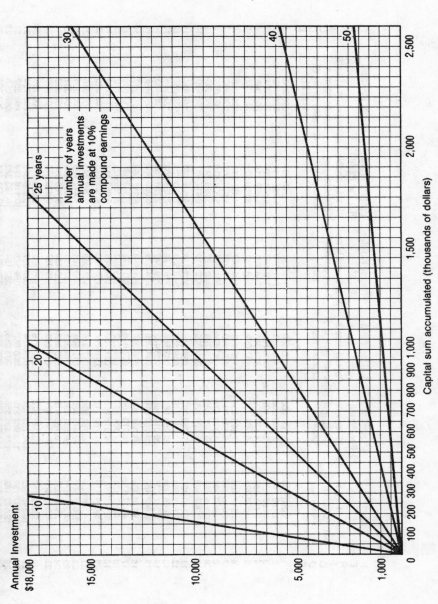

Annual investments to accumulate capital (to $2,600,000) at 10%

Rate of 9%

PERIODS	Amount of 1 — How $1 left at compound interest will grow.	Amount of 1 Per Period — How $1 deposited periodically will grow.	Sinking Fund — Periodic deposit that will grow to $1 at future date.	Present Worth of 1 — What $1 due in the future is worth today.	Present Worth of 1 Per Period — What $1 payable periodically is worth today.	Partial Payment — Annuity worth $1 today. Periodic payment necessary to pay off a loan of $1.
1	1.090 000	1.000 000	1.000 000	.917 431	.917 431	1.090 000
2	1.188 100	2.090 000	.478 468	.841 679	1.759 111	.568 468
3	1.295 029	3.278 100	.305 054	.772 183	2.531 294	.395 054
4	1.411 581	4.573 129	.218 668	.708 425	3.239 719	.308 668
5	1.538 623	5.984 710	.167 092	.649 931	3.889 651	.257 092
6	1.677 100	7.523 334	.132 919	.596 267	4.485 918	.222 919
7	1.828 039	9.200 434	.108 690	.547 034	5.032 952	.198 690
8	1.992 562	11.028 473	.090 674	.501 866	5.534 819	.180 674
9	2.171 893	13.021 036	.076 798	.460 427	5.995 246	.166 798
10	2.367 363	15.192 929	.065 820	.422 410	6.417 657	.155 820
11	2.580 426	17.560 293	.056 946	.387 532	6.805 190	.146 946
12	2.812 664	20.140 719	.049 650	.355 534	7.160 725	.139 650
13	3.065 804	22.953 384	.043 566	.326 178	7.486 903	.133 566
14	3.341 727	26.019 189	.038 433	.299 246	7.786 150	.128 433
15	3.642 482	29.360 916	.034 058	.274 538	8.060 688	.124 058
16	3.970 305	33.003 398	.030 299	.251 869	8.312 558	.120 299
17	4.327 633	36.973 704	.027 046	.231 073	8.543 631	.117 046
18	4.717 120	41.301 337	.024 212	.211 993	8.755 625	.114 212
19	5.141 661	46.018 458	.021 730	.194 489	8.950 114	.111 730
20	5.604 410	51.160 119	.019 546	.178 430	9.128 545	.109 546
21	6.108 807	56.764 530	.017 616	.163 698	9.292 243	.107 616
22	6.658 600	62.873 338	.015 904	.150 181	9.442 425	.105 904
23	7.257 874	69.531 938	.014 381	.137 781	9.580 206	.104 381
24	7.911 083	76.789 813	.013 022	.126 404	9.706 611	.103 022
25	8.623 080	84.700 896	.011 806	.115 967	9.822 579	.101 806
26	9.399 157	93.323 976	.010 715	.106 392	9.928 972	.100 715
27	10.245 082	102.723 134	.009 734	.097 607	10.026 579	.099 734
28	11.167 139	112.968 216	.008 852	.089 548	10.116 128	.098 852
29	12.172 182	124.135 356	.008 055	.082 154	10.198 282	.098 055
30	13.267 678	136.307 538	.007 336	.075 371	10.273 654	.097 336

N	$(1+i)^N$	$\dfrac{(1+i)^N - 1}{i}$	$\dfrac{i}{(1+i)^N - 1}$	$(1+i)^{-N}$	$\dfrac{1-(1+i)^{-N}}{i}$	$\dfrac{i}{1-(1+i)^{-N}}$
31	14.461 769	149.575 217	.006 685	.069 147	10.342 801	.096 685
32	15.763 328	164.036 986	.006 096	.063 438	10.406 240	.096 096
33	17.182 028	179.800 315	.005 561	.058 200	10.464 440	.095 561
34	18.728 410	196.982 343	.005 076	.053 394	10.517 835	.095 076
35	20.413 967	215.710 754	.004 635	.048 986	10.566 821	.094 635
36	22.251 225	236.124 722	.004 235	.044 941	10.611 762	.094 235
37	24.253 835	258.375 947	.003 870	.041 230	10.652 993	.093 870
38	26.436 680	282.629 782	.003 538	.037 826	10.690 819	.093 538
39	28.815 981	309.066 463	.003 235	.034 702	10.725 522	.093 235
40	31.409 420	337.882 445	.002 959	.031 837	10.757 360	.092 959
41	34.236 267	369.291 865	.002 707	.029 208	10.786 568	.092 707
42	37.317 531	403.528 132	.002 478	.026 797	10.813 366	.092 478
43	40.676 109	440.845 664	.002 268	.024 584	10.837 950	.092 268
44	44.336 959	481.521 774	.002 076	.022 554	10.860 505	.092 076
45	48.327 286	525.858 734	.001 901	.020 692	10.881 197	.091 901
46	52.676 741	574.186 020	.001 741	.018 983	10.900 180	.091 741
47	57.417 648	626.862 762	.001 595	.017 416	10.917 597	.091 595
48	62.585 236	684.280 411	.001 461	.015 978	10.933 575	.091 461
49	68.217 908	746.865 648	.001 338	.014 658	10.948 234	.091 338
50	74.357 520	815.083 556	.001 226	.013 448	10.961 682	.091 226
51	81.049 696	889.441 076	.001 124	.012 338	10.974 021	.091 124
52	88.344 169	970.490 773	.001 030	.011 319	10.985 340	.091 030
53	96.295 144	1058.834 942	.000 944	.010 384	10.995 725	.090 944
54	104.961 707	1155.130 087	.000 865	.009 527	11.005 252	.090 865
55	114.408 261	1260.091 795	.000 793	.008 740	11.013 993	.090 793
56	124.705 005	1374.500 057	.000 727	.008 018	11.022 011	.090 727
57	135.928 455	1499.205 062	.000 667	.007 356	11.029 368	.090 667
58	148.162 016	1635.133 518	.000 611	.006 749	11.036 118	.090 611
59	161.496 598	1783.295 534	.000 560	.006 192	11.042 310	.090 560
60	176.031 291	1944.792 132	.000 514	.005 680	11.047 991	.090 514

Source: Financial Compound Interest and Annuity Tables, 5th ed. (Boston: Financial Publishing Co., 1970).

Rate of 9%

PERIODS	Amount of 1 How $1 left at compound interest will grow.	Amount of 1 Per Period How $1 deposited periodically will grow.	Sinking Fund Periodic deposit that will grow to $1 at future date.	Present Worth of 1 What $1 due in the future is worth today.	Present Worth of 1 Per Period What $1 payable periodically is worth today.	Partial Payment Annuity worth $1 today. Periodic payment necessary to pay off a loan of $1.	PERIODS
61	191.874 108	2120.823 424	.000 471	.005 211	11.053 202	.090 471	61
62	209.142 777	2312.697 533	.000 432	.004 781	11.057 984	.090 432	62
63	227.965 627	2521.840 311	.000 396	.004 386	11.062 370	.090 396	63
64	248.482 534	2749.805 939	.000 363	.004 024	11.066 395	.090 363	64
65	270.845 962	2998.288 473	.000 333	.003 692	11.070 087	.090 333	65
66	295.222 099	3269.134 436	.000 305	.003 387	11.073 474	.090 305	66
67	321.792.088	3564.356 535	.000 280	.003 107	11.076 582	.090 280	67
68	350.753 376	3886.148 623	.000 257	.002 851	11.079 433	.090 257	68
69	382.321 179	4236.901 999	.000 236	.002 615	11.082 048	.090 236	69
70	416.730 086	4619.223 179	.000 216	.002 399	11.084 448	.090 216	70
71	454.235 793	5035.953 265	.000 198	.002 201	11.086 650	.090 198	71
72	495.117 015	5490.189 059	.000 182	.002 019	11.088 669	.090 182	72
73	539.677 546	5985.306 075	.000 167	.001 852	11.090 522	.090 167	73
74	588.248 525	6524.983 622	.000 153	.001 699	11.092 222	.090 153	74
75	641.190 893	7113.232 148	.000 140	.001 559	11.093 782	.090 140	75
76	698.898 073	7754.423 041	.000 128	.001 430	11.095 213	.090 128	76
77	761.798 900	8453.321 115	.000 118	.001 312	11.096 525	.090 118	77
78	830.360 801	9215.120 015	.000 108	.001 204	11.097 730	.090 108	78
79	905.093 273	10045.480 816	.000 099	.001 104	11.098 834	.090 099	79
80	986.551 668	10950.574 090	.000 091	.001 013	11.099 848	.090 091	80
81	1075.341 318	11937.125 758	.000 083	.000 929	11.100 778	.090 083	81
82	1172.122 036	13012.467 076	.000 076	.000 853	11.101 631	.090 076	82
83	1277.613 020	14184.589 113	.000 070	.000 782	11.102 414	.090 070	83
84	1392.598 192	15462.202 133	.000 064	.000 718	11.103 132	.090 064	84
85	1517.932 029	16854.800 325	.000 059	.000 658	11.103 791	.090 059	85
86	1654.545 911	18372.732 355	.000 054	.000 604	11.104 395	.090 054	86
87	1803.455 044	20027.278 267	.000 049	.000 554	11.104 950	.090 049	87
88	1965.765 998	21830.733 311	.000 045	.000 508	11.105 458	.090 045	88
89	2142.684 937	23796.499 309	.000 042	.000 466	11.105 925	.090 042	89
90	2335.526 582	25939.184 247	.000 038	.000 428	11.106 353	.090 038	90

N	$(1+i)^N$	$\dfrac{(1+i)^N - 1}{i}$	$\dfrac{i}{(1+i)^N - 1}$	$(1+i)^{-N}$	$\dfrac{1-(1+i)^{-N}}{i}$	$\dfrac{i}{1-(1+i)^{-N}}$	N
91	2545.723 974	28274.710 829	.000 035	.000 392	11.106 746	.090 035	91
92	2774.839 132	30820.434 803	.000 032	.000 360	11.107 106	.090 032	92
93	3024.574 654	33595.273 936	.000 029	.000 330	11.107 437	.090 029	93
94	3296.786 373	36619.848 590	.000 027	.000 303	11.107 740	.090 027	94
95	3593.497 146	39916.634 963	.000 025	.000 278	11.108 019	.090 025	95
96	3916.911 889	43510.132 110	.000 022	.000 255	11.108 274	.090 022	96
97	4269.433 960	47427.044 000	.000 021	.000 234	11.108 508	.090 021	97
98	4653.683 016	51696.477 960	.000 019	.000 214	11.108 723	.090 019	98
99	5072.514 487	56350.160 976	.000 017	.000 197	11.108 920	.090 017	99
100	5529.040 791	61422.675 464	.000 016	.000 180	11.109 101	.090 016	100
101	6026.654 463	66951.716 256	.000 014	.000 165	11.109 267	.090 014	101
102	6569.053 364	72978.370 719	.000 013	.000 152	11.109 419	.090 013	102
103	7160.268 167	79547.424 084	.000 012	.000 139	11.109 559	.090 012	103
104	7804.692 302	86707.692 252	.000 011	.000 128	11.109 687	.090 011	104
105	8507.114 609	94512.384 554	.000 010	.000 117	11.109 805	.090 010	105
106	9272.754 924	103019.499 164	.000 009	.000 107	11.109 912	.090 009	106
107	10107.302 868	112292.254 089	.000 008	.000 098	11.110 011	.090 008	107
108	11016.960 126	122399.556 957	.000 008	.000 090	11.110 102	.090 008	108
109	12008.486 537	133416.517 083	.000 007	.000 083	11.110 185	.090 007	109
110	13089.250 325	145425.003 621	.000 006	.000 076	11.110 262	.090 006	110
111	14267.282 855	158514.253 947	.000 006	.000 070	11.110 332	.090 006	111
112	15551.338 312	172781.536 802	.000 005	.000 064	11.110 396	.090 005	112
113	16950.958 760	188332.875 114	.000 005	.000 058	11.110 455	.090 005	113
114	18476.545 048	205283.833 874	.000 004	.000 054	11.110 509	.090 004	114
115	20139.434 103	223760.378 923	.000 004	.000 049	11.110 559	.090 004	115
116	21951.983 172	243899.813 026	.000 004	.000 045	11.110 604	.090 004	116
117	23927.661 657	265851.796 199	.000 003	.000 041	11.110 646	.090 003	117
118	26081.151 207	289779.457 857	.000 003	.000 038	11.110 685	.090 003	118
119	28428.454 815	315860.609 064	.000 003	.000 035	11.110 720	.090 003	119
120	30987.015 749	344288.063 879	.000 002	.000 032	11.110 752	.090 002	120

Source: Financial Compound Interest and Annuity Tables, 5th ed. (Boston: Financial Publishing Co., 1970).

Rate of 10%

PERIODS	Amount of 1 — How $1 left at compound interest will grow.	Amount of 1 Per Period — How $1 deposited periodically will grow.	Sinking Fund — Periodic deposit that will grow to $1 at future date.	Present Worth of 1 — What $1 due in the future is worth today.	Present Worth of 1 Per Period — What $1 payable periodically is worth today.	Partial Payment — Annuity worth $1 today. Periodic payment necessary to pay off a loan of $1.	PERIODS
1	1.100 000	1.000 000	1.000 000	.909 090	.909 090	1.100 000	1
2	1.210 000	2.100 000	.476 190	.826 446	1.735 537	.576 190	2
3	1.331 000	3.310 000	.302 114	.751 314	2.486 851	.402 114	3
4	1.464 100	4.641 000	.215 470	.683 013	3.169 865	.315 470	4
5	1.610 510	6.105 100	.163 797	.620 921	3.790 786	.263 797	5
6	1.771 561	7.715 610	.129 607	.564 473	4.355 260	.229 607	6
7	1.948 717	9.487 171	.105 405	.513 158	4.868 418	.205 405	7
8	2.143 588	11.435 888	.087 444	.466 507	5.334 926	.187 444	8
9	2.357 947	13.579 476	.073 640	.424 097	5.759 023	.173 640	9
10	2.593 742	15.937 424	.062 745	.385 543	6.144 567	.162 745	10
11	2.853 116	18.531 167	.053 963	.350 493	6.495 061	.153 963	11
12	3.138 428	21.384 283	.046 763	.318 630	6.813 691	.146 763	12
13	3.452 271	24.522 712	.040 778	.289 664	7.103 356	.140 778	13
14	3.797 498	27.974 983	.035 746	.263 331	7.366 687	.135 746	14
15	4.177 248	31.772 481	.031 473	.239 392	7.606 079	.131 473	15
16	4.594 972	35.949 729	.027 816	.217 629	7.823 708	.127 816	16
17	5.054 470	40.544 702	.024 664	.197 844	8.021 553	.124 664	17
18	5.559 917	45.599 173	.021 930	.179 858	8.201 412	.121 930	18
19	6.115 909	51.159 090	.019 546	.163 507	8.364 920	.119 546	19
20	6.727 499	57.274 999	.017 459	.148 643	8.513 563	.117 459	20
21	7.400 249	64.002 499	.015 624	.135 130	8.648 694	.115 624	21
22	8.140 274	71.402 749	.014 005	.122 845	8.771 540	.114 005	22
23	8.954 302	79.543 024	.012 571	.111 678	8.883 218	.112 571	23
24	9.849 732	88.497 326	.011 299	.101 525	8.984 744	.111 299	24
25	10.834 705	98.347 059	.010 168	.092 295	9.077 040	.110 168	25
26	11.918 176	109.181 765	.009 159	.083 905	9.160 945	.109 159	26
27	13.109 994	121.099 941	.008 257	.076 277	9.237 223	.108 257	27
28	14.420 993	134.209 936	.007 451	.069 343	9.306 566	.107 451	28
29	15.863 092	148.630 929	.006 728	.063 039	9.369 605	.106 728	29
30	17.449 402	164.494 022	.006 079	.057 308	9.426 914	.106 079	30

N	$(1+i)^N$	$\dfrac{(1+i)^N - 1}{i}$	$\dfrac{i}{(1+i)^N - 1}$	$(1+i)^{-N}$	$\dfrac{1-(1+i)^{-N}}{i}$	$\dfrac{i}{1-(1+i)^{-N}}$	N
31	19.194 342	181.943 424	.005 496	.052 098	9.479 013	.105 496	31
32	21.113 776	201.137 767	.004 971	.047 362	9.526 375	.104 971	32
33	23.225 154	222.251 544	.004 499	.043 056	9.569 432	.104 499	33
34	25.547 669	245.476 698	.004 073	.039 142	9.608 574	.104 073	34
35	28.102 436	271.024 368	.003 689	.035 584	9.644 158	.103 689	35
36	30.912 680	299.126 805	.003 343	.032 349	9.676 508	.103 343	36
37	34.003 948	330.039 485	.003 029	.029 408	9.705 916	.103 029	37
38	37.404 343	364.043 434	.002 746	.026 734	9.732 651	.102 746	38
39	41.144 777	401.447 777	.002 490	.024 304	9.756 955	.102 490	39
40	45.259 255	442.592 555	.002 259	.022 094	9.779 050	.102 259	40
41	49.785 181	487.851 811	.002 049	.020 086	9.799 137	.102 049	41
42	54.763 699	537.636 992	.001 859	.018 260	9.817 397	.101 859	42
43	60.240 069	592.400 691	.001 688	.016 600	9.833 997	.101 688	43
44	66.264 076	652.640 760	.001 532	.015 091	9.849 088	.101 532	44
45	72.890 483	718.904 836	.001 391	.013 719	9.862 807	.101 391	45
46	80.179 532	791.795 320	.001 262	.012 472	9.875 279	.101 262	46
47	88.197 485	871.974 852	.001 146	.011 338	9.886 618	.101 146	47
48	97.017 233	960.172 337	.001 041	.010 307	9.896 925	.101 041	48
49	106.718 957	1057.189 571	.000 945	.009 370	9.906 295	.100 945	49
50	117.390 852	1163.908 528	.000 859	.008 518	9.914 814	.100 859	50
51	129.129 938	1281.299 381	.000 780	.007 744	9.922 558	.100 780	51
52	142.042 931	1410.429 319	.000 709	.007 040	9.929 598	.100 709	52
53	156.247 225	1552.472 251	.000 644	.006 400	9.935 998	.100 644	53
54	171.871 947	1708.719 477	.000 585	.005 818	9.941 817	.100 585	54
55	189.059 142	1880.591 424	.000 531	.005 289	9.947 106	.100 531	55
56	207.965 056	2069.650 567	.000 483	.004 808	9.951 914	.100 483	56
57	228.761 562	2277.615 623	.000 439	.004 371	9.956 286	.100 439	57
58	251.637 718	2506.377 186	.000 398	.003 973	9.960 260	.100 398	58
59	276.801 490	2758.014 904	.000 362	.003 612	9.963 873	.100 362	59
60	304.481 639	3034.816 395	.000 329	.003 284	9.967 157	.100 329	60

Source: *Financial Compound Interest and Annuity Tables*, 5th ed. (Boston: Financial Publishing Co., 1970).

Rate of 10%

PERIODS	Amount of 1 How $1 left at compound interest will grow.	Amount of 1 Per Period How $1 deposited periodically will grow.	Sinking Fund Periodic deposit that will grow to $1 at future date.	Present Worth of 1 What $1 due in the future is worth today.	Present Worth of 1 Per Period What $1 payable periodically is worth today.	Partial Payment Annuity worth $1 today. Periodic payment necessary to pay off a loan of $1.	PERIODS
61	334.929 803	3339.298 034	.000 299	.002 985	9.970 142	.100 299	61
62	368.422 783	3674.227 838	.000 272	.002 714	9.972 857	.100 272	62
63	405.265 062	4042.650 622	.000 247	.002 467	9.975 324	.100 247	63
64	445.791 568	4447.915 684	.000 224	.002 243	9.977 567	.100 224	64
65	490.370 725	4893.707 252	.000 204	.002 039	9.979 607	.100 204	65
66	539.407 797	5384.077 978	.000 185	.001 853	9.981 461	.100 185	66
67	593.348 577	5923.485 776	.000 168	.001 685	9.983 146	.100 168	67
68	652.683 435	6516.834 353	.000 153	.001 532	9.984 678	.100 153	68
69	717.951 778	7169.517 789	.000 139	.001 392	9.986 071	.100 139	69
70	789.746 956	7887.469 567	.000 126	.001 266	9.987 337	.100 126	70
71	868.721 652	8677.216 524	.000 115	.001 151	9.988 488	.100 115	71
72	955.593 817	9545.938 177	.000 104	.001 046	9.989 535	.100 104	72
73	1051.153 199	10501.531 995	.000 095	.000 951	9.990 486	.100 095	73
74	1156.268 519	11552.685 194	.000 086	.000 864	9.991 351	.100 086	74
75	1271.895 371	12708.953 713	.000 078	.000 786	9.992 137	.100 078	75
76	1399.084 908	13980.849 085	.000 071	.000 714	9.992 852	.100 071	76
77	1538.993 399	15379.933 993	.000 065	.000 649	9.993 502	.100 065	77
78	1692.892 739	16918.927 393	.000 059	.000 590	9.994 092	.100 059	78
79	1862.182 013	18611.820 132	.000 053	.000 537	9.994 629	.100 053	79
80	2048.400 214	20474.002 145	.000 048	.000 488	9.995 118	.100 048	80
81	2253.240 236	22522.402 360	.000 044	.000 443	9.995 561	.100 044	81
82	2478.564 259	24775.642 596	.000 040	.000 403	9.995 965	.100 040	82
83	2726.420 685	27254.206 856	.000 036	.000 366	9.996 332	.100 036	83
84	2999.062 754	29980.627 541	.000 033	.000 333	9.996 665	.100 033	84
85	3298.969 029	32979.690 295	.000 030	.000 303	9.996 968	.100 030	85
86	3628.865 932	36279.659 325	.000 027	.000 275	9.997 244	.100 027	86
87	3991.752 525	39907.525 258	.000 025	.000 250	9.997 494	.100 025	87
88	4390.927 778	43899.277 783	.000 022	.000 227	9.997 722	.100 022	88
89	4830.020 556	48290.205 562	.000 020	.000 207	9.997 929	.100 020	89
90	5313.022 611	53120.226 118	.000 018	.000 188	9.998 117	.100 018	90

N	$(1+i)^N$	$\dfrac{(1+i)^N - 1}{i}$	$\dfrac{i}{(1+i)^N - 1}$	$(1+i)^{-N}$	$\dfrac{1-(1+i)^{-N}}{i}$	$\dfrac{i}{1-(1+i)^{-N}}$
91	5844.324 873	58433.248 730	.000 017	.000 171	9.998 288	.100 017
92	6428.757 360	64277.573 603	.000 015	.000 155	9.998 444	.100 015
93	7071.633 096	70706.330 963	.000 014	.000 141	9.998 585	.100 014
94	7778.796 406	77777.964 060	.000 012	.000 128	9.998 714	.100 012
95	8556.676 046	85556.760 466	.000 011	.000 116	9.998 831	.100 011
96	9412.343 651	94113.436 512	.000 010	.000 106	9.998 937	.100 010
97	10353.578 016	103525.780 163	.000 009	.000 096	9.999 034	.100 009
98	11388.935 818	113879.358 180	.000 008	.000 087	9.999 121	.100 008
99	12527.829 399	125268.293 998	.000 007	.000 079	9.999 201	.100 007
100	13780.612 339	137796.123 398	.000 007	.000 072	9.999 274	.100 007
101	15158.673 573	151576.735 738	.000 006	.000 065	9.999 340	.100 006
102	16674.540 931	166735.409 311	.000 005	.000 059	9.999 400	.100 005
103	18341.995 024	183409.950 243	.000 005	.000 054	9.999 454	.100 005
104	20176.194 526	201751.945 267	.000 004	.000 049	9.999 504	.100 005
105	22193.813 979	221928.139 794	.000 004	.000 045	9.999 549	.100 004
106	24413.195 377	244121.953 773	.000 004	.000 040	9.999 590	.100 004
107	26854.514 915	268535.149 150	.000 003	.000 037	9.999 627	.100 003
108	29539.966 406	295389.664 065	.000 003	.000 033	9.999 661	.100 003
109	32493.963 047	324929.630 472	.000 003	.000 030	9.999 692	.100 003
110	35743.359 351	357423.593 519	.000 002	.000 027	9.999 720	.100 002
111	39317.695 287	393166.952 871	.000 002	.000 025	9.999 745	.100 002
112	43249.464 815	432484.648 158	.000 002	.000 023	9.999 768	.100 002
113	47574.411 297	475734.112 974	.000 002	.000 021	9.999 789	.100 002
114	52331.852 427	523308.524 272	.000 001	.000 019	9.999 808	.100 001
115	57565.037 669	575640.376 699	.000 001	.000 017	9.999 826	.100 001
116	63321.541 436	633205.414 369	.000 001	.000 015	9.999 842	.100 001
117	69653.695 580	696526.955 806	.000 001	.000 014	9.999 856	.100 001
118	76619.065 138	766180.651 387	.000 001	.000 013	9.999 869	.100 001
119	84280.971 652	842799.716 525	.000 001	.000 011	9.999 881	.100 001
120	92708.068 817	927080.688 178	.000 001	.000 010	9.999 892	.100 001

Source: *Financial Compound Interest and Annuity Tables*, 5th ed. (Boston: Financial Publishing Co., 1970).

Rate of 11%

PERIODS	Amount of 1 — How $1 left at compound interest will grow.	Amount of 1 Per Period — How $1 deposited periodically will grow.	Sinking Fund — Periodic deposit that will grow to $1 at future date.	Present Worth of 1 — What $1 due in the future is worth today.	Present Worth of 1 Per Period — What $1 payable periodically is worth today.	Partial Payment — Annuity worth $1 today. Periodic payment necessary to pay off a loan of $1.
1	1.110 000	1.000 000	1.000 000	.900 900	.900 900	1.110 000
2	1.232 100	2.110 000	.473 933	.811 622	1.712 523	.583 933
3	1.367 631	3.342 100	.299 213	.731 191	2.443 714	.409 213
4	1.518 070	4.709 731	.212 326	.658 730	3.102 445	.322 326
5	1.685 058	6.227 801	.160 570	.593 451	3.695 897	.270 570
6	1.870 414	7.912 859	.126 376	.534 640	4.230 537	.236 376
7	2.076 160	9.783 274	.102 215	.481 658	4.712 196	.212 215
8	2.304 537	11.859 434	.084 321	.433 926	5.146 122	.194 321
9	2.558 036	14.163 972	.070 601	.390 924	5.537 047	.180 601
10	2.839 420	16.722 008	.059 801	.352 184	5.889 232	.169 801
11	3.151 757	19.561 429	.051 121	.317 283	6.206 515	.161 121
12	3.498 450	22.713 187	.044 027	.285 840	6.492 356	.154 027
13	3.883 280	26.211 637	.038 150	.257 514	6.749 870	.148 150
14	4.310 440	30.094 918	.033 228	.231 994	6.981 865	.143 228
15	4.784 589	34.405 358	.029 065	.209 004	7.190 869	.139 065
16	5.310 894	39.189 948	.025 516	.188 292	7.379 161	.135 516
17	5.895 092	44.500 842	.022 471	.169 632	7.548 794	.132 471
18	6.543 552	50.395 935	.019 842	.152 822	7.701 616	.129 842
19	7.263 343	56.939 488	.017 562	.137 677	7.839 294	.127 562
20	8.062 311	64.202 832	.015 575	.124 033	7.963 328	.125 575
21	8.949 165	72.265 143	.013 837	.111 742	8.075 070	.123 837
22	9.933 574	81.214 309	.012 313	.100 668	8.175 739	.122 313
23	11.026 267	91.147 883	.010 971	.090 692	8.266 431	.120 971
24	12.239 156	102.174 150	.009 787	.081 704	8.348 136	.119 787
25	13.585 463	114.413 307	.008 740	.073 608	8.421 744	.118 740
26	15.079 864	127.998 771	.007 812	.066 313	8.488 058	.117 812
27	16.738 649	143.078 635	.006 989	.059 741	8.547 800	.116 989
28	18.579 901	159.817 285	.006 257	.053 821	8.601 621	.116 257
29	20.623 690	178.397 187	.005 605	.048 487	8.650 109	.115 605
30	22.892 296	199.020 877	.005 024	.043 682	8.693 792	.115 024

N	$(1+i)^N$	$\frac{(1+i)^N - 1}{i}$	$\frac{i}{(1+i)^N - 1}$	$(1+i)^{-N}$	$\frac{1-(1+i)^{-N}}{i}$	$\frac{i}{1-(1+i)^{-N}}$	N
31	25.410 449	221.913 174	.004 506	.039 353	8.733 146	.114 506	31
32	28.205 598	247.323 623	.004 043	.035 453	8.768 600	.114 043	32
33	31.308 214	275.529 222	.003 629	.031 940	8.800 540	.113 629	33
34	34.752 118	306.837 436	.003 259	.028 775	8.829 316	.113 259	34
35	38.574 851	341.589 554	.002 927	.025 923	8.855 239	.112 927	35
36	42.818 084	380.164 405	.002 630	.023 354	8.878 594	.112 630	36
37	47.528 073	422.982 490	.002 364	.021 040	8.899 634	.112 364	37
38	52.756 162	470.510 564	.002 125	.018 955	8.918 589	.112 125	38
39	58.559 339	523.266 726	.001 911	.017 076	8.935 666	.111 911	39
40	65.000 867	581.826 066	.001 718	.015 384	8.951 050	.111 718	40
41	72.150 962	646.826 933	.001 546	.013 859	8.964 910	.111 546	41
42	80.087 568	718.977 896	.001 390	.012 486	8.977 396	.111 390	42
43	88.897 201	799.065 465	.001 251	.011 248	8.988 645	.111 251	43
44	98.675 893	887.962 666	.001 126	.010 134	8.998 780	.111 126	44
45	109.530 241	986.638 559	.001 013	.009 129	9.007 910	.111 013	45
46	121.578 568	1096.168 801	.000 912	.008 225	9.016 135	.110 912	46
47	134.952 210	1217.747 369	.000 821	.007 410	9.023 545	.110 821	47
48	149.796 953	1352.699 579	.000 739	.006 675	9.030 220	.110 739	48
49	166.274 618	1502.496 533	.000 665	.006 104	9.036 235	.110 665	49
50	184.564 826	1668.771 152	.000 599	.005 418	9.041 653	.110 599	50
51	204.866 957	1853.335 978	.000 539	.004 881	9.046 534	.110 539	51
52	227.402 323	2058.202 936	.000 485	.004 397	9.050 931	.110 485	52
53	252.416 578	2285.605 259	.000 437	.003 961	9.054 893	.110 437	53
54	280.182 402	2538.021 838	.000 394	.003 569	9.058 462	.110 394	54
55	311.002 466	2818.204 240	.000 354	.003 215	9.061 678	.110 354	55
56	345.212 737	3129.206 706	.000 319	.002 896	9.064 574	.110 319	56
57	383.186 138	3474.419 444	.000 287	.002 609	9.067 184	.110 287	57
58	425.336 614	3857.605 583	.000 259	.002 351	9.069 535	.110 259	58
59	472.123 641	4282.942 197	.000 233	.002 118	9.071 653	.110 233	59
60	524.057 242	4755.065 839	.000 210	.001 908	9.073 561	.110 210	60

Source: Financial Compound Interest and Annuity Tables, 5th ed. (Boston: Financial Publishing Co., 1970).

Rate of 12%

PERIODS	Amount of 1 — How $1 left at compound interest will grow.	Amount of 1 Per Period — How $1 deposited periodically will grow.	Sinking Fund — Periodic deposit that will grow to $1 at future date.	Present Worth of 1 — What $1 due in the future is worth today.	Present Worth of 1 Per Period — What $1 payable periodically is worth today.	Partial Payment — Annuity worth $1 today. Periodic payment necessary to pay off a loan of $1.	PERIODS
1	1.120 000	1.000 000	1.000 000	.892 857	.892 857	1.120 000	1
2	1.254 400	2.120 000	.471 698	.797 193	1.690 051	.591 698	2
3	1.404 928	3.374 400	.296 348	.711 780	2.401 831	.416 348	3
4	1.573 519	4.779 328	.209 234	.635 518	3.037 349	.329 234	4
5	1.762 341	6.352 847	.157 409	.567 426	3.604 776	.277 409	5
6	1.973 822	8.115 189	.123 225	.506 631	4.111 407	.243 225	6
7	2.210 681	10.089 011	.099 117	.452 349	4.563 756	.219 117	7
8	2.475 963	12.299 693	.081 302	.403 883	4.967 639	.201 302	8
9	2.773 078	14.775 656	.067 678	.360 610	5.328 249	.187 678	9
10	3.105 848	17.548 735	.056 984	.321 973	5.650 223	.176 984	10
11	3.478 549	20.654 583	.048 415	.287 476	5.937 699	.168 415	11
12	3.895 975	24.133 133	.041 436	.256 675	6.194 374	.161 436	12
13	4.363 493	28.029 109	.035 677	.229 174	6.423 548	.155 677	13
14	4.887 112	32.392 602	.030 871	.204 619	6.628 168	.150 871	14
15	5.473 565	37.279 714	.026 824	.182 696	6.810 864	.146 824	15
16	6.130 393	42.753 280	.023 390	.163 121	6.973 986	.143 390	16
17	6.866 040	48.883 674	.020 456	.145 644	7.119 630	.140 456	17
18	7.689 965	55.749 714	.017 937	.130 039	7.249 670	.137 937	18
19	8.612 761	63.439 680	.015 763	.116 106	7.365 776	.135 763	19
20	9.646 293	72.052 442	.013 878	.103 666	7.469 443	.133 878	20
21	10.803 848	81.698 735	.012 240	.092 559	7.562 003	.132 240	21
22	12.100 310	92.502 583	.010 810	.082 642	7.644 645	.130 810	22
23	13.552 347	104.602 893	.009 559	.073 787	7.718 433	.129 559	23
24	15.178 628	118.155 241	.008 463	.065 882	7.784 315	.128 463	24
25	17.000 064	133.333 870	.007 499	.058 823	7.843 139	.127 499	25
26	19.040 072	150.333 934	.006 651	.052 520	7.895 659	.126 651	26
27	21.324 880	169.374 006	.005 904	.046 893	7.942 553	.125 904	27
28	23.883 866	190.698 887	.005 243	.041 869	7.984 422	.125 243	28
29	26.749 930	214.582 753	.004 660	.037 383	8.021 806	.124 660	29
30	29.959 922	241.332 684	.004 143	.033 377	8.055 183	.124 143	30

N	$(1+i)^N$	$\dfrac{(1+i)^N - 1}{i}$	$\dfrac{i}{(1+i)^N - 1}$	$(1+i)^{-N}$	$\dfrac{1-(1+i)^{-N}}{i}$	$\dfrac{i}{1-(1+i)^{-N}}$
31	33.555 112	271.292 606	.003 686	.029 801	8.084 985	.123 686
32	37.581 726	304.847 719	.003 280	.026 608	8.111 594	.123 280
33	42.091 533	342.429 445	.002 920	.023 757	8.135 352	.122 920
34	47.142 517	384.520 979	.002 600	.021 212	8.156 564	.122 600
35	52.799 619	431.663 496	.002 316	.018 939	8.175 503	.122 316
36	59.135 573	484.463 116	.002 064	.016 910	8.192 414	.122 064
37	66.231 842	543.598 690	.001 839	.015 098	8.207 512	.121 839
38	74.179 663	609.830 532	.001 639	.013 480	8.220 993	.121 639
39	83.081 223	684.010 196	.001 461	.012 036	8.233 029	.121 461
40	93.050 970	767.091 420	.001 303	.010 746	8.243 776	.121 303
41	104.217 086	860.142 390	.001 162	.009 595	8.253 372	.121 162
42	116.723 137	964.359 477	.001 036	.008 567	8.261 939	.121 036
43	130.729 913	1081.082 615	.000 924	.007 649	8.269 588	.120 924
44	146.417 503	1211.812 528	.000 825	.006 829	8.276 418	.120 825
45	163.987 603	1358.230 032	.000 736	.006 098	8.282 516	.120 736
46	183.666 116	1522.217 636	.000 656	.005 444	8.287 961	.120 656
47	205.706 050	1705.883 752	.000 586	.004 861	8.292 822	.120 586
48	230.390 776	1911.589 802	.000 523	.004 340	8.297 162	.120 523
49	258.037 669	2141.980 579	.000 466	.003 875	8.301 038	.120 466
50	289.002 189	2400.018 248	.000 416	.003 460	8.304 498	.120 416
51	323.682 452	2689.020 438	.000 371	.003 089	8.307 587	.120 371
52	362.524 346	3012.702 891	.000 331	.002 758	8.310 346	.120 331
53	406.027 268	3375.227 237	.000 296	.002 462	8.312 809	.120 296
54	454.750 540	3781.254 506	.000 264	.002 199	8.315 008	.120 264
55	509.320 605	4236.005 047	.000 236	.001 963	8.316 971	.120 236
56	570.439 078	4745.325 652	.000 210	.001 753	8.318 724	.120 210
57	638.891 767	5315.764 731	.000 188	.001 565	8.320 289	.120 188
58	715.558 779	5954.656 499	.000 167	.001 397	8.321 687	.120 167
59	801.425 833	6670.215 278	.000 149	.001 247	8.322 935	.120 149
60	897.596 933	7471.641 112	.000 133	.001 114	8.324 049	.120 133

Source: Financial Compound Interest and Annuity Tables, 5th ed. (Boston: Financial Publishing Co., 1970).

Rate of 13%

PERIODS	Amount of 1 How $1 left at compound interest will grow.	Amount of 1 Per Period How $1 deposited periodically will grow.	Sinking Fund Periodic deposit that will grow to $1 at future date.	Present Worth of 1 What $1 due in the future is worth today.	Present Worth of 1 Per Period What $1 payable periodically is worth today.	Partial Payment Annuity worth $1 today. Periodic payment necessary to pay off a loan of $1.	PERIODS
1	1.130 000	1.000 000	1.000 000	.884 955	.884 955	1.130 000	1
2	1.276 900	2.130 000	.469 483	.783 146	1.668 102	.599 483	2
3	1.442 897	3.406 900	.293 521	.693 050	2.361 152	.423 521	3
4	1.630 473	4.849 797	.206 194	.613 318	2.974 471	.336 194	4
5	1.842 435	6.480 270	.154 314	.542 759	3.517 231	.284 314	5
6	2.081 951	8.322 705	.120 153	.480 318	3.997 549	.250 153	6
7	2.352 605	10.404 657	.096 110	.425 060	4.422 610	.226 110	7
8	2.658 444	12.757 263	.078 386	.376 159	4.798 770	.208 386	8
9	3.004 041	15.415 707	.064 868	.332 884	5.131 655	.194 868	9
10	3.394 567	18.419 749	.054 289	.294 588	5.426 243	.184 289	10
11	3.835 861	21.814 316	.045 841	.260 697	5.686 941	.175 841	11
12	4.334 523	25.650 177	.038 986	.230 705	5.917 647	.168 986	12
13	4.898 011	29.984 700	.033 350	.204 164	6.121 811	.163 350	13
14	5.534 752	34.882 711	.028 667	.180 676	6.302 488	.158 667	14
15	6.254 270	40.417 464	.024 741	.159 890	6.462 378	.154 741	15
16	7.067 325	46.671 734	.021 426	.141 496	6.603 875	.151 426	16
17	7.986 077	53.739 060	.018 608	.125 217	6.729 092	.148 608	17
18	9.024 267	61.725 138	.016 200	.110 812	6.839 905	.146 200	18
19	10.197 422	70.749 406	.014 134	.098 063	6.937 969	.144 134	19
20	11.523 087	80.946 828	.012 353	.086 782	7.024 751	.142 353	20
21	13.021 089	92.469 916	.010 814	.076 798	7.101 550	.140 814	21
22	14.713 830	105.491 005	.009 479	.067 963	7.169 513	.139 479	22
23	16.626 628	120.204 836	.008 319	.060 144	7.229 657	.138 319	23
24	18.788 090	136.831 465	.007 308	.053 225	7.282 883	.137 308	24
25	21.230 542	155.619 555	.006 425	.047 101	7.329 984	.136 425	25
26	23.990 512	176.850 098	.005 654	.041 683	7.371 668	.135 654	26
27	27.109 279	200.840 610	.004 979	.036 887	7.408 555	.134 979	27
28	30.633 485	227.949 890	.004 386	.032 644	7.441 199	.134 386	28
29	34.615 838	258.583 376	.003 867	.028 888	7.470 088	.133 867	29
30	39.115 897	293.199 215	.003 410	.025 565	7.495 653	.133 410	30

N	$(1+i)^N$	$\dfrac{(1+i)^N - 1}{i}$	$\dfrac{i}{(1+i)^N - 1}$	$(1+i)^{-N}$	$\dfrac{1-(1+i)^{-N}}{i}$	$\dfrac{i}{1-(1+i)^{-N}}$
31	44.200 964	332.315 113	.003 009	.022 623	7.518 277	.133 009
32	49.947 090	376.516 077	.002 655	.020 021	7.538 298	.132 655
33	56.440 211	426.463 167	.002 344	.017 717	7.556 016	.132 344
34	63.777 439	482.903 379	.002 070	.015 679	7.571 695	.132 070
35	72.068 506	546.680 818	.001 829	.013 875	7.585 571	.131 829
36	81.437 412	618.749 325	.001 616	.012 279	7.597 851	.131 616
37	92.024 275	700.186 737	.001 428	.010 866	7.608 717	.131 428
38	103.987 431	792.211 013	.001 262	.009 616	7.618 334	.131 262
39	117.505 797	896.198 445	.001 115	.008 510	7.626 844	.131 115
40	132.781 551	1013.704 243	.000 986	.007 531	7.634 375	.130 986
41	150.043 153	1146.485 794	.000 872	.006 664	7.641 040	.130 872
42	169.548 763	1296.528 948	.000 771	.005 898	7.646 938	.130 771
43	191.590 102	1466.077 711	.000 682	.005 219	7.652 157	.130 682
44	216.496 815	1657.667 814	.000 603	.004 619	7.656 776	.130 603
45	244.641 401	1874.164 629	.000 533	.004 087	7.660 846	.130 533
46	276.444 784	2118.806 031	.000 471	.003 617	7.664 481	.130 471
47	312.382 606	2395.250 815	.000 417	.003 201	7.667 683	.130 417
48	352.992 344	2707.633 422	.000 369	.002 832	7.670 515	.130 369
49	398.881 349	3060.625 766	.000 326	.002 507	7.673 022	.130 326
50	450.735 925	3459.507 116	.000 289	.002 218	7.675 241	.130 289
51	509.331 595	3910.243 041	.000 255	.001 963	7.677 204	.130 255
52	575.544 702	4419.574 637	.000 226	.001 737	7.678 942	.130 226
53	650.365 514	4995.119 340	.000 200	.001 537	7.680 480	.130 200
54	734.913 031	5645.484 854	.000 177	.001 360	7.681 840	.130 177
55	830.451 725	6380.397 885	.000 156	.001 204	7.683 044	.130 156
56	938.410 449	7210.849 610	.000 138	.001 065	7.684 110	.130 138
57	1060.403 807	8149.260 059	.000 122	.000 943	7.685 053	.130 122
58	1198.256 302	9209.663 867	.000 108	.000 834	7.685 888	.130 108
59	1354.029 622	10407.920 170	.000 096	.000 738	7.686 626	.130 096
60	1530.053 473	11761.949 792	.000 085	.000 653	7.687 280	.130 085

Source: Financial Compound Interest and Annuity Tables. 5th ed. (Boston: Financial Publishing Co., 1970).

Rate of 14%

PERIODS	Amount of 1 — How $1 left at compound interest will grow.	Amount of 1 Per Period — How $1 deposited periodically will grow.	Sinking Fund — Periodic deposit that will grow to $1 at future date.	Present Worth of 1 — What $1 due in the future is worth today.	Present Worth of 1 Per Period — What $1 payable periodically is worth today.	Partial Payment — Annuity worth $1 today. Periodic payment necessary to pay off a loan of $1.	PERIODS
1	1.140 000	1.000 000	1.000 000	.877 192	.877 192	1.140 000	1
2	1.299 600	2.140 000	.467 289	.769 467	1.646 660	.607 289	2
3	1.481 544	3.439 600	.290 731	.674 971	2.321 632	.430 731	3
4	1.688 960	4.921 144	.203 204	.592 080	2.913 712	.343 204	4
5	1.925 414	6.610 104	.151 283	.519 368	3.433 080	.291 283	5
6	2.194 972	8.535 518	.117 157	.455 586	3.888 667	.257 157	6
7	2.502 268	10.730 491	.093 192	.399 637	4.288 304	.233 192	7
8	2.852 586	13.232 760	.075 570	.350 559	4.638 863	.215 570	8
9	3.251 948	16.085 346	.062 168	.307 507	4.946 371	.202 168	9
10	3.707 221	19.337 295	.051 713	.269 743	5.216 115	.191 713	10
11	4.226 232	23.044 516	.043 394	.236 617	5.452 733	.183 394	11
12	4.817 904	27.270 748	.036 669	.207 559	5.660 292	.176 669	12
13	5.492 411	32.088 653	.031 163	.182 069	5.842 361	.171 163	13
14	6.261 349	37.581 065	.026 609	.159 709	6.002 071	.166 609	14
15	7.137 937	43.842 414	.022 808	.140 096	6.142 167	.162 808	15
16	8.137 249	50.980 352	.019 615	.122 891	6.265 059	.159 615	16
17	9.276 464	59.117 601	.016 915	.107 799	6.372 859	.156 915	17
18	10.575 169	68.394 065	.014 621	.094 561	6.467 420	.154 621	18
19	12.055 692	78.969 234	.012 663	.082 948	6.550 368	.152 663	19
20	13.743 489	91.024 927	.010 986	.072 761	6.623 130	.150 986	20
21	15.667 578	104.768 417	.009 544	.063 826	6.686 956	.149 544	21
22	17.861 039	120.435 995	.008 303	.055 987	6.742 944	.148 303	22
23	20.361 584	138.297 035	.007 230	.049 112	6.792 056	.147 230	23
24	23.212 206	158.658 620	.006 302	.043 080	6.835 137	.146 302	24
25	26.461 915	181.870 827	.005 498	.037 790	6.872 927	.145 498	25
26	30.166 584	208.332 743	.004 800	.033 149	6.906 076	.144 800	26
27	34.389 905	238.499 327	.004 192	.029 078	6.935 154	.144 192	27
28	39.204 492	272.889 232	.003 664	.025 507	6.960 662	.143 664	28
29	44.693 121	312.093 725	.003 204	.022 374	6.983 037	.143 204	29
30	50.950 158	356.786 847	.002 802	.019 627	7.002 664	.142 802	30

N	$(1+i)^N$	$\dfrac{(1+i)^N-1}{i}$	$\dfrac{i}{(1+i)^N-1}$	$(1+i)^{-N}$	$\dfrac{1-(1+i)^{-N}}{i}$	$\dfrac{i}{1-(1+i)^{-N}}$
31	58.083 180	407.737 005	.002 452	.017 216	7.019 880	.142 452
32	66.214 826	465.820 186	.002 146	.015 102	7.034 983	.142 146
33	75.484 901	532.035 012	.001 879	.013 247	7.048 230	.141 879
34	86.052 787	607.519 914	.001 646	.011 620	7.059 851	.141 646
35	98.100 178	693.572 702	.001 441	.010 193	7.070 045	.141 441
36	111.834 203	791.672 880	.001 263	.008 941	7.078 987	.141 263
37	127.490 991	903.507 083	.001 106	.007 843	7.086 830	.141 106
38	145.339 730	1030.998 075	.000 969	.006 880	7.093 711	.140 969
39	165.687 292	1176.337 806	.000 850	.006 035	7.099 746	.140 850
40	188.883 513	1342.025 098	.000 745	.005 294	7.105 040	.140 745
41	215.327 205	1530.908 612	.000 653	.004 644	7.109 685	.140 653
42	245.473 014	1746.235 818	.000 572	.004 073	7.113 758	.140 572
43	279.839 236	1991.708 833	.000 502	.003 573	7.117 332	.140 502
44	319.016 729	2271.548 069	.000 440	.003 134	7.120 466	.140 440
45	363.679 071	2590.564 799	.000 386	.002 749	7.123 216	.140 386
46	414.594 142	2954.243 871	.000 338	.002 411	7.125 628	.140 338
47	472.637 321	3368.838 013	.000 296	.002 115	7.127 744	.140 296
48	538.806 546	3841.475 335	.000 260	.001 855	7.129 600	.140 260
49	614.239 463	4380.281 882	.000 228	.001 628	7.131 228	.140 228
50	700.232 988	4994.521 346	.000 200	.001 428	7.132 656	.140 200
51	798.265 606	5694.754 334	.000 175	.001 252	7.133 909	.140 175
52	910.022 791	6493.019 941	.000 154	.001 098	7.135 008	.140 154
53	1037.425 982	7403.042 733	.000 135	.000 963	7.135 971	.140 135
54	1182.665 620	8440.468 715	.000 118	.000 845	7.136 817	.140 118
55	1348.238 807	9623.134 336	.000 103	.000 741	7.137 559	.140 103
56	1536.992 240	10971.373 143	.000 091	.000 650	7.138 209	.140 091
57	1752.171 153	12508.365 383	.000 079	.000 570	7.138 780	.140 079
58	1997.475 115	14260.536 536	.000 070	.000 500	7.139 281	.140 070
59	2277.121 631	16258.011 652	.000 061	.000 439	7.139 720	.140 061
60	2595.918 659	18535.133 283	.000 053	.000 385	7.140 105	.140 053

Source: *Financial Compound Interest and Annuity Tables*, 5th ed. (Boston: Financial Publishing Co., 1970).

INDEX

Addressograph-Multigraph, 162

Advertising (commercials), 17, 87, 88

Alimony, 101–2, 143–44

Annuities, 169–73, 186, 192

Antiques, investing in, 163, 164

Apartments, 28–29, 30, 34–35, 52, 74. *See also* Condominiums; Housing; Renting

Automobiles, 3, 15, 18, 20, 51, 55, 63, 89, 91, 97, 153, 176, 177, 184, 196, 199; depreciation, 19; insurance, 48; loans and, 22; twenties age group (marrieds) and, 15, 19, 22, 24–25, 29, 48; twenties (singles), 48, 51, 63; thirties, 89, 91, 97

Babies. *See* Children

Baldwin-United annuities, 172

Bank failures, 161

Bank loans, 21–23, 80–81; applications for, 21, 22; collateral and creditworthiness and, 22; for education, 80–81; loan officers and, 21–22. *See also* Mortgages

Bank money market funds, 63, 164–65, 166, 167, 192–93

Bequests to children, 193–94

Blue-collar workers, rate of pay increases and, 14

Bonds, investing in, 62, 93–94, 105, 162–63, 165–67, 191–93; municipals, 166–67; mutual funds, 166; U.S. Treasury, 162–63, 165–66

Borrowing (loans), 6–7, 16, 20–25, 146, 148; banks and, 21–23, 80–81 *(see also* Bank loans); education costs and, 80–81, 90, 128, 129, 139–40; homeownership and, 31–34, 41, 106 *(see also* Mortgages); interest payments and, 22–23; shopping for, 22–23;

twenties age group (marrieds) and, 16–25

Capital accumulation, investments and interest rates and (charts), 199–219. *See also* Savings; specific aspects, developments, problems

Career changes, 63, 70–71

Cars. *See* Automobiles

Catastrophic illness, 190. *See also* Health care

Cattle, tax shelters and, 59–61

Certificates of deposit (CDs), 58, 60, 61, 62, 63, 93, 94, 105, 131, 165, 166, 167, 168

Children, child-rearing costs and, 3, 8–9, 27–43, 47, 49, 57, 65, 78–86, 90, 121–31; basic rules for, 82–84; bequests and, 193–94; divorce and *(see* Divorce); education and, 78–81 *(see also* Education); female "householders" and, 144–45; and help with family income, 128–31, 145, 148, 196; homeownership and *(see* Housing); and insurance, 43; statistics, 82–84

Child support, 101–2, 143–44

Clothing expenditures, 15, 51, 52, 55, 63, 84, 91, 132, 153, 176

Coins, investing in, 163, 164

Collectibles, investing in, 164

College education, 2, 3, 6, 7–8, 49, 121–31, 139–40; children sharing cost of, 128–31, 148; costs, statistics, 122–23; gifts, loans, and scholarships, 81, 128–29, 139–40; value of, 126, 127, 130–31. *See also* Education

Commercials. *See* Advertising

Competition, labor market and, 66–71, 124, 156–58

Computer stocks, investing in, 162

Condominiums (condos), 24, 31, 33–34, 39, 45, 56–57, 74, 108. *See also* Apartments; Housing
Consumption function, 5–9, 65–71. *See also* Expenditures; specific aspects, kinds, problems
Convalescent homes, 173–74
Co-ops, 31–34, *See also* Apartments; Condominiums; Housing
Corporate bonds, 162–63. *See also* Bonds
Credit cards, 21

Declining industries and geographic areas, pay growth and, 67–68, 69
Defined Benefit Plans, 167
Diamonds, investing in, 164
Dividends, investing in stocks and, 161–62, 186
Divorce, 7–8, 88–90, 101–3, 196, 142–45, 196; alimony and child support and, 101–2, 143–44; financial implications of, 77, 78, 88–90, 101–2, 143–45; financial stress and, 88–90, 142–44; rise in, statistics, 78, 88, 101–2, 144–45. *See also* Single mothers; Working women
Dow-Jones Industrial Average, 31, 106, 161–62
Dwellings (shelter), 27–43. *See also* Housing, specific developments, kinds, problems

Earnings, 4–9, 11–29, 53, 105; competition and, 66–71, 124, 156–58; education and *(see* Education and knowledge); expenditures and, 4–9, 15–53, 45–64, 65–71 *(See also* Expenditures); "function," 5; homeownership and, 30–31, 34–43 *(see also* Housing); life-style and *(see* Life-style; specific aspects, developments); marrieds and singles and, 47–49, 50; part-time and second jobs and, 35–36, 37, 53–54, 55; pay growth and 11–15 *(see also* Pay); productivity and, 11–15 *(see also* Productivity); twenties (marrieds) and, 11–29 *passim,* 30–31, 34–43, 45–58 *passim,* 111–12; twenties (singles) and, 45–64 *passim,* 111–12; thirties, 74, 76, 77, 79–92 *passim,* 102–3, 105–6, 108, 111–20; thirties as peak in growth of, 111–20; forties (marrieds), 123–35, 138, 143; forties

(singles); 141–42, 143; fifties, 156–59, 175; sixties and seventies (retirees), 183; upgrading, 35–36, 37, 53–54, 55, 66 *(see also* specific aspects, developments, methods); working women and, 36–37 *(see also* Working women). *See also* Income; Pay; specific aspects, developments, kinds, problems
Economic and financial statistics, economic health and, 6. *See also* specific aspects, developments, kinds
Education, child-rearing and costs of, 75, 76, 77, 78–81, 90, 91, 121–31, 153, 176, 196; borrowing and, 80–81, 90; college, 121–31 *(see also* College education); private schools, 78–81, 94, 196, 199; public schools, 28, 78–81, 122–23; rise in, 78–81, 122–23; saving on, 79–81, 128–29 *(see also* specific aspects, developments)
Education and knowledge, income growth and, 14, 35–36, 37, 53, 58, 66, 109, 112–17, 118, 123 126, 127, 142, 180; part-time schooling (classes) and, 35, 37, 53, 54; productivity and *(see* Productivity). *See also* College education; Education
Entertainment costs, 63. *See also* Recreation expenses; Vacations
Expenditures (consumption, expenses, spending), 4–9, 15–43, 45–64, 65–71; borrowing and *(see* Borrowing); children and child-rearing and, 27–43, 82–86, 90 *(see also* Children); consumption "function" and, 5–9, 65–71; homeownership and, 27–43 *(see also* Housing); income and, 4–9, 15–26, 46, 65–71, 74–91 *(see also* Income; specific developments, kinds); luxury bracket creep and, 147–48; marriage stresses and divorce and, 88–90 *(see also* Divorce; specific aspects, developments); savings and, 16–20, 26 *(see also* Savings); singles *vs.* marrieds and, 45–64 *passim;* twenties age group (marrieds) and, 15–43, 45–56, 65–71; twenties (singles), 45–64, 65–71; thirties, 74–92 *passim,* 93–99, 120; forties, 121–34, 139–40, 141–53; fifties, 158–60, 175–77, 180–81; sixties and seventies (retirees), 184–87. *See also* specific aspects, developments, kinds, problems

Finance companies, loans and, 22, 80–81
Financial crises (money worries), avoiding, 1–9, 195–97; four parts of, 7–9; ten commandments for, 196–97. *See also* specific aspects, developments, kinds, problems
Food costs, 17, 18, 29, 91, 153, 176, 184. *See also* Meals away from home
Furniture (appliances, furnishings), 15, 18, 19, 20–21, 76, 89, 91, 153, 176; loans and, 20–21

Gifts, 52. *See also* Bequests to children
Gold, investing in, 161, 163–64; bullion, 161; coins, 163–64
Government assistance, education costs and, 128, 129
Government employment, 66–67
Grants, college, 128

Health care, 18, 55, 91, 153, 174, 176, 177, 184, 190; insurance, supplemental coverage, 190; Medicare program, 173–74, 181, 184, 187, 190; nursing and convalescent homes, 173–74, 181; retirement and, 190
Hiring freezes, 67
Home (household) expenses, 74, 132, 153. *See also* specific kinds
"Householder," female, 144–45
Housing (homeownership), 2, 8, 18, 27–43, 52–58, 63, 75–76, 88, 90, 91, 106–10, 149–50, 196, 199; appreciation and sales value, 150, 188–89; banks (mortgages) and, 21, 29, 30, 31–34, 41, 42 *(see also* Mortgages); children (child-rearing) and, 27–43, 79, 196; costs, 27–43; income and, 30–31, 34–43, 45, 75–76, 91, 106–10; investment aspects of, 31, 32–34, 106, 188–89 *(see also* Real estate); renting and, 6, 28–29, 149 *(see also* Rent); rule for cost of buying, 107; savings and, 31–32, 33–34, 42, 52, 57; tax shelter aspects of, 32–34, 150; twenties age group (marrieds) and, 18, 24, 27–43, 45, 55; twenties (singles), 45, 52, 55–58, 63; thirties, 75–76, 80, 90, 91, 98, 106–10; forties, 149–50, 153; fifties, 175, 176; sixties and seventies (retirees), 187–89. *See also* specific aspects, developments, kinds

Illness, catastrophic, 190. *See also* Health care
Income, 4–9, 26, 65–71; children (child-rearing costs) and, 82–86 *(see also* Children); divorce and *(see* Divorce); education costs and *(see* Education); employment competition and, 66–71, 124, 156–58; expenditures and, 4–9, 15–26 *(see also* Expenditures); homeownership and, 30–31, 34–43 *(see also* Housing); inflation and *(see* Inflation); investing and *(see* Investing; specific kinds); life-style and *(see* Life-style); luxury bracket creep and, 147–48; marrieds and singles and, 47–49, 50; retirement and, 136–40, 183–94 *passim (see also* Retirement); savings and *(see* Savings); twenties age group (marrieds) and, 11–15, 23, 24, 34–43, 45–58, 65–71; twenties (singles), 45–64, 65–71; thirties, 74–92 *passim,* 97, 102–3, 105–6, 107–10, 111–20; forties (marrieds), 121–34, 135–40; forties (singles), 141–53 *passim;* fifties, 156–77 *passim,* 179–81; sixties and seventies (retirees), 183–94 *passim;* working women and, 36–37, 85–86, 102–3, 114–17, 118–19 *(see also* Working women); zero-sum situation and, 159. *See also* Earnings; Pay; specific aspects, developments, kinds
Indebtedness, 19, 20–25, 120, 139–40; twenties age group and, 19, 20–25. *See also* Borrowing; Credit cards; Mortgages; Time, buying on
Inflation, 191–93; automatic hedging and, 167–69, 191–93; borrowing and, 146; debt instruments and, 167–69, 173; homeownership and, 31, 42; interest income and, 16–17, 136–38 *(see also* Interest); retirement income and, 136–38, 191–93; wage increases and, 14–15, 16
Insurance, 18, 43, 91, 133, 153, 174, 176, 177, 185; auto, 48; health care, 190 *(see also* Medicare program); life *(see* Life insurance); retirement and, 174, 190 *(see also* Pension plans; Social Security)
Insurance companies, annuities and, 171, 172
Insured investments, 164–68, 173
Interest (interest rates), 186, 199; annuities and, 170–73; capital

accumulation (charts) and, 200–19; inflation and *(see* Inflation); loans and mortgages and, 22, 23, 29, 31, 33–34, 74, 75–76, 129; investments and, 162, 165–69; on savings, compounding and, 6, 16–17, 137–40, 151, 152, 153

Internal Revenue Service (IRS), tax shelters and, 59, 61, 132

Investing (investments), 59–64, 74, 93–94, 105–6, 131–32, 160, 161–75, 189, 191–93, 196; annuities, 169–73; automatic inflation hedging and, 167–69, 191–93; and capital accumulation (charts), 200–3; safety and liquidity and, 61–64, 93–94, 105–6, 131–32, 160, 161–75, 191–93; savings and, 59–64, 93–94, 160, 161 *(see also* specific kinds); short-term, 165–69, 191–93; sleeping point rule for, 105; thirties age group and, 93–94, 105–6; forties, 131–32; fifties, 160, 161–75; sixties and seventies (retirees), 191–92. *See also* specific aspects, developments, kinds

IRA plans, 125, 131, 167, 175

Job changes, 63, 70–71

Keogh plans, 125, 131, 167, 175
Knight, Frank, 128

Labor market (work force), 66–71; competition and, 66–71, 124, 156–58; married women and, 36–37 *(see also* Working women); pay (earnings, income) and, 11–15, 26, 66–71 *(see also* Pay; specific aspects, developments); twenties age group and, 11–15, 26, 35–36, 45; thirties *(see under* Earnings); forties, 141–42; fifties, 156–58

Life insurance, 94–96; term, 94–95, 96; universal, 95–96; variable, 95–96; whole life, 94, 95, 96

Life-style (standard of living), 9, 15, 86–91, 196; divorce and, 88–90, 143–44; financial planning and, 9; inflation and, 15 *(see also* Inflation); luxury bracket creep and, 147–48; marriage stresses and, 90; twenties age group and, 15–21; thirties, 86–91, 98; fifties, 175–77, 180–81

Limited partnerships, investing in, 164
Liquidity and safety, investing and, 61–

64, 93–94, 105–6, 131–32, 160, 161–75, 191–93

Loans. *See* Borrowing (loans)

Marriage, 47–49, 88–90; financial stresses and, 88–90; and income growth, 47–49; statistics, 45, 88, 101–2, 179; and working women, 36–37 *(see also* Working women). *See also* Children; Divorce; Single mothers; specific aspects, developments

MasterCard, 50

Meals away from home (restaurant meals), 15, 18, 29, 51, 55, 63, 80, 91, 153, 175, 176, 184

Medicare program, 174, 184, 187, 190; supplementing, 190

Money market funds, 62–63, 93, 131, 164–65, 166, 167–68, 173, 192–93; bank funds, 63, 164–65, 166, 167–68, 192–93; mutual funds, 62–63, 165, 167–68, 192–93

Mortgages, 29, 30; education costs and, 80–81; homeownership and, 29, 30, 31–34, 41, 42, 75–76, 80–81, 91, 106, 149–50, 153, 176, 184; second (refinancing), 80–81. *See also* Borrowing (loans)

Municipal bonds, investing in, 166–67, 168, 186

Nursing homes, 173–74, 181

Parents, nursing homes and, 173–74, 181
Parochial school education, costs of, 80, 81

Part-time jobs, 36, 54, 85, 129–30, 139, 145. *See also* Second jobs

Passbook savings accounts, 58, 162, 173

Pay (pay levels, promotions, salaries, wages), 11–15, 66–71; labor market and *(see* Labor market); productivity and *(see* Productivity); twenties age group and, 11–15, 35–37, 39–40, 47–48, 53, 63, 66–70; thirties, 74, 77, 85–86, 90, 92, 102–3, 109, 111–19; forties (marrieds), 123–24, 143; forties (singles), 141–42, 143; fifties, 156–59, 179–80. *See also* Earnings; Income; specific aspects, developments

Penn Square Bank, failure of, 161

Pension plans, 18, 91, 153, 170, 175, 185,

186; contributions to, 18, 91, 153, 176, 177. *See also* specific plans

Precious stones, investing in, 163–64

Private schools, 78–81, 94, 196, 199

Productivity (expertise, skills), income and, 11–15, 35, 36, 37, 47, 54, 66, 112, 113–14, 115–17, 123–24, 196; education and *(see* Education and knowledge); income growth curve and, 112, 113–14, 115–17; twenties age group and, 11–15, 35, 36, 37, 53; forties, 123–24;

"Project notes," investing in, 167·

Public schools, 28, 78–81; colleges and universities, 122–23 *(see also* College education)

Real estate (land deals), investing and, 94, 105, 132, 150, 164. *See also* Housing

Recreation expenses, 18, 19, 20, 51, 52, 55, 91, 133–34, 153, 176. *See also* Travel; Vacations

Rent (renting), housing and, 6, 28–29, 30, 34–35, 36, 40, 42–43, 48, 52, 91, 106, 107, 149, 150, 153, 176, 189; retirement and, 189. *See also* Housing

Restaurant meals. *See* Meals away from home

Retirement, 3–4, 135–40, 183–94, 196; annuities and, 169–73, 186, 192, 193–94; bequests to children and, 193–94; compounding of interest and income and, 136–40; facts and fallacies, 184–87; forties age group and, 123, 134, 135–40, 151; fifties, 160, 161, 163–75, 180–81; sixties and seventies and, 183–94, government assistance and, 185–86; homeownership and, 187–89; inflation and, 136–40, 191–93; investing and, 160, 161–75 *(see also* Investing)

Robot labor, 113

Roommates (shared housing), 52–53

Salaries. *See* Pay

Savings (saving), 6, 8, 9, 36–37, 46, 49–50, 58–64, 103–5; balance between spending and, 24; children and education costs and, 79–81 *(see also* Children; Education); compounded interest and, 6, 16–17, 36–37, 137–40, 151, 152, 153, 199, 200–19; freedom (independence) and, 49–50; general

rules for, 103–5; growth chart (late thirties age group), 120; homeownership and, 31–32, 33–34, 42, 52, 57 *(see also* Housing); interest rates and capital accumulation (charts), 199, 200–19; investing and, 59–64 *(see also* Investing); lifetime expenditures and, 6, 8, 9 *(see also* Expenditures); marrieds *vs.* singles and, 46, 49–64; retirement and *(see* Retirement); safety and liquidity and, 61–64, 93–94, 105–6, 131–32, 160, 161–75, 191–93; twenties age group (marrieds) and, 16–20, 21, 24, 25, 26, 46, 53; twenties (singles), 46, 49–50, 58–64, 93; thirties, 74, 76, 77, 79–92 *passim*, 93, 99, 103–5, 120; forties, 137–40, 152–53, 169–77 *passim*, 159, 160, 167, 169–77 *passim*, 180–81; sixties and seventies (retirees), 184–94 *passim*

Savings accounts, passbook, 58, 162, 173

Scholarships, 81, 128, 139

Second jobs, 35–36, 53–54, 55. *See also* Part-time jobs

Seniority, pay levels and, 125, 142

Shelter. *See* Housing

Silver, investing in, 163–64

Single mothers (single women), 101–4, 196; divorce and, 101–3, 144–45 *(see also* Divorce); homeownership and, 103–4, 105–6, 108–10, 111; and pay increases, 112–14. *See also* Working women; specific aspects, developments, problems

Social Security, 3, 151, 170, 185, 186, 190

Spending (expenses). *See* Expenditures

Statistics, financial, economic health and, 6

Stocks, investing in, 61, 62, 63, 74, 93–94, 105–6, 131, 161–63; growth stocks, 61; hi tech, 63

Stress (strains), financial, divorce and, 88–90

Taxes, 91; child-rearing costs and, 84–85; retirement income and, 186

Tax shelters, 59–61, 105, 132, 150; cattle, 59–61; homeownership and, 32–34, 150; IRA and Keogh plans, 125, 131, 167, 175; IRS and, 59, 61, 132; municipal bonds, 166–67; real estate, 105, 150

Teaching, pay for, 67, 69, 70–71

Teenagers, and help with family income, 128–30, 145, 148, 196
Telephone bills, 52, 91, 153, 176
Time, buying on, 15, 76. *See also* Credit cards; specific aspects
Transportation costs, 18, 29, 55, 91, 97, 153; marrieds *vs.* singles and, 55. *See also* Automobiles; Travel
Travel, 21, 51, 52, 63. *See also* Automobiles; Recreation; Transportation costs; Vacations
Tuition assistance, financial, 81–82. *See also* Education; specific aspects

Unions, seniority and pay and, 125, 142
United States Treasury obligations, 162–63, 165–66, 167
Utilities, costs of, 52, 91, 153, 176

Vacations, 15, 18, 19, 21, 24. *See also* Recreation; specific aspects
Veterans Administration, 173

Wages. *See* Pay
White-collar employees, rate of pay increases and, 14
Working women, 36–37, 78, 85–86, 102–4, 114–17, 118–19, 141–42, 156–58, 180; income growth curve and, 114–17, 118–19, 141–42. *See also* Single mothers (single women); specific developments, problems
Work-study plan, college, 128, 129

Zero-sum situation, personal income and, 159